MW00999135

The wood I walk in on this mild M(*foliage of the oaks between me and the blue sky, the white star-flowers and the blue-eyed speedwell and the ground ivy at my feet – what grove of tropic palms, what strange ferns or splendid broad-petalled blossoms, could ever thrill such deep and delicate fibres within me as this home-scene? These familiar flowers, these well remembered bird-notes, this sky with its fitful brightness, these furrowed and grassy fields, each with a sort of personality given to it by the capricious hedgerows – such things as these are the mother tongue of our imagination, the language that is laden with all the subtle inextricable associations the fleeting hours of our childhood left behind them. Our delight in the sunshine on the deep-bladed grass today might be no more than the faint perception of wearied souls if it were not for the sunshine and the grass in the far-off years which still live in us and transform our perception into love.*

George Eliot, *The Mill on the Floss*, 1.5

A tree gives glory to God simply by being a tree.

Thomas Merton, *New Seeds of Contemplation*

For these sins, the land trembles and the people mourn. Amos 8:8
If the people of God are silent, the very stones will shout out! Luke 19:40
We confess our silence. This disaster leaves us speechless;
Lord, give us the courage to repent with our lips, and with our actions.
The earth is the Lord's, and all that is in it.
Hear the cries of your servants, O Lord.
Deliver your creation from this peril,
and put a new and right spirit within us. Psalm 51:10

from *Prayer of Confession*,
written at 2010 Duke Divinity School's
Summer Institute for Reconciliation

Nature as Spiritual Practice

Steven Chase

William B. Eerdmans Publishing Company
Grand Rapids, Michigan / Cambridge, U.K.

Published 2011 by
Wm. B. Eerdmans Publishing Co.
2140 Oak Industrial Drive N.E., Grand Rapids, Michigan 49505 /
P.O. Box 163, Cambridge CB3 9PU U.K.

Printed in the United States of America

16 15 14 13 12 11   7 6 5 4 3 2 1

Library of Congress Cataloging-in-Publication Data

Chase, Steven.
    Nature as spiritual practice / Steven Chase.
        p.   cm.
    Includes bibliographical references and index.
    ISBN 978-0-8028-4010-3 (pbk.: alk. paper)
    1. Nature — Religious aspects — Christianity.
    2. Spiritual life — Christianity.   I. Title.

BT695.5.C44   2011
248 — dc22
                                    2011008452

www.eerdmans.com

Dedicated to my daughter, Rachel Renée Chase

"The earth is not an inheritance from our parents,
but is given in trust to hand on to our children."

Attributed to Chief Si'ahl (Sealth),
Leader of Suquamish and Duwamish Tribes
of the Salish Peoples, 1854

Contents

Acknowledgments

A sabbatical stay at the Collegeville Institute of Ecumenical and Cultural Research, on the grounds of St. John's Abbey and St. John's University in Collegeville, Minnesota, made the completion of this book possible and pleasurable. The Benedictine monks of the abby set a tone of hospitality that permeates and bonds an eclectic community: a community of monks, scholars, students, artisans, land, sky, animals, plants, fish, birds, air, water, and yes, even extreme cold! It was a blessing to be a part of this community. During my time at the institute, I was able to pray with the monks, walk the land, and write this book — what more could I ask? I would like to thank all those who made my stay there the productive delight that it was, including Fr. Kilian McDonnell, O.S.B., the founder of CIECR, Donald Ottenhoff, its executive director, Elisa Schneider, its manager, and Carla Durand-Demarais, its program coordinator.

Students in the classes I offered with the same title as this book helped me understand that there are as many perspectives to nature as there are pairs of eyes to look, and even more importantly, as there are pairs of eyes to *see* nature. I would especially like to thank one student, Ryan Ende, who had a particularly sensitive and caring spirit. It is a great sorrow that Ryan is no longer with us. Often I think of him returned to dust, and in his return how he is even now humanizing the earth.

Finally, I would like to thank my father, Harry Chase, a trained forester who, when I was with him as a young boy, simply could not pass a tree without "testing" me by asking me to identify it. We lived in the Pacific Northwest of the United States. There are a lot of trees in the Pacific Northwest.

How to Use This Book

I expect by very ridicule and contempt to be called a man of very fruitful brain and copious fancy, but they are welcome to it. I am not ashamed to own that I believe that the whole universe, heaven and earth, air and seas . . . [and] . . . holy Scriptures, be full of images of divine things, as full as language is of words.

Jonathan Edwards, *Typological Writings*[1]

Intentions

Nature *is* spiritual practice.

A friend once showed me an old cottonwood, its trunk hollowed with age, but still standing, still putting out leaves each spring and letting them go in the fall. "Stand in the inside," my friend said. I felt good in the hollow, comforted: looking up, I could see open sky. Then the wind blew in from the north, quite sharp, and I could hear a deep tone as if the cottonwood were the reed of a wind instrument, deepening a quarter, a fifth in the wind shift. Embraced in the old cottonwood, I stood for some time. Walking home, I said to my friend, "It's almost like the wind and the tree were talking to me."

"Almost?" she said. We walked on a bit.

"And what did the sky say?" she asked.

Nature *is* Christian practice: she is the teacher and she is material and she is spiritual — the everyday and the sacramental.

---

1. *Typological Writings*, in *The Works of Jonathan Edwards*, ed. Wallace Anderson et al. (New Haven: Yale University Press, 1993), 11:152.

Creation speaks, and the language of creation shapes, forms, and transforms relationships. Our human/creation relationship is born of our common parentage; the relationship is realized in practice. Still pulsing through the lifeblood of this human/creation connection are common genes — common genes whose function seems to be the nurturing of mindful attention, wonder, and shared longings to return to their Creator. Through the eyes of the senses and the eyes of wisdom and the eyes of faith, we behold the Easter in the ordinary, the mundane in the sacred. Jonathan Edwards saw and heard: this "whole universe, heaven and earth, air and seas," is "full of images of divine things, as full as language is of words." Listen. The whole universe is a language more complex and full of words than any holy text, any Scripture. The whole universe is God's tongue speaking, speaking in a language more ancient than Torah, more ancient than the Bhagavad Gita, more ancient than any Testament. Thomas Merton is known for one of his great insights: "Scripture is like a lake with no bottom." Creation *is* the lake; creation *is* the no bottom; creation *is* a scripture.

Most religious traditions honor and revere their holy texts. I am frightened, even horrified, by our lack of reverence for creation. Imagine a Muslim throwing her Koran in a polluted lake. Imagine the Christian pope, instead of kissing the Gospels, setting them on fire. Imagine a rabbi announcing to his flock that the Torah is extinct.

There are many modes of spiritual practices that draw us toward God: the reading of Scripture, feasting together, prayer, acts of kindness, building soaring cathedrals, music and art and film, hoping, worshiping, relationships, and dreams. *Nature as Spiritual Practice* (and the accompanying *Field Guide to Nature as Spiritual Practice*) acknowledges and encourages all these while attending primarily to the shared experiences, reciprocal perceptions, and cumulative wisdoms of the human/nature relationship. In part, this book is about remembering: separated as we have been from the natural world for generations, relearning our shared language with creation is a slow but essential prayer that draws memory back into the present. Scripture, the tradition, worship, prayer, and other formational practices serve as a kind of grammar for these memories. But the primary teacher in this book is nature itself. Nature, of which we are a part, draws ancient memories and wisdom into the present through a language of its own.

Formation, relationship, family, and language can be difficult: taken seriously, they are in fact disciplines. They require practice, even a little sweat and dirt and blood and trust and disappointment. But one hope I have for this book is that those who are captured by and give attention to nature will be blessed with Jonathan Edwards's "very fruitful brain and copious fancy . . . full of divine things." My prayer is that conscious attentiveness, mindfulness, and open wonder toward nature will bring, not "ridicule and contempt," but patterns of creation practice that lead you closer to its Creator, help you become more familiar with yourself, guide you into recommitted love of neighbor, instill reverence for and companionship with nature, and awaken you to the imperative of creation care.

Toward these ends, *Nature as Spiritual Practice* has four primary goals:

Making Connections with Nature

Humans are material and spiritual beings. Nature is material and spiritual. The material (what I primarily call "ecological" in this book) and the spiritual (what I usually refer to as "sacramental") need each other like a body needs a soul and a soul needs a body. We were formed from material clay and given a soul of divine breath. Humans are thus connected to nature both in their material embodiment and in their spiritual natures: creation and humanity are brothers and sisters of a common parent. Reconnection with nature requires that we relearn this deep kinship between humanity and creation and recognize the organically patterned process through which Christ is reconciling *all things* to God (Col. 1:20).

Recognizing the Creator in the Created

Every leaf and flower bear the marks and give witness to their Creator. Illustrated by Jonathan Edwards, perception of this reality requires contemplative attention, the eyes of the heart, and the wonder of a child. This is not a book on natural theology (proving the existence of God on the basis of nature), nor does it attempt to sort out issues of pantheism (all creation is God) or panentheism (God is in all created things). It is a book that assumes that the glory of the Creator is discernible in creation's ecological, material, sacramental, and spiritual realities.

Participating with Nature as Spiritual Practice

Nature as practice makes us aware of the fact that nature is a formative influence on Christian identity, that nature draws us closer to our true selves and thus closer to God, and that within nature is an imperative of moral response, of earth care. Touching the earth brings solace to the suffering; reconnecting to the earth brings healing, compassion, and ethical engagement; recognizing the Creator in the created leads to praise, worship, and doxology. Thus is spiritual practice as much about contemplation, attention, and prayer as it is about wonder (see below), moral response to nature in the everyday, and praise.

Reawakening Attention, Wonder, and Moral Response

The artist Katharine Houk writes: "My work is re-enchantment. It is about waking up, seeing life and the world anew, creating conditions such that we have an opportunity to experience the grace of our emergent universe."[2] *Nature as Spiritual Practice* seeks to awaken attentiveness in such a way that you may find enchantment surrounding you in nature. In many ways such attentive wonder contains the logic of play. The educator Jerome Berryman says that "[p]reschool children juxtapose bits and pieces of the world and language in novel ways. They associate things by similar sounds or relate events that happen together by chance as being connected by cause and effect."[3] Both attention and wonder, as used in this book, will help us reexperience nature in this enchanted, essentially contemplative way. Adults have an added dimension to such enchantment: you and I will inevitably experience a shift from enchantment to recognition of what this book calls "the dark night of the planet." Yet, in the attention required and the wonder experienced in moral response to ecological degradation, we come full circle, back to the possibility of a renewed, environmentally responsible "earth-enchantment."

2. Cited in Christine Valters Painter, *Illuminating Mystery: Creativity as a Spiritual Practice* (Seattle: Abby of the Arts Press, 2009), 6.

3. Jerome W. Berryman, *Godly Play: A Way of Religious Education* (San Francisco: Harper, 1991), 94-95.

Creation as Practice: How to Use This Book

> *Woven together, Christian practices form a way of life. . . . [Prac-*
> *tices are] like a tree whose branches reach out toward the future,*
> *even when the earth is shaking, because it is nourished by living*
> *water.*
>   Craig Dykstra and Dorothy C. Bass, in *Practicing Our Faith*[4]

Many fine books — both ancient and contemporary — have been written
about practice and spiritual formation. Many equally fine books have been
written on a wide range of subjects having to do with creation, earth, and
nature. Together, this book and the *Field Guide* accompanying it differ
from others in that they present theological, scriptural, historical, and cultural discussions of creation *and* nature-practice.

The interweaving of text (theory) in *Nature as Spiritual Practice* and
practice in both the book and the *Field Guide* reflects an ancient partner-
ship grounded in Greek philosophy, later assimilated in new ways by early
mothers and fathers of the Christian church, and today undergoing long-
neglected retrieval and revival. Practice deepens reflective and critical theory at the same time that theory deepens experiential practice. Together,
they engage mind, body, and spirit in a holistic way that leaves us open and
receptive to the dynamics of change, need, desire, and renewal. This is especially true regarding the formational quality of the natural world, where,
as Bass and Dykstra suggest, participative practices are organic ways of
thinking about and experiencing creation as what creation indeed is: a way
of life.

Field Guides

Traditionally, field guides are books designed to help seek out, find, and
identify particular aspects of creation. There are, for instance, field guides
to help the curious find and identify birds (some by region or song), shells,
butterflies, rocks and minerals, animal tracks, trees and shrubs, reptiles
and amphibians, wildflowers, stars and planets, insects, edible plants,

---

4. Craig Dykstra and Dorothy C. Bass, "A Way of Thinking about a Way of Life," in *Practicing Our Faith: A Way of Life for a Searching People*, ed. Dorothy C. Bass (San Francisco:
Jossey-Bass, 1997), 203.

fishes, weather and clouds, geological forms or structures, mushrooms, and much more. Most are keyed to particular locations and obvious identifying marks. Depending on the field guide, details may include seasons, habitat, species, identifying shapes, colors, sounds and habits, food sources, means of reproduction, means of identifying similar species, and, again, much more. In themselves, field guides are wonderful ways to get out into nature, to begin observing closely, or simply to wander — often noticing characteristics or other aspects of nature within a particular habitat. It is very difficult, for instance, to use a field guide for wildflowers and not notice things like butterflies, insects, seeds, soil composition, birds, and much more.

The *Field Guide to Nature as Spiritual Practice* functions in a similar way to any field guide. It will get you into nature; it will encourage you to pay attention to details large and small; it will awaken curiosity; it will invite you to reacquaint yourself with wonder and astonishment and beauty in nature; it will lead you into wanderings, serendipitous experiences, surprises, perhaps even into getting lost; and it will inform your decisions about how to live responsibly and with care on the earth on which you walk. (Just don't take a nap in the poison ivy!) The *Field Guide*, should you choose to use it, is designed to be taken with you into the "field."

A Word on the Practices[5]

Whether you or I notice it or not, we are always situated in some place within creation. Though contemporary culture does its best to make creation more predictable, at any moment in any place, creation is still capable of shifting, even shattering, our expectations. This organic patterning and chaotic potential are a part of what makes creation such a good teacher. And it is also the reason why each of the practices in this book begins with an "intention." Beginning with an "intention," the practices never have a goal as such. (The shifts and patterns and potentials of nature also preclude a goal: as a first practice, you might ask yourself, "What is the goal of creation?") The practices are suggestions, experiments in spiritual formation, and invitations. After the "intention," nature becomes its own adventure.

---

5. See Appendix A at the back of this book on the nature of specifically Christian practice.

Using Nature as Spiritual Practice *and the* Field Guide *Together*

Note on Organization: In *Nature as Spiritual Practice,* about one-quarter of the suggested practices are given in full. The "title" of the practice and the "intention" of each practice not given in full is also included in *Nature as Spiritual Practice.* The *Field Guide* contains all of the practices in complete form: those given in full in *Nature as Spiritual Practice* and the complete practice for which only the "title" and "intention" are given in *Nature as Spiritual Practice.* You will find that the full practices in the *Field Guide* are arranged in the order you find them in *Nature as Spiritual Practice,* and they are keyed numerically according to the chapters. The arrangement of text and practices will give you maximum flexibility for reading, practice, and prayer at home or school or coffee shop, or for reading, practice, and prayer in nature.

Nature as Spiritual Practice and *Field Guide to Nature as Spiritual Practice* are intended to be read and practiced together, and are integrated in a way that makes this possible. The intentional placement of practices will broaden and enhance understanding and discussion of the text, while textual reflection will, in a circular way, deepen the impact of your experience of the practice.

You will want to find your own schedule and pace for doing the practices and for moving between text and practice. *Nature as Spiritual Practice* can be read straight through as you might read any "regular" book; or you can open it to what interests you and read it in parts. Many of the practices are valuable as reading material even if you do not immediately put them into practice. The reason for this, I think, is twofold: (1) Your creative imagination is a valuable resource for experiencing nature as practice; often, as you read through a practice, you will creatively imagine doing the practice, which in itself will be informative, formative, and experiential. (2) Your memory is also a valuable resource for experiencing nature as practice. Often you can read through a practice that you do not have the time to do right away, or one where you know of a particular location you would like to do the practice at a later date. Later, when you do the practice, memory of the earlier reading will enhance your experience. In addition, you will find many times that, as you explore the natural world, you will remember the practice you have done in the past or have only read, and you may wish to repeat the practice or portions of it even if you do not have the description of the practice with you. Even more serendipitously, in the midst of your time in nature you may suddenly realize that you are in fact doing the practice!

Speaking of serendipity, always allow yourself to be playful with the practices. Assimilate the intention and the details of the practice, follow them, and then allow your attention and wonder to be guided by creation herself. The *Field Guide* is intended to be taken with you into the "field," referred to as needed, then — as with any good field guide — you can essentially forget about it, as attention to, wonder about, and contemplation of nature themselves capture you and begin to guide you. It is my hope that your *Field Guide* will become ragged, torn, dirt-smudged, and berry- or bug-stained over time as you carry it into the field, alternately leafing through it and meditating on it, pocketing it and dropping it, and taking it home for another day. I often fall asleep while reading my field guides to medicinal plants, wildflowers, and trees.

Some practices are intended to be done only once, others over the course of some days or weeks or months, still others over a lifetime. But again, every practice itself is simply a point of entry to be followed only to the point where nature herself begins to guide you. You will want to work through some of the practices systematically; others will be more "organic" in structure. But when you notice that Something Else is guiding you, make it a practice to follow it.

The practices are also flexible with regard to personal or group use. Regardless of how they are described, most of the practices in *Nature as Spiritual Practice* and in the *Field Guide* can be adapted for personal use, for use in small groups, or for use in retreats focused on nature. A sample retreat is provided at the end of the practices in the *Field Guide*.

On Journaling, Photography, Art, Canoeing, Hiking, Identifying

All of us have our own ways of seeing, attending to, and being astonished by nature. One way of thinking about how you can see nature more clearly is to think about a phrase used by Gerald May that I will return to later in the book. May writes that there is something within nature that evokes "the power of the slowing." What he means by this is that, if we give careful attention to nature, it has the ability to slow us down to its pace. (On the other hand, unless manipulated by humans, nature is singularly reluctant to convenience us by stepping up to our pace.) What will help you enter this "power of the slowing" in nature? Ask yourself what slows you down, what helps you pay attention, what cultivates a contemplative form of listening and seeing and hearing and responding. For some, journaling is a powerful way to pay careful attention to nature and also provides a record of nature experiences and practices. For others, photography works in much the same way, using different powers of the senses, mind, and concentration. Still others find that canoeing or hiking develops the power of the slowing. Artistic drawing helps others, while still others are brought into the power of the slowing by gardening or by bird watching or using a field guide to identify wildflowers or trees. Different forms of prayer, meditation, and contemplation in nature slow us down to the pace and rhythms of nature. You may find that chopping wood or watching rain brings on the power of the slowing. There are many, many possibilities.

Since there are so many possibilities and so many personalities, my suggestion of journaling in *Nature as Spiritual Practice* and in the *Field Guide* is a kind of a code that invites you to do any of the many possible things that help you most easily enter the power of the slowing.

"Creation" and "Nature" as Used in This Book

In this book, city and nature are not antithetical. Nature thrives in cities; cities are enhanced by nature; and God is present in both. "Creation" and "nature" are used in the broadest possible sense in this book. This means that when the text and the practices refer to nature or creation, it is just as legitimate to think of them being embodied in a city park as it is in the Gates of the Arctic National Park in northern Alaska. It can be just as potentially formative to work in a backyard garden as it is to contemplate or write about a tree growing in Brooklyn. Thus, whether it be on farms or in city parks, on cross-country ski trails through national forests, from the remotest wilderness area to what remains of the North American Midwest prairie, you can encounter and interact with "creation" and "nature" in the ways *Nature as Spiritual Practice* intends: as local, personal, relational, experiential, material, sensual, spiritual, and as "fruit" for the imagination, memory, intellect, body, creativity, and moral integrity. There will be a different tone to a remote wilderness than there will be to your own backyard, but both join you in creation and nature.

Using This Book for Personal Practice

Depending on your own personality, needs, interests, "smarts" (see below), and desires at this time in your life, you can read this book organically or systematically. You may choose to read a section or do a practice as they attract you for whatever reason (organically), or you may choose to read through a chapter or set of sections from beginning to end, taking time to do the practices as they are arranged (systematically). You will probably find that some combination of these two approaches is most helpful. With text or practice, you may initially pick several practices and do them over time, returning to the text as you feel the need; or you may expand one exercise over the duration of a few days or weeks or months. However you proceed, you will soon become aware that, though your experience may be personal, it is never personal in the sense of being individual or isolated: creation practice teaches that personal identity formation is also always formation in community.

It is also important to speak aloud your formational encounter with creation. Sharing what we learn and experience in nature is often difficult, because we have neglected the spiritual arts of these connective practices in nature for so long. But in sharing and verbalizing your journey, you will begin to experience the heartbeat of nature as a vast web of connection. Ideally, you will have a friend, pastor, spiritual director, spouse, or group with whom you can begin exploring how to communicate and refine your kinship with nature. You may wish to begin each exercise acknowledging your desire to grow in connection with nature, yourself, others, and God. You can do this in prayer, or through some ritual, or via a simple acknowledgment of your intention before God.

Spiritual practice in nature changes and transforms the mind and body and soul. As I have observed above, it is not the practice that instigates change and transformation: it is the spirit of Christ working through creation. The organic reality of nature disassembles even our best intentions. Therefore, the intention of this book is really to learn to let go of our intentions and to embrace creation's more dynamic, organic ways of being.

Finally, in your own way, know and believe that the divine is accompanying you on this journey of formation and discovery.

Using This Book with Multiple Ways of Learning

Each of the practices in this book is intended to be very flexible, especially with respect to the different ways of learning that are unique to each person. The now widely accepted theory of multiple intelligences, developed in 1983 by Howard Gardner, a professor of education at Harvard University, came about largely as a result of his dissatisfaction with the standard IQ tests that measure only certain ways of knowing or learning. Gardner instead proposes seven types of learning or intelligences to account for the broader range of human ways of knowing. The simple and quick evaluation instrument provided in Appendix B will help you assess the two or three intelligence types (or "smarts") that best describe how you learn and understand the world around you. As you work through the practices, allow your own particular ways of processing information to guide you in following the practices as given or, perhaps, adapting them in ways that are better suited to your own "smarts."[6]

Since humans access nature in so many individual ways, it is not surprising that Gardner has, since his earlier work, suggested an eighth intelligence: "nature smart" (naturalist intelligence). Work in this type of intelligence has just begun, but Leslie Owen Wilson, of the University of Wisconsin, has developed a list of descriptors for this eighth kind of intelligence.[7] Wilson finds that people who are "nature smart" have keen sensory skills, including sight, sound, smell, taste, and touch, that help them notice and categorize things from the natural world. They enjoy outside activities such as gardening, nature walks, or field trips geared toward observing nature or natural phenomena, and they readily notice patterns from their surroundings — differences, similarities, and anomalies. People who are "nature smart" notice things in the environment that others often miss. Such people show heightened awareness of and concern for the environment and endangered species, for example, and they easily learn characteristics, names, categorizations, and data about objects or species found in the natural world.

The text and practices in this book are intended to exercise our "nature smarts" in ways that contribute to Christian identity formation. Once again, be creative with your practice and your time in nature. Allow your own "multiple intelligences" to interact with your growing "nature smarts" in ways that serve to reconnect you with the entirety of creation.

---

6. "Nature smarts" was not included in the original seven types of intelligences and so is not a part of the inventory in Appendix B.

7. The descriptors are listed in Richard Louv, *The Last Child in the Woods: Saving Our Children from Nature-Deficit Disorder* (Chapel Hill, NC: Algonquin Books, 2005), 72-73. Chap. 6 in Louv's book (pp. 70-84) is devoted to this eighth intelligence.

Using This Book in Group Settings

Meaning in the natural world is often found in solitude. But meaning in the natural world is also often found in community, which is not surprising, given creation's own intricate, communal webs of meaning. The gentle movement between solitude and community is a foundational lesson of creation: transition, as nature teaches, is a practice. The practices in this book can and should be exercised in solitude and also as a part of a community or group as needed. Practices can be adapted to either personal explorations or group settings. Whether entirely personal, initially personal with later "processing" in small groups, or practiced and processed in community, the practices can be formed to fit the needs of church or parish education and formation, academic courses, or personal or group retreats. The material is intended for the laity, pastors, priests, rabbis, and religious educators as well as undergraduate, seminary, or graduate courses, or anyone with an awakening sense of the mystery and pattern of creation. Regardless of who receives them, the gifts of nature will also, inevitably, raise awareness of and commitment to creation care, ecological restoration, and lifestyles that honor and sustain creation resources. For retreats — personal or group — the practices can be grouped in any number of ways that will help focus and deepen the broader intention of the retreat. A sample retreat is suggested in the *Field Guide*.

If you are facilitating a retreat or the use of practices in a group setting, identify the relative need for text (theory) and practice (experience) that is most appropriate for your group. Take some time to think about "learner outcomes," but do not be tied to these. Nature is one place where agendas and learner outcomes are entirely unpredictable. Also, if you are leading the group, be familiar with the details of the practice so that you can explain them clearly to participants. It will be most helpful for each participant to have the *Field Guide to Nature as Spiritual Practice* to refer to during any given practice and *Nature as Spiritual Practice* as a tool to help participants begin to think about the implications of their experience in nature. It is often helpful to gather in a circle beforehand to read the complete practice, to let everyone know the time frame for a particular practice, and to pray. If your group is covenanting to explore creation practice or formation over time, offer one or two practices to be done between meetings and discuss the participants' experience of these at the next gathering. Whatever the structure of your group, it is important to find a balance between opportunities to spend time in solitude in nature, opportunities to move from experiences of solitude to a processing of those experiences with others, and opportunities to reflect on the experiences by reading and discussing *Nature as Spiritual Practice.*

For processing practices: (1) ensure that each participant can commit to the entire process to allow sufficient trust to be built; (2) allow all to contribute actively, but maintain boundaries that are appropriate and safe; (3) allow all group members to share equally in discussion or processing; (4) do not offer advice or try to "fix" another's perspective or ideas; and (5) maintain strict group confidentiality.

The most important aspect of the dynamics of doing and processing spiritual practice in groups is the art of contemplative listening, which is essential both in nature and when gathered together in a group. What Elizabeth Liebert writes about contemplative listening in groups can also be applied to "listening" to creation: "Contemplative listening seeks to honor the presence of the Holy Spirit in the speaker and between listener and speaker. Such listening rests in warm, loving, engaged, and prayerful silence, which often needs few or no words."[8] You will find that creation, too, has much to teach you about listening.

Finally, as with any practice or retreat, factor in time for "wandering," that is, rest with no agenda at all. Nature will provide one! And the most important thing to remember in using this material is to turn your hunger for a deepening relationship with God . . . toward nature. In doing so, you will find that creation shares exactly the same hunger.

---

8. Elizabeth Liebert, *The Way of Discernment: Spiritual Practices for Decision Making* (Louisville: Westminster John Knox, 2008), xix. Liebert's introduction contains an excellent section on participating in and leading retreats.

On Earth as It Is

CHAPTER ONE

"Thy Will Be Done, on Earth as It Is . . ."

For no part of Creation is left void of Him [Christ, Word of God].

Athanasius, *On the Incarnation of the Word*[1]

As a part of the prayer that Jesus taught, "on earth as it is" stops just short of the eschatological, heavenly hope. Without denying this eschatological dimension, this book is focused "on earth as it is." Not only is "earth as it is" good enough; it is all we have at present. And it is much in need of attention and reverence — just "as it is." What has been given us, what we have, and what we pass on to future generations is "earth as it is."

In the sections and practices that follow, we will explore how attention to creation and a reawakening of the capacity for wonder in creation forms and shapes Christian identity. In the process we will explore how God abides in places within creation and how nature itself is spiritual practice. Nature is too often ignored or forgotten in contemporary culture; in this book she will be our primary teacher and guide.

The more time we spend in the natural world, the more we recognize that nature herself, "on earth as it is," directs and guides formation, discernment, and healing. As Athanasius says in the above quotation, "No part of creation is left void of the Word of God." We participate with creation in formation, discernment, and healing in ways similar to our participation in Christ. Jesus himself lived and died "on earth as it is." Today, as

---

1. Athanasius, *On the Incarnation of the Word (De Incarnatione Verbi Dei)*, 8.1, 8.3, in Philip Schaff, ed., *Nicene and Post-Nicene Fathers*, 2nd ser. (New York: The Christian Literature Company, 1892), 4:40, 41.

we are branches from a vine, this same Christ still abides within us: "I am the true vine, and my Father is the vine grower. . . . Abide in me as I abide in you. Just as the branch cannot bear fruit by itself unless it abides in the vine, neither can you unless you abide in me" (John 15:1, 4). The very words of Jesus' teaching and hope originate in and are etched with ordinary images of this "earth as it is."

PRACTICE 1.1

Ah!

INTENTION   The intention of this practice is to begin to notice and respond to nature "on earth as it is."

PRACTICE   The theologian Dorothée Sölle identifies five possible "responses on seeing a flower":

> Ah!
> Oh, beautiful — I want it, but I will let it be!
> Oh, beautiful — I want it, I will take it!
> Oh, beautiful — I can sell it!
> So?[2]

- Find something in the natural world that captures your attention or recall your past experiences. Reflect honestly on how you respond to this object: in other words, how do you "respond on seeing a flower"?
- The following are key concepts developed in this and the chapters that follow. How, at this time, do each of the following affect your possible responses to nature?
  - No part of creation is left void of the Word of God.
  - There is no place we can learn but from the place itself.
  - Creation is both seen (ecological and material) and unseen (sacramental and relational).
  - Every creature knows its Creator and reaches back to the Lord.
  - If we listen, we find that nature has its own way of speaking.
  - We are accustomed to separating nature and human perception into two realms; they are, in fact, indivisible.

---

2. Dorothée Sölle, *Christianity and Crisis,* cited in Nancy Roth, *Organic Prayer: A Spiritual Gardening Companion* (New York: Seabury Books, 2007), 114.

- Today the earth is suffering.
- At the same time that the earth is suffering, it still provides healing, solace, and guidance.
- Christ is not here (within the tomb where he was laid) because he is now everywhere.
- How would you *like* to respond to creation — "on earth as it is"?

God Resides in Places

There is no way to learn to live in a place but from the place itself.
Freeman House, *Totem Salmon*

The scientist and environmentalist Freeman House lives "on earth as it is" with an intensity of connection to nature that is rare. His passion and work brings him in close contact with the wild salmon of the Columbia River watershed. The salmon themselves and salmon ecology serve as his teachers and guides. Creation guides and forms him so thoroughly in the art of attention that he slowly becomes conscious of how creation itself affects how he sees and hears and feels. Having spent hours, days, weeks, even years with the salmon, he is conscious of how nature shapes and forms even the way he perceives the world around him. They form, he says, "empathy . . . the long practice of cumulative attentiveness . . . reciprocal perception," and "there is no way to learn to live in a place but from the place itself."[3] Rainer Maria Rilke, in his own more poetic way, writes of this same reciprocity and in so doing manages to make even the ordinary sacred. Of the creatures of the earth he writes: "[Y]ou built a temple deep inside their hearing."[4] In *Nature as Spiritual Practice*, we will find that the Christian tradition — as well as our own experience and knowledge — also points toward cumulative attentiveness and reciprocal perception in which we are called to hear with our ears, where God has created a holy temple deep within our own hearing.

In nature, God resides in places. It is simultaneously true, however, that

3. Freeman House, *Totem Salmon: Life Lessons from Another Species* (Boston: Beacon Press, 1999), 99.

4. Rainer Maria Rilke, *The Sonnets to Orpheus,* in *Ahead of All Parting: The Selected Poetry and Prose of Rainer Maria Rilke,* trans. Stephen Mitchell (New York: Modern Library, 1995), 411.

while God resides *in* places, the same God is *beyond* all residing, beyond any place. Nature thus has its hand in divine paradox and mystery. In theological terms, God in and at the same time beyond all places is stated in terms of God's simultaneous immanence and transcendence.

Theologians are accustomed to making necessary adjustments and fine-tuning theology as it bends and swerves through the centuries, and so it is with the mystery of immanence and transcendence. In patristic and medieval times, theologians often smoothed over this paradox by using the metaphor of "the bridge of Christ," which crossed the chasm between heaven and earth, between immanence and transcendence. But as this bridge began to collapse in the early seventeenth century, as theologian William Placher has written, "since they [theologians] did not want to think of God as utterly beyond their comprehension, they thought of God's otherness in terms of distance and remoteness from the world."[5] Distance and remoteness are transcendent characteristics of God, and for the most part, since the early seventeenth century, divine transcendence has been emphasized at the expense of divine immanence. But distance and remoteness are less satisfactory visions of God than the paradox it tries to solve.

More recent writers, such as theologian Kathryn Tanner, have reestablished the balance, speaking of divine immanence, in Tanner's felicitous phrase, as "God's positive fellowship with the world." Tanner, in effect, helps us see divine immanence and transcendence from the human perspective of relationship rather than reason. Her perspective of relationship helps to make even transcendence amenable to relationship. She adds that "a radical transcendence does not exclude God's positive fellowship with the world or presence within it. God's transcendence alone [over against created beings, who risk losing distinctiveness in relationship] is one that may be properly exercised in the radical immanence by which God is said to be nearer to us than we are to ourselves."[6] Humans risk loss of identity in intimacy; God does not. God resides in places — closer to us than we are to ourselves — while at the same time retaining that identity of being radically "other" than creation.

Nature as spiritual and formational practice begins to take shape as we

5. William C. Placher, *The Domestication of Transcendence: How Modern Thinking about God Went Wrong* (Louisville: Westminster John Knox, 1996), 111.

6. Kathryn Tanner, *God and Creation in Christian Theology: Tyranny or Empowerment* (Oxford: Basil Blackwell, 1988), 79.

participate in a God who is both placed and placeless — in theological terms, both immanent and transcendent. Such practice is possible precisely because we experience personal *sharing* in the divine intimacy of God's residing in places. Another way of saying this is that practice in nature is "solitude shared," which is another rational paradox, but not a relational one. The great medieval theologian Thomas Aquinas speaks of "solitude shared" in this way: "[A]ll things other than God are not their own being, but are beings by participation [in God] . . . for whatever is found in anything by participation, must be caused in it by that to which it belongs essentially, as iron becomes ignited by fire."[7] Just as a person's being or essence is intimate with itself — you are intimate with yourself, I am intimate with myself — so God is intimate to each person or thing of creation. God resides in places where even solitude is found, in places where divine intimacy is shared.

PRACTICE 1.2

God Resides in Places: Attention as Contemplative Prayer

INTENTION In this section we learned that God is simultaneously transcendent (beyond all things) and immanent (known through all things). This practice focuses on the immanent nature of the divine, with the intention of assimilating the phrase "God resides in places" on an experiential level and to allow the experience to become prayer.

Creation Consoles

> *I will be like the dew to Israel;*
> *he shall blossom like the lily,*
> *he shall strike root like the forests of Lebanon.*
> *His shoots shall spread out;*
> *his beauty shall be like the olive tree,*
> *and his fragrance like that of Lebanon.*

---

7. Thomas Aquinas, *Summa Theologica*, I, q. 44, art. 1, trans. Fathers of the English Dominican Province (London: Burns, Oates and Washbourne, 1921), vol. 2, 214.

They shall again live beneath my shadow,
  they shall flourish as a garden;
they shall blossom like the vine,
  their fragrance shall be like the wine of Lebanon.

Hosea 14:5-7

This beautiful passage from the prophet Hosea is a fountain overflowing with images of hope and well-being and abundance — all drawn from creation. Each line contains objects, places, and sensations in nature that taken together recreate in our minds and hearts a second — more hopeful — garden of Eden. We are captured by this word picture of beauty and peace, a beauty and peace that we recognize in part because, though not in its completeness, we have already experienced it here "on earth as it is."

There is another aspect of this passage, another mood that nature can evoke or capture. I am fortunate — even privileged — that, as a part of my responsibilities at the seminary where I teach, I also do individual and group spiritual direction. On one particular occasion, during a group spiritual direction session, a participant told us of her week of grief and sorrow. The group sat with her sorrow and gently explored her grief in the context of her spiritual journey. During our time together, someone asked the group, almost offhandedly, where each of us went — a physical place we could name — when we felt sorrow, grief, loss, or pain. Though I know it was not the original intent of the question, in a very short time the question provoked what became an avalanche of conversation, all of it focused on nature. One student said that when she felt sadness or grief, she invariably made her way to a certain wilderness place where she knew she would not be disturbed, where the earth, the vegetation, the cyclical dynamics of growth, decay, death, and resurrection seemed to absorb her sorrow. Another student said he would always go to water; pressed, the student specified the ocean as the place where he felt most safe with his sorrow, where he could even share it in a way that comforted him and, as he said, even seemed to comfort the waves and beach. Yet another student remembered that only rivers really functioned to sweep away pain or loss or grief. And another student said that he found solace as a little boy for the early loss of his mother when he was with his father hiking and camping in the desert in the far northeastern corner of his state. The exploration continued throughout that session and, I know, after and beyond it.

All members of that group, normally highly verbal and relational with other people, had at certain times in their lives found silence and solitude shared in nature in ways that provided space for solace, absorbed sorrow, and brought some consolation for grief and loss. As Hosea demonstrates, creation is a place of beauty and hope, and perhaps precisely because of that, it is also a natural place for mourning, grief, sadness, and sorrow.

Gerald May, a contemplative psychoanalyst, also knows of the formative, healing, and consoling power of creation. As May was writing his last book, which he entitled *Wisdom of Wilderness,* he knew he was dying. Toward the end of the book, with barely enough strength but with a soul newly tuned to the wild, May speaks of digging a shallow hole in loamy soil, a hole just large enough to surround and enclose him comfortably. He settles into this hole and experiences it, he writes, as both a womblike memory and as a tomblike embrace. In a very real sense, the earth is womb and tomb for all creation on earth. Reminding us of the Latin word *humus* (meaning "earth" or "ground"), May goes on to say that in this experience of being embraced by the earth, he became simultaneously truly human and truly humble.[8] In his experience of the human and the humble, of the womb and the tomb, he found deep and abiding consolation in the face of his impending death.

PRACTICE 1.3

Consolation, Grief, and Loss

INTENTION   The intention of this practice is to recover in your memory places in nature you have gone for consolation and to return there or find new places in the natural world that comfort you.

PRACTICE   There are two aspects of this practice that are important to notice: (1) where you go when you feel pain, suffering, or loss; (2) noticing what about nature has the ability to "consume" grief, bringing comfort, calm, equilibrium, and peace.

- Recall places or a place in nature where in the past you have gone when you were feeling sadness or grief. If you can't think of a particular place, recall the last few times you were sad, then think back, remembering places you went during that time.

8. Gerald G. May, *The Wisdom of Wilderness: Experiencing the Healing Power of Nature* (San Francisco: HarperSanFrancisco, 2006), 180.

- As you look back, is there a particular landscape or part of creation that comforts you during times of grief and loss? What is the most consoling environment you have experienced?
- What is it about a particular place that attracts you when you are sad, in mourning, or hurting? Simply recall places you have been with nature in sadness. Recall what you were doing at the time: walking, sitting, running, writing, kayaking, crying, photographing. Again, what part of your grief was absorbed by this place in nature?
- If you can, return to this place if it is near. What does it feel like to you now, and what do you notice about it?
- We all suffer grief or loss, more so at certain periods in our lives, less at other times. Consciously seek a place in nature that soothes and comforts you. You may find yourself on a bench in a city park, or aggressively chopping wood, or gathering blackberries, or sitting on a beach.
- Notice how nature "sits" with you as it consoles and comforts. How is nature an active partner in consolation? Nature may calm; it may help put into perspective a particular sorrow; its very "isness," or presence, may redirect sorrow in a healing direction. Let yourself absorb this healing. How did — or does — nature bring solace? How would you describe or communicate it?
- How can you be present to another person in the way nature has been present to you in sorrow? How can you be present to nature in the same way?

On the Constant Work of Sustaining Shells and Dragonflies

If God should take back her spirit to herself, and gather to herself her breath, all flesh would perish together, and all mortals return to dust.

Job 34:14-15

Spiritual theologians have listened closely to nature. One of nature's most primary formational lessons is that God is so thoroughly engaged in the world that were God to withdraw, the universe would cease to be. It would collapse. As the book of Job puts it, if God should withdraw God's Spirit or breath, all flesh would perish and in an instant all "mortals return to dust." Creation is divinely sustained moment to moment to moment: "[F]or from him and through him and to him are all things" (Rom. 11:36). In the seventh century, Pseudo-Dionysius said that "God is the Source and the Cause of all life and of all being, for out of God's goodness God commands all things to be and keeps them going."[9] For the Reformer John Calvin, not only did God create the universe, God is still in the process of creating it, "constantly at work" sustaining, governing, and cherishing creation: "For it is certain that inasmuch as God sustains the world by his power, governs it by his providence, cherishes and even propagates all creatures, he is constantly at work."[10] Calvin adds that creation is sustained in and through the fact that it is constantly praising God, and "if God should withdraw his hand a little, all things would immediately perish and dissolve into nothing."[11]

Contemporary writers, too, catch something of the importance of this divine, constant work that is so essential, lest we perish and dissolve into nothing. David Abram reminds us of the sustaining power of sacred breath in Hebrew cosmology when he writes that "sacred breath enters not just into human beings, . . . it also animates and sustains the whole of the sensible world. . . . [W]ithout the continual outflow of God's breath, all of the letters that stand within the things of this world — all the letter combinations embodied in particular animals, plants, and stones — would be . . . extinguished."[12]

All this is fairly abstract until we actually join our own hearts to nature in place and space and time. Let's say, for instance, that I find myself walking on a beach and pause to pick up a shell. I hold the shell in my hands, note its shape and coloring, imagine that it was a tiny house for some small sea creature for some short time, a refuge, a stronghold, a place to dwell. If I am lucky, the shell is relatively new to the beach and not too worn, and I can look at and feel intricate detail, sublime symmetries, precise whorls and spirals. Even if it is worn by wave and sand and wind, such a shell still holds its own kind of degenerating beauty.

And I pause to realize that, were the sacred breath not at work constantly to sustain this tiny shell and bless and keep it, it would collapse into

9. Pseudo-Dionysius, *The Divine Names*, in *Pseudo-Dionysius: The Complete Works*, trans. Colm Luibheid (New York: Paulist Press, 1987), 3:51.

10. John Calvin, *Commentaries on the First Book of Moses Called Genesis*, trans. John King, *Calvin's Commentaries* (Grand Rapids: Baker, 1989), 1:103.

11. Calvin, *Commentaries on Genesis*, 1:103.

12. David Abram, *The Spell of the Sensuous: Perception and Language in a More-Than-Human World* (New York: Pantheon Books, 1996), 246.

nothing in an instant. In fact, the collapsing would not even be in an "instant," since God is also constantly at work sustaining instants, sustaining time.

Or here is a second example. I love to watch dragonflies as they dart and hover around the edges of lakes, along riverbanks and over wetlands. I don't know a lot about them, but they do always delight me when I see them. And how they can fly! Better and quicker than any human-constructed helicopters: they zig this way, then zag that way, reverse their course from any angle, hover stock-still, then shoot backward, alight on some water lily, cattail, or blade of wild rice, then in an instant catapult up, down, right, left — this way or that. Their colors are brilliantly electric and varied, partly, I think, because of the way sunlight reflects off their bodies (and as shadowed souls to their bodies, through their wings) at different angles as they change course with such speed. As quickly as I see their colors, they are usually gone, and though I have tried many times to catch a dragonfly in my hands, I have never come close. They are quicker than houseflies — and much quicker than my hands.

I usually forget that every wingbeat, every new and quick direction change, every slight shadow they etch across the water, every sheen of color, every mating in every new season, even every tiny, tiny breath gathered into and expelled from minute lungs — all are gathered and sustained in the hands of God's constant creating. Out of some goodness and beauty and truth beyond imagining, God breathes into the nostrils of each living dragonfly, governing, cherishing, embodying, and making of each a prayer. I found this old Hasidic prayer:

> See your prayer as arousing the letters
>   through which heaven and earth
>   and all living things were created.
> The letters are the life of all;
>   when you pray through them,
>   all Creation joins with you in prayer.
> All that is around you can be uplifted;
>   even the song of a passing bird
>   may enter into such a prayer.

The Fertility of Silence

INTENTION   One of the beautiful antiphons of Lent is: "May the fertility of silence give life and power to our words and deeds — Lord, give us hope." In this section I have suggested that creation is a kind of "visible hope" that emerges and is sustained by God out of what we might call a "fertility of silence." In this practice we meditate on what it might be like if this were not the case.

Scripture and Nature: Stories Told Together

> *But ask the animals, and they will teach you;*
> *the birds of the air, and they will tell you;*
> *ask the plants of the earth, and they will teach you;*
> *and the fish of the sea will declare to you.*
>
> Job 12:7-8

Throughout this book we will see how Scripture is saturated on virtually every page with the Creator's creation. Yet even people very familiar with Scripture often miss this central role that creation plays. The earth/creation/nature is, in fact, a *major* character in the drama of God's people. Scripture draws not only on images and messages from the natural world; it describes for us a creation inebriated with love, intoxicated with longing and joy, and in constant praise for its Creator. Creation can even teach us, in fact, what Paul's injunction to "pray without ceasing" (1 Thess. 5:17) means: creation is constant prayer. Creation is also a place of mourning: as Paul says in Romans 8, it is actively groaning; it is a place in bondage to decay. Perhaps it is this very reason — that creation itself is so practiced in mourning — that enables nature to become a place of consolation that so willingly and without condition absorbs human grief and loss and pain. Scripture tells the story of a people always on the move *from* a land, *through* a land, *to* a land. Through this story Scripture gives us new eyes to read nature just as nature herself provides new and fresh ways to read Scripture. Both narrate a story of God and God's ways, one to the other.

Many people would say that they love Scripture. In Scripture we learn that creation is not an object; it is a subject, something to be loved and something that gives love in return. What else should we expect from a creation sustained and redeemed by Love? The poet Wendell Berry captures this subjective quality of nature that draws us into Love:

> When despair for the world grows in me
> and I wake in the night at the least sound
> in fear of what my life and my children's lives may be,
> I go and lie down where the wood drake
> rests in his beauty on the water, and the great heron feeds.
> I come into the peace of wild things
> who do not tax their lives with forethought
> of grief. I come into the presence of still water.
> And I feel above me the day-blind stars
> waiting with their light. For a time
> I rest in the grace of the world, and am free.
>
> Wendell Berry, "The Peace of Wild Things"

PRACTICE 1.5

God Was Pleased

> Do you not say, "Four months more, then comes the harvest"? But I tell you, look around you, and see how the fields are ripe for harvesting.
>
> John 4:35

INTENTION   Scripture and nature tell God's story, one to the other. In this passage from John, Jesus sees all things two ways, simultaneously: he sees both what is and what will be. He sees "ripeness" now, and he sees the "ripeness" of the harvest time. Notice that Christ communicates this "double vision" via a story that includes nature and her seasons. In fact, this "double vision" is possible only through a reciprocating attention between the book of nature and the book of Scripture. As an example of "double vision" made possible by the intersection between Scripture and nature, the intention of this practice is to participate in Jesus' own "double-sighted" vision of creation.

PRACTICE   Meditate on the above passage from John 4. Notice that, though Jesus recognizes that the harvest will arrive in four months, he also sees that in some important way these same fields are already ripe for harvesting now!

- Walk into the natural world into a place that attracts you. Spend time there noting the season, noting when leaves may fall or berries may become ripe or the first snow may fall — sometime in the future. In doing so, you are a human engaged in the cycles of creation. In exactly the same way, Christ was a human engaged in the cycles of the seasons.
- Now take a closer look around you. What is "ripe for harvesting" now? One way to put this metaphor plainly is: What do you experience as sacred (ripe) now? How can you be present, as was Jesus, to creation in both her ecological and sacramental realities? It might help to recall Moses' experience with the burning bush: it was on fire, yet the bush was not consumed. The bush remained precisely what it was ecologically even as it raged with a fire of the sacred. Practice experiencing nature in this way. It may also help, as it did for Moses, to remove your shoes.
- Again, Jesus sees the time of natural harvesting in four months at the same time that he points out the sacred harvest of the field here and now. Practice joining Jesus in this "dual vision" of creation.
- How do the "double stories" of Scripture and creation help complete this vision?

CHAPTER TWO

Definitions and Intentions

"Nature," "Earth," and "Creation" in *Nature as Spiritual Practice*

Seemingly simple, a mountain can be difficult to define. Just one single mountain can mean many things, depending on the context. To an indigenous people, the mountain is sacred history and ecology; to a mining company, it is a valuable commodity; to a highway engineer, it is an obstacle; to a vacationer, it is a much-needed place of quiet and peace; to a bird watcher, it is a chance to catch sight of a rare bird; to a biologist, it is a unique ecosystem to preserve and study; to a hunter, it is prime location for deer; to an astronomer, it is a unique location free of "light pollution"; to a lumberjack, it is a paycheck; to a conservationist, it is the last preserve of a rare and elsewhere extinct species of owl; to a farmer, it is perfect soil, altitude, and climate for a certain crop; to a monk, it is a hermitage; to an otherwise drab city, it is a singular reminder of beauty and hope.

If it is difficult to define a mountain — and we have just begun. How can we possibly define something much more complex, like the "earth"? Obviously, a definitive answer is not possible. Certain words and ideas are just difficult to pin down. Reams of paper and much ink, for instance, have been devoted to a discussion of the meaning of words such as "nature," "earth," "creation," "place," "land," "landscape," "space," "wilderness," "geography," and "ecology." These definitions and distinctions are important, but they need not be hard and fast for the purposes of this book. (Readers interested in exploring distinctions that have been made between these terms will find a list of resources in Appendix C.)

I have maintained just a few important distinctions between "nature," "earth," and "creation" in this book. In both the practices and the text, "nature" refers only to the planet earth with its surrounding biosphere (and whatever comes into contact with the planet from the universe). In both the practices and the text, "earth" might best be experienced as both that planet photographed from the Apollo missions as a blue-and-white sphere against a backdrop of black and as that place where you live and walk. And likewise in both practices and text, "creation" refers both to the planet and to the entire created order: the universe, the cosmos. Theologically, "creation" carries an explicit reference to its Creator, Redeemer, and Sustainer — the triune God of Abraham and Sarah — whereas "nature" may or may not. Both "nature" and "creation" include humanity.

PRACTICE 2.1

Finding a Place Not Sacred?

INTENTION   One of the real disagreements in discussions about "nature," "earth," and "creation" is about what is sacred in these places and what is not. This practice involves a few simple imaginary games: (1) to suggest that we can, in fact, choose to find the sacred in nature; (2) to suggest that from a certain perspective, through attentiveness or awareness, it is possible to recognize that any created place is sacred; and (3) to suggest that an "ordinary" place is "ordinary" only because we participate in it in an "ordinary" way.

Ecology: The Household of the World

In a beautifully written and illustrated book on the great prairie regions of the Northern Hemisphere, Candice Savage teaches as much about natural history as she does about the modern meaning of "ecology."[1] After detailing the sadly stark decimation of Great Plains ecology, she reminds us that we cannot really blame our European ancestors for lack of ecological

---

1. The majority of the discussion that follows on "ecology" is adapted from Candace Savage, *Prairie: A Natural History* (Vancouver/Toronto/Berkeley: Greystone Books, 2004), 19-29.

awareness: "ecology" as we know it had not yet been invented. The science of the period of greatest ecological devastation of the prairies was more focused on fixing life to a pin — with species laid out, labeled, and safely dead, in straight rows and separate compartments — than with anything that we would today think of as ecological science.

Around the middle of the nineteenth century, things slowly began to change. In 1866, the German physician and philosopher Ernst Haeckel joined together two Greek root words — *oikos* (meaning "household") and *ologie*, (meaning "study of") — to describe what turned out to be a radical new approach to the study of the natural world. Haeckel described his new approach as "the study of natural selection in action; the investigation of the total relations of the animal both to its inorganic and organic environment." In other words, the essence of life did not lie in a static, pinned species but in this tangled web of interconnections that was, in effect, more home ("household") than microscope.

Ecology truly began as a science when Frederic Clements began to ground the new field in observation and hands-on evidence — two poles of classic empiricism. In a study published in 1916, he concluded that the prairie was a self-healing system in which, given the chance, groups of plants grew back in an orderly sequence, each wave creating the conditions required for the next, until the vegetation once again reached a stable condition. Based on his observations, Clements argued that not only the Great Plains grasslands but the entire living world was sustained by these self-organized, internally motivated processes of renewal.

The study of "ecology" was bolstered when Arthur Tansley, in 1935, introduced the concept of the "ecosystem": the idea that the earth operates as a series of self-organized complexes in which all components (both living and nonliving) are linked. Tansley's real advancement was his integration of the study of nature with new advances in math and systems theory. Previously only described in terms of "relationship" or "community," ecology suddenly gained respect and functional support through the vocabulary of the physical sciences. Tansley himself wrote that "the systems we isolate mentally are not only included as parts of larger ones, but they also overlap, interlock and interact with one another." The task of trying to map these complex, adaptive, open, nonlinear, overlapping, and fluid systems remains a major preoccupation of ecologists.

Ecosystem Game

INTENTION Arthur Tansley writes that ecological systems "are not only included as parts of larger ones, but they also overlap, interlock and interact with one another." Using a group ecosystem game, the intent of this practice is to experience ecology as an interdependent, self-organizing, internally motivated, and interlocking system.

What Is Christian Practice?

Christian Formation

Christian formation is a function of Christian practice. And Christian formation is as notoriously difficult to define as, say, nature. One way of thinking about spiritual formation is as personal formation that has as its goal conscious awareness of the presence of God through ministry to others. Or even more simply, personal formation is a process of being present to others through ministry. Given the dynamics of Christian practice, formation is an open-ended journey that happens over time. Christian practice is more "immediate," more "primal"; practice can be thought of as a "first-order experience," while formation is a "second-order experience." "Experience" of any kind is also a notoriously slippery concept, but *Nature as Spiritual Practice* intends the more immediate "first-order" experience of practice. Since formation in creation happens and is often seen more clearly as the "result" of practice, a few words on Christian formation will help clarify what this book means by *practice*.

Two basic, contrasting methods are evident in the history and practice of Christian formation. One method has particular goals and purposes: to "form" a functioning, devoted, active member of a specific religious community or way of life. That is, its function is to "form" a Methodist or to "form" a Roman Catholic Benedictine monk or to "form" a Lutheran or to "form" a Romanian Orthodox layperson. Betraying my preference, I refer to this method as "formation by constriction": it takes into account few of the unique qualities and gifts of persons and communities. A second method I refer to as "formation by liberation," where "liberation" refers to the freedom of persons or communities to grow and *trans*-form into the persons they are created to be. This second method thus liberates the true self as an image of God, likewise liberates the true self in community, and frees the true community to blossom and to grow in the "sun" of divine love through ministry to others, whether those others be humans or nature. Though these two methods, in fact, never function independently of each other, this latter, more organic, method is much closer to the method of formation delivered and taught by nature itself.

Values Orientation and Nature

The researchers Florence Kluckhohn and Fred Strodtbeck have worked to develop models of values orientation that direct human actions related to common human relationships. These, in turn, have significance for the meaning of spiritual practice.[2] One of the five primary relationships confronting all cultures, according to these researchers, is the relationship between humans and nature.[3] Accordingly, all cultures approach the human/nature issue in one or more of three ways:

1. *Subjugation to nature:* humans have no control over nature and are subject to the inevitable effects of nature.
2. *Harmony with nature:* humans are united with nature in a precarious balance so that their actions affect nature and themselves in turn.
3. *Mastery over nature:* Nature is made up of impersonal objects and forces that humans can or should manipulate for their own purposes.

In the first approach, humans feel helpless against nature, and they feel that their actions accordingly can do little or nothing to alter nature. In the

2. Florence R. Kluckhohn and Fred L. Strodtbeck, *Variations in Value Orientations* (Westport, CT: Greenwood Publishers, 1973). The following discussion focusing on the human/nature relationship, as described by Kluckhohn and Strodtbeck, is summarized in Ronald A. Simkins, *Creator and Creation: Nature in the Worldview of Ancient Israel* (Peabody, MA: Hendrickson Publishers, 1994), 31-40.

3. The four problems to which all humans have had to find a solution, in addition to the relationship between humans and nature, include the character of innate human nature, the temporal focus of life (past, present, future), the modality of human activity (being, being-in-becoming, doing), and the modality of human relationships. See Simkins, *Creator and Creation*, 32.

third alternative, nature is an impersonal object controlled by humans, with technology the key to controlling nature.[4] It is this third view that sociologists and others have recognized as the dominant Western worldview. Unfortunately, in the context of global economies and technologies, this worldview is no longer dominantly Western.

Regardless of its origin and dissemination, this third worldview is represented by four prominent assumptions:[5]

1. People are fundamentally different from all other creatures on earth, over which they have dominion.
2. People are masters of their destiny: they can choose their goals and learn to do whatever is necessary to achieve them.
3. The world is vast and thus provides unlimited opportunities for humans.
4. The history of humanity is one of progress: for every problem there is a solution, and thus progress need never cease.

Mastery over nature and these concurrent worldviews are the assumptions that this book seeks to undermine, dismantle, and ultimately abandon. In their place, *Nature as Spiritual Practice* advocates spiritual practice in a context of a values orientation in which both human flourishing and nature flourishing are in harmony. As we will see, this is not a naïve denial of violence, loss, and death in nature; instead, it is an integrative vision of nature's ability to hold life cycles and death cycles in balance.

Psychological Perspectives on Identity Formation and Nature

In her jointly edited book *Identity and the Natural Environment*, Susan Clayton says that "identity can be described as a way of organizing information about the self." She goes on to propose that "an environmental identity is one part of the way in which people form their self-concept: a sense of connection to some part of the nonhuman natural world."[6] *Nature as Spiritual*

4. See Simkins, *Creator and Creation*, 38.

5. William R. Catton and Riley E. Dunlap, "A New Ecological Paradigm for Post-Exuberant Sociology," *American Behavioral Scientist* 24 (1980): 15-47.

6. Susan Clayton and Susan Opotow, eds., *Identity and the Natural Environment: The Psychological Significance of Nature* (Cambridge, MA: MIT Press, 2003), 45. Though presenting a psychological perspective of identity formation in nature, the editors are scrupulous in

Practice takes the position that there is a subjective quality to the natural world that allows the environment to organize information about itself and in so doing inform humans about who and what they are. This subjective quality is evident in Scripture, the Christian tradition, and what we experience in nature as spiritual practice. Three areas of psychological research have been especially productive in assessing this reciprocal relationship based on intersubjectivity.[7] The first is the *developmental and psychoanalytic perspective,* in which the crucial developmental stage of differentiation "involves the infant's becoming aware of himself as differentiated not only from his human environment but also from his nonhuman environment."

A second approach is *place theory,* as formulated in humanistic geography and environmental psychology. From the place theory perspective, the natural world forms identity not in a general or abstract way but through interaction with a particular place that in effect "imprints" itself on body, mind, and spirit. A Tennessee mountaineer commenting on what a particular place means to him captures the essence of this approach when he says of hills and valleys of his home that it is "where you can feel you're you, and no one else." A third category of writers and researchers assessing identity and nature are exploring *the links among identity, ethics, and action.* One contemporary writer notes about this category: "For many, a sense of personal relationship to nature or place evokes an ethical commitment to practical action to protect and care for the natural environment — that is, environmental identity can lead directly to an identity as an environmental*ist*."[8]

Based on research to date, essential psychological points of intersection between human identity formation and the natural world include:

- The primal importance of bodily or kinesthetic self-awareness in conditioning one's sense of identity

---

introducing contemporary work in other fields, which support Clayton's claim that "environmental identity is one way in which people form their self-concept." Most of the following discussion about identity formation in nature is based on Clayton and Opotow's introductory survey.

7. Clayton and Opotow review the most contemporary theories of identity formation, all of which can be identified with two fundamentally different perspectives: 1) that identity, when formed, is a relatively stable phenomenon; 2) that identity is inherently a quality of the human person that is constantly in "flux." See Clayton and Opotow, *Identity and the Natural Environment,* 5ff.

8. Steven J. Holmes, "Some Lives and Some Theories," in Clayton and Opotow, *Identity and the Natural Environment,* 29-41.

- A sense of continuity across the life span, especially the integration of childhood memory in adult self-image
- Environmental experiences in growth and maintenance of individuality or uniqueness
- Self-definition and self-worth through assertion, work, and achievement
- The importance for identity of communal or regional identity and of moral and political commitment
- "Ecological identity," or felt relationships with natural beings, places, and processes on their own terms

These perspectives on spiritual formation and identity formation in the context of nature all contribute meaning to what I mean by "Christian practice" in this book. A more formal survey of what is meant by Christian practice is offered in Appendix B. But the primary way to *understand* Christian practice is to experience the practices themselves. In a very real sense, the practices and your experiences of them form identity within that space held and nurtured within the human subject/creation subject relationship.

Mindfulness, Attentiveness, and Wonder in Nature

What we pay attention to defines who we are. "Mindfulness," meaning open, centered, and attentive awareness, is today associated primarily with Buddhism. It is a sad commentary on Christian "mindfulness" that precisely what early Christian mothers and fathers advocated and practiced is now mostly forgotten. Those early Christians focused their attention on God, on themselves, on others, on virtue, and on spiritual practice. With the intensity of a laser, they also focused attention on the earth. A fundamental goal of this book is to promote Christian mindfulness in nature, and to remind ourselves that this is not a concept that is alien to Christian spiritual traditions. In Greek, the word for "attentiveness" or "watchfulness," which are both cognates of mindfulness, is *nipsis*. In the early Christian tradition of desert spirituality, desert-based Christians are often referred to as the "niptic" fathers or mothers, that is, as the ones who watched, who paid attention, and who practiced "Christian mindfulness" — and in so doing cultivated a capacity for wonder.

Both traits — attention and wonder — are core practices promoted by nature and practiced in *Nature as Spiritual Practice.* As one desert monk, Hesychios the Priest, put it, in creation one finds that "continuity of attention produces inner stability; inner stability produces a natural intensification of watchfulness; and this intensification gradually and in due measure gives way to contemplative mystery and insight."[9]

PRACTICE 2.3

Attention as Contemplative Reawakening[10]

INTENTION People become animated talking about even brief connections with nature. The intention of this practice is — "intentionally" — to awaken us from perceptual sleepiness to an awareness (contemplation) of our place in nature and to our habitual connection to it.

PRACTICE Our awareness is shaped by what we choose to pay attention to. When we focus our attention primarily on human-made things and activities, our consciousness of creation naturally diminishes. In fact, consciousness itself diminishes.

- Identify an object or location in nature that attracts your attention. This could be as close as your own backyard, a nearby park, a tree outside your bedroom window, a bird singing at sunrise — any thing or place that "speaks" to you.
- Illuminate or "shine" your awareness on this object or location. Illuminate it with your senses by looking, listening, smelling, touching. As you are ready, "shine" your memory and imagination and intuition on this object or location. In other words, consume this location to the utmost of your attentive powers.
- For several consecutive days, return to study this same object or place, and each time seek to notice some other aspect of it that previously escaped your attention.
- Pay attention to the tremendous variations and subtleties of the relationship that form over time. You might wish to go to a place in nature during different times of the year, taking photographs of the same scene each

---

9. Hesychios the Priest, "On Watchfulness and Holiness," in *The Philokalia: The Complete Text,* trans. and ed. G. E. H. Palmer et al., vol. 1 (New York: Faber and Faber, 1979), 163.

10. This practice is given in part in Philip Sutton Chard, *The Healing Earth: Nature's Medicine for the Troubled Soul* (Minnetonka, MN: NorthWord Press, 1994), 37.

time. Noticing the changes over time in this way can sometimes be startling. A lake or river can awaken you in new ways no matter how many times you visit it. On the other hand, be prepared for the fact that at times, even with your senses open, you will sense nothing new, numinous, or — perhaps at times — even anything very interesting at all. At other times, moments that you share with nature with a purely open and wandering mind can be refreshing in themselves. At still other times, you will find yourself enfolded in sacred matters.

- To be honest, at times nature will simply bore you. Boredom is a part of a relationship. Talk with nature about being bored!
- Over time, and as you are taken by nature and nature by you, you will find that nature opens your senses and enlivens your soul. Creation becomes a kind of gift, an offering prepared by God for awakening and illuminating our bodies and minds and spirits.

"A Tree Is Just a Tree": An Emerging Miracle

> *Looking into the face of nature is not really that different from looking into the face of God: both are miracles, and both are mirrors. You just have to be prepared for what you might see.*
>
> A friend — after a day at the ocean

A coastal redwood *(sequoia sempervirens)* is just a tree — just a tall, beautiful tree of a certain height and girth and age and color and odor, supporting and supported by a particular enveloping biosystem. It is also an emerging miracle: it is just a burning bush.

Nature forms us in this kind of "bi-focal" vision: the visible and the invisible, the mundane and the sacred, the ecological and the sacramental. Each of these apparent oppositions actually enhances the other, each heightens the reality of the other. This is the true "code of nature": not survival, as is often said, but simply that a tree is just a tree, an emerging miracle. Nature can certainly be violent, and all things do die; but as emerging miracle and within its imperative of truth, nature also forms a kind of mirror that gives us nowhere to hide. Within the mirror of this more gentle code, nature invites us to find our true selves. The naturalist and nature writer Terry Tempest Williams says: "Wildness reminds us what it means to be human, what we are connected to rather than separate from. . . . If the desert is holy, it is because it is a forgotten place that allows us to re-member the sacred. Perhaps that is why every pilgrimage to the desert is a pilgrimage to the self. There is no place to hide and so we are found."[11] Like woman and man, nature bears the impress of God; pilgrimage into nature is a pilgrimage into the true self. At the still point of our true self an emerging miracle occurs: we are found by creation wisdom.

Sitting at ease, my back propped against a gentle giant of a coastal red-wood, wrapped in fog, my feet in sword fern and moss, my mind associating the cry of a blue jay with the few crumbs I have for a lunch, I am as likely to encounter the demons of death and decay that consume nature as I am the angels of fire and life that burn but do not consume. The odor of redwood, like cedar, once burned into the senses, is impossible to forget with shoes off and bare feet in sword fern and moss.

This burning redwood bush props the back and grounds the toes, as much a burning bush as it is a good backrest for a nap on a warm summer afternoon. Nature as spiritual practice elicits a response: constantly emerging doxology, constantly emerging praise.

> Praise the Lord!
> Praise the Lord, all the angels;
>   praise the Lord, all the hosts!
> Praise the Lord, sun and moon;
>   praise the Lord, all you shining stars!
> Praise the Lord from the earth,
>   you sea monsters and all deeps,
> Fire and hail, snow and frost,
>   stormy wind fulfilling his command!
> Mountains and all hills,
>   fruit trees and all cedars!
> Wild animals and all cattle,
>   creeping things and flying birds!
>
> Psalm 148:1-3, 7-10

Praise is creation's language of spiritual practice. The poet Walt Whitman heard this language as a visible invitation to participate in that emerging miracle that turns all creation into . . . simply what it is:

---

11. Terry Tempest Williams, *Red: Passion and Patience in the Desert* (New York: Vintage Books, 2002), 75, 77.

I believe a leaf of grass is no less than the journey-work
     of the stars. . . .
And the running blackberry would adorn the parlors of heaven,
And the narrowest hinge in my hand puts to scorn all machinery,
And the cow crunching with depress'd head surpasses any statue,
And a mouse is miracle enough to stagger sextillions of infidels.

Walt Whitman, Song of Myself (1855)

PRACTICE 2.4

De-Creating Genesis

INTENTION   The intention of this practice is to experience creation, not as transferred, imagistic, or symbolic, but as ecological (material) and sacramental (spiritual) reality. We will do this by using the first Genesis creation story, reading it in reverse. Two phases of meditation are used for each day, starting from the seventh day: (1) we first enter guided meditation on what was created on this day as described in Genesis; (2) we then move through guided meditation, imagining that God did not, in fact, create that day or any of its creations. The guided meditation takes us back to the time before God "began" creation. The intention of the practice is this: in stripping creation of all we "imagine" it to be, we will see it as it is, as pure doxology.

Sacramental Ecology

CHAPTER THREE

The Sacred Matters

The Holy Spirit warmed the waters with a kind of vital warmth, even bringing them to a boil through intense heat in order to make them fertile. The action of a hen is similar. It sits on its eggs, making them fertile through the warmth of incubation. Here then, the Holy Spirit foreshadows the sacrament of holy baptism, prefiguring its arrival, so that the waters made fertile by the hovering of the same divine Spirit gave birth to the children of God.

Ephrem the Syrian, *Commentary on Genesis* 1

In creation the sacred matters. A redwood forest, for instance, makes a difference; it is important. It matters whether a redwood forest is destroyed or preserved. T. S. Eliot says: "Love is most nearly itself/When here and now cease to matter." In one sense in which Eliot uses the word "matter," the fact that the sacred matters means that the sacred in a redwood forest counts for something; it is a thing of consequence. Eliot also alludes to one of the reasons the sacred matters in creation: "love" is also "most nearly itself" in creation.

However, in another sense, a redwood forest is physical, material, substantial, a diversified ecology of organic and inorganic materials. In this sense, the sacred "matters" as physical material: it is something to touch, to smell, to see, to feel, to walk on, and to breathe. Redwood forests thrive on a mixture of matter, including sun, fog, mists, and rains; wide-ranging and intertwining roots share the soil and ground cover with fungi, microscopic invertebrates, burrowing squirrels and chipmunks. High-tannin bark protects the trees from fire and insects. Cut, the redwood is fragrant even be-

31

yond cedar. Left to grow on its own, the redwood adds growth rings century after century after century. The marbled murrelet, an enterprising ocean-shore bird, actually moves into the redwood forest to nest and raise its young. Redwoods make up forests by sharing their space with Douglas fir, madrone, rhododendron, tan oak, trilliums, salal, and varieties of mosses, ferns, and lichen. All this is "matter," something that occupies space and time. If we say, then, that "the sacred matters," we mean that what is holy, spiritual, divine, and sacred is so only through matter, material, and substance. The sacred emerges in the here and now of the material matter that is a redwood forest. The invisible and the visible, the spiritual and the material, converge as sacred ecology.

We can also say in this sense that God "matters." It is at this point that *Nature as Spiritual Practice* will be passionately at odds with the implications of a second interpretation of Eliot's lines. A slight — but admittedly audacious — alteration to Eliot's lines makes the point: "Love is most nearly itself/When here and now *begin* to matter." "Here" and "now" are what creation is; we don't have much else. And it is in this here and now that not only the material, but the sacred, matters. In the beginning God "mattered"; God is "mattering"; God will continue to "matter." As the sacred matters in creation, the here and the now are as essential to love as they are to the redwood forest, which is *only* itself as the here and now begin to matter. The eyes and breath and flesh of a lover, the bark and aroma and lofty green of a redwood — only in the here and now, on earth as it is, does the sacred begin to matter.

Yes, we reach a kind of paradox: the more we attend to the physical matter of creation, the more the sacred emerges; at the same time, the more we attend to the spiritual matter of creation, the more we enter the here and now of physical matter. The ninth-century Celtic Christian theologian and philosopher John Scotus Eriugena regarded the whole world as a theophany, that is, a "thin place," a manifestation of God, literally a place where the God of light illuminates and enlightens "ordinary" matter. On the other hand, Eriugena recognized that the more we behold physical creation, the more we are beheld by God.[1]

I look out my window and see two large puffed, grayish cotton-ball clouds edged in bright white against the blue sky. The shades of gray show imperceptible movement into shallow yellows all the way into deep purples

---

1. See, for instance, Eriugena's *Periphyseon* as discussed by J. Philip Newell, *Listening for the Heartbeat of God: A Celtic Spirituality* (New York: Paulist Press, 1997), 34-37.

in the denser center of the cloud. The clouds are moving slowly with the wind across the sky. In the sacramental ecology of the sacred matters, the here and now also begin to matter, much like the bread and the wine. In the epigraph that opens this chapter, Ephrem the Syrian is surprisingly prophetic of contemporary science: from vital warmth infused into the seas by the Holy Spirit, life evolved, prefiguring sacred, material water as the living sacrament that would give new life to the children of God.

PRACTICE 3.1

The Sacred Matters

INTENTION   Acknowledging that the sacred matters.

PRACTICE   In this practice, be astonished by nature as you are called to do so, or simply be with nature in a more detached but open way.

- Explore the physical and spiritual characteristics of nature. Notice what and how nature incorporates your attention and wonder: possibilities are as diverse as a rock or the wind or how sunlight strikes the ground or how the fish are biting or how you experience some interconnected features of nature. It will involve using all your perceptions, thoughts, memories, intuitions, feelings, imaginings, creativity, hopes, dreams, faith, body, soul, and love. You can attend to nature in ways that appeal to you: through journaling, photography, drawing, or using a field guide to focus in on particular features of nature.
- Explore what captures your attention in its material nature.
- Similarly, explore how nature offers you its sacred aspect.
- Notice the here and now, the how, where, and when of material nature, then whether and/or how this same material nature takes on sacred qualities.
- Similarly, notice the here and now, the how, where, and when of sacred nature as it is or becomes material.
- How do the material and the spiritual (the ecological and the sacramental) mutually enhance one another?
- As you experience this, is one possible without the other?
- Try to behold the sacred and material in balance. As they move out of balance, as they inevitably will (for instance, you begin to notice only the sound of a cedar waxwing as sound, or as one series of notes in a sacred creation-symphony of bird song), be attentive to the shift. Can you con-

trol the shift? Notice what you experience as balance between sacred and matter in nature over time.

- Practice this form of contemplative attention (by yourself and in nature) at random times. How does your sensitivity to the material and the spiritual qualities of nature evolve?

Sacramental Wonder and Ecological Attentiveness

We truly use this kind of contemplation when by means of visible things we are raised up to speculation of invisible things.
Richard of Saint Victor, *The Mystical Ark* (I.vi)

For nature is all good and fair in itself.
Julian of Norwich, *Showings of Love* (63)

As the sacred matters, the natural world is both sacramental (sacred or spiritual) and ecological (physical or material). As such, nature is a sacramental ecology. For our part, to experience nature as sacramental ecology requires the ongoing practices of wonder and attentiveness. I will return again and again to these two essential practices of 1) developing a capacity for astonishment — that is, wonder, and 2) using and refining our powers of paying attention — being watchful and mindful — to the natural world. Richard of Saint Victor is an example of a response to the sacramental quality of nature: the visible, material things of creation lead those who are contemplative to the invisible, spiritual things of God. Julian of Norwich responds to the ecological quality of nature: nature is "all" and "good" and "fair," and in these attributes nature is what it is "in itself." Together, Richard and Julian illustrate how the ecological and material aspects of nature are complete in themselves; yet we recognize that even this completeness offers the possibility of more. This *more* has a reciprocating quality: attention and wonder to the details and structures of the material aspects of creation opens us to the invisible, spiritual, sacred qualities of creation; reciprocally, as we are drawn into the spiritual, sacred realities of creation, we begin to appreciate and notice in a more comprehensive way the material, relational, visible qualities of creation. The sacred matters in both these "ecological" and "sacramental" realities of creation. Each carries its own independence, while each needs the other to become fully alive.

As spiritual practice, I will associate the "ecological" realities of creation with the various forms of the practice of attention and the "sacramental" realities of creation with those varieties of practices that cultivate wonder, mystery, and astonishment. Ecological aspects of nature evoke wonder, and sacramental aspects of nature certainly capture our attention. But as the sacred matters, our discussion and practices will be more understandable as we keep our focus on "ecological attention" and "sacramental wonder."

We can observe this relationship of ecological attention and sacramental wonder from the perspective of, say, a white-oak leaf. On earth as it is, the sacramental and ecological do not compete for the affections of a white-oak leaf: the leaf is pleased to present itself to us as both. The oak leaf is material and physical; it is sacred and sacramental. The sacramental and ecological qualities of a white-oak leaf are not in competition.

A short description of a white-oak leaf from a reliable handbook on trees reads as follows:

Obvate, to 8 in (20 cm) long and 4 (10 cm) across, tapered at the base, deeply cut into four lobes on each side, pink-tinged and white-hairy becoming bright green above, blue-green beneath, turning purple-red in autumn.[2]

Let's assume that we are holding a white-oak leaf in our hands; you might want to find a white oak that is close by and ask for one of its leaves. Failing that, any leaf will do.

Examine the leaf, then read the above description again. Is the handbook describing the ecological or the sacramental reality of the leaf? The writer probably intended the description to be matter-of-fact, to the point, objective, biological, and ecological. In order to write such a description, the writer has had to observe the leaf very closely, to be watchful of the leaf through its seasons, to be mindful of a whole list of names for the shapes of leaves in order to name this one "obvate," and to be attentive to small details of shape and color and size and location and season. The writer's attentiveness indicates that he or she could have written much more and, based on this very short description, we are left in little doubt that the writer would agree with Julian of Norwich's claim that "nature is all good and fair in itself." If you are mindful of and attentive to the leaf you are

2. Allen J. Combes, *Trees: Smithsonian Handbooks,* 2nd ed. (New York: Dorling Kindersley, 2002), 158.

holding, you, too, could write as much or more about that physical, eco-logical, good, and blessed thing in your hand.

But with the leaf still in our hands, its "objective" description still in our minds, let's approach it from a slightly different angle of vision. In his book *The Sacred Lantern*, Ronald Rolheiser calls for a recovery from the Christian contemplative traditions of what he calls an "ancient instinct for astonish-ment." In essence, Rolheiser is inviting us to wake up to wonder: "According to the great mystics within [the Christian contemplative tradition], we gen-erally lack the purity of heart necessary to see God because normal aware-ness is both very reduced and muddied by unhealthy self-concern and with restless distractions. God is present but we are, for the most part, asleep, dis-tracted, and unaware of that presence."[3] Rolheiser's words allude to the words of Jesus: "Blessed are the pure of heart, for they shall see God" (Matt. 5:8), a concise summation of what it means to be open to wonder.

You have a leaf in your hands.

Can we see this leaf with purity of heart? In doing so, we are not only at-tentive, but we have allowed the leaf to awaken within us an instinct for as-tonishment and wonder. Look again at the leaf: "Obvate, to 8 in (20 cm) long and 4 (10 cm) across." It is measurable, and it is holy and astonishing. As we enter the sacramental-holy through the ecological present, we expe-rience purity of heart as a blessing: we "see the face of God" in the midst of the ecological-holy.

Richard of Saint Victor writes of precisely this kind of purity of heart or contemplative awakening: "We truly use this kind of contemplation when by means of visible things we are raised up to speculation of invisible things." Through contemplation of a white-oak leaf, we are "raised" in wonder into the holy and the sacred. The leaf is not a *symbol* of God; it is not trapped in a prison house of language or metaphor. The leaf is a leaf, and as a leaf it is a work of wonder. Julian's reminder is a blessing: "Nature is all good and fair in itself." Richard of Saint Victor's own definition of contemplation is "the free, attentive gaze of the soul hovering with wonder in the visible showings of wisdom."[4] The leaf is "all good and fair in itself," and it is a visible showing of divine wisdom, a wonder. It is a showing of the sacramental ecology of divine wisdom.

---

3. Ronald Rolheiser, *The Shattered Lantern: Rediscovering the Felt Presence of God* (New York: Crossroad, 2001), 78.

4. Richard of St. Victor, *De arca mystica*, I.iv, in *Patrologiae Latinae* 196, ed. J.-P. Migne (my translation). The Latin *mens* can be translated as "mind" or "soul"; in this case it is best con-ceived as encompassing both.

An Ecological Perception of Place

INTENTION   One of the best ways to awaken wonder and attentiveness to nature is to know your environment. The intention of this practice is just that: to get to know your local environment more thoroughly in all its variety and specificity. As you do so, you will notice its beauty. You will also notice some other things: how nature is being degraded by human actions, and also how — in nature — violence, death, and renewal must become a part of your attention and wonder.

Nature as Praise

> *Wonder or radical amazement is the chief characteristic of the religious man's attitude toward history or nature.*
>
> Abraham Joshua Heschel[5]

According to Hebrew and Christian scriptures, nature's primary spiritual practice is praise. By practicing attention and wonder in the sacred matters of nature, we begin to see for ourselves how the matter of praise is practiced within creation. The history of the word "matter" helps us see creation's practice of praise even more clearly.

Our English word "matter" has evolved from a complex of meanings. Its etymological roots are also found in "forest" and "wood": indeed, the original Greek word for "matter" originally meant "forest." As Latin evolved, the Greek word meaning "forest" became *materia,* which has the same root as the word *mater* ("mother"). Civilization emerged and evolved as much from a complex relationship with forests as it did from a complex relationship with mothers! As the birthplace of civilization, *mater* connotes both a forest ecology and a sacramental birth.[6] And it begins to show its proclivity for praise.

In his book about Saint Francis of Assisi, G. K. Chesterton begins to

---

5. Abraham Joshua Heschel, *God in Search of Man* (New York: Straus and Giroux, 1955), 45.

6. For a fuller etymological history of the word "matter," see Robert Pogue Harrison, *Forests: The Shadow of Civilization* (Chicago: University of Chicago Press, 1992), 28.

hint at creation praise through the eyes of a Christian saint: "For there is no way in which a man can earn a star or deserve a sunset. . . . The transition from a good man to the saint is a sort of revolution; by which one for whom all things illustrate and illuminate God becomes one for whom God illustrates and illuminates all things."[7] In our contemporary culture of consumption, it is easy to forget this simple yet cosmic insight: "There is no way we can earn a star or deserve a sunset." The "mother" in "matter" is seen by the pure in heart just as a star or sunset is seen as an illustration and illumination of God. I'm not sure one needs to be a saint to see stars or sunsets equivalent to the "love that moves the sun and the stars," as Dante says in the last line of his *Divine Comedy*. I do believe, though, that while we don't earn or deserve nature, our closest relationship as humans to the created world is through praise. What is left, after all, but praise as one comes to see that either all things illustrate and illuminate God, or that God illustrates and illuminates all things? Ecologically and sacramentally, creation is a doxological fire: "Praise the Lord from the earth, you sea monsters and all deeps, fire and hail, snow and frost, stormy wind fulfilling his command . . ." (Ps. 148:7-8). "Make a joyful noise to the Lord, *all the earth*" (Ps. 100:1). "The Lord is king! Let the earth rejoice; let the many coastlands be glad" (Ps. 97:1).

PRACTICE 3.3

Nature as Praise

INTENTION   The intention of this practice is to begin to notice how nature is in constant praise of God and to join nature in that praise. If this praise awakens "wonder" and "radical amazement" as well, so much the better!

----

7. G. K. Chesterton, *St. Francis of Assisi* (London: Hodder and Stoughton, 1924), 80, 85, 86.

Creation Education: Nature as Teacher

> *By wisdom the Lord laid the earth's foundations,*
>   *by understanding the Lord set the heavens in place;*
> *by the Lord's knowledge the deeps were divided,*
>   *and the clouds let drop the dew.*
>
> Proverbs 3:19-21

The best teachers teach what they are. The best guides guide by the light that sustains them. The best place to turn, then, for education and guidance in nature's sacramental ecology is to creation herself: creation invites us into her own formative wisdom and divine showings. Turned to creation in this way, we are in for the education of our lives.

In his Gospel, John relates how Jesus prays that all may become one with the Father as Jesus himself is one with the Father: "I in them and Thou in me" (John 17:23). And as Paul writes in Colossians, through Christ "God was pleased to reconcile to himself all things, whether on earth or in heaven" (Col. 1:20). Creation, along with you and me, exists with Christ in us as God (Thou) is in Christ. "In each *thou* we address the eternal *Thou*," says Martin Buber, and "through contact with every *thou* we are stirred with a breath of the *Thou*, that is, eternal life."[8] As subjects, we turn to nature as a subject (not as an object); as thou, we turn to nature as thou. We find that thus connected, thou to thou, in creation we encounter the eternal Thou, both materially (ecologically) and spiritually (sacramentally).

In such intimacy with nature we are free to draw our own conclusions and lessons about who we are, what creation is, who God is: the hospitality in the gift of another, the "thou," invites this free choosing. As with any gift, the hospitality of nature, inviting us into her wisdom, may be received or may be ignored. But choosing to receive the gift of nature's guidance is always a lesson in wisdom and love, a lesson in death and resurrection. The idea that nature loves us as much as we are capable of loving nature should not be surprising: we (humanity) and nature share a common Thou, a common parentage, and "everyone who loves is born of God and knows God," because "God is love" (1 John 4:7-8).

How do we face this thou created and sustained by the Thou, as a guide and teacher in Christian spiritual formation? In fact, we are never sure of the

---

8. Martin Buber, *I and Thou*, trans. Ronald Gregor Smith, 2nd ed. (New York: Scribner, 1958), 6, 101.

particular face that nature will turn to us: a languid walk on a sharply cold autumn day may open the soul, or it may just make a person cold and lonely. Yet this is exactly the point: the guidance and the teaching of nature are formational practices only as we accept the risk and uncertainty of nature's pedagogy. The word "education" comes from the Latin *ducere* ("to lead or guide"); the *e* is very important because it indicates that *e*-ducation leads and guides us "from" one thing to another, from one way of knowing to another. Nature is educational then to the extent that we allow it to lead and guide us out of ourselves and into its own thou. This certainly involves risk, but a choice for risk is also a choice for the possibility of the Thou, the possibility of Love. In a real sense, nature educates in the arts of *belonging:* relationship and belonging; transformation and belonging; power, wisdom, goodness, and belonging; loneliness and belonging; solitude and belonging; decay, savagery, pain, and belonging; beauty, synthesis, desire, and belonging; interdependence, participation, gift, and belonging; death and belonging.

Why do we miss the *e*-ducation of the pink-purple, bee-seducing wild bergamot in the pounding sun of July while an approaching cold front, slow as Bach's *Mass in B Minor,* clears the crest of the Rockies? Habit. We are habituated to not belonging to creation. Without allowing nature to be our education — our formation in Christ — we presume to reshape nature in our own image, an image that is only about concealing; we fail to see the Thou staring us in the face. We make a habit of missing both the sacred *and* the matter.

Habit and formation in creation has deep kinship with the habit and formation in Christ. Nature herself has made Christ her form and her habit. In the second century, Bishop Irenaeus of Lyons wrote:

> Because [Christ] is himself the Word of God . . . who in His invisible form pervades us universally in the whole world, and encompasses its length and breadth and height and depth . . . the Son of God was also crucified in these, imprinted in the form of a cross on the universe.[9]

The smallest grain of sand, the deepest black hole in the universe, the smile on a lover's face, the clarity of the desert are all forms and habits "imprinted in the form of a cross."

9. G. B. Ladner, *God, Cosmos, and Humankind: The World of Early Christian Symbolism,* trans. Thomas Dunlap (Berkeley: University of California Press, 1995), 99, cited in Douglas Burton-Christie, "Nature," in *The Blackwell Companion to Christian Spirituality,* ed. Arthur Holder (Oxford: Blackwell, 2005), 478.

I sit on the wooded banks of an upper Minnesota lake as August dusk turns to dark. I am sitting on the fallen branch of a maple. I've collected a bouquet of wildflowers from a nearby open field. The lake is shallow and warm, and lily pads grow tens of meters out from the shore. There is a beaver dam off on the wetland side of the lake that I see for the first time. I have had to climb down a steep rise off the main trail to arrive at this narrow beach. Facing west, I note that the sky echoes the color of the bouquet of flowers I have collected. Though I know that there is decay all around me — I am in fact sitting on a branch of decay — beauty and contentment and well-being and tranquility are my companions. But, as always, death is a companion as well. The colors to the west begin to fade as the evening grows cooler, and I sit as the sky blackens and, with no moon, stars appear where they did not exist just an instant before. I am faced: I belong alike with the loon and the slight odor of fish rising from the lake as the air moistens and the breath of a wind signals the shift to night. This is becoming a habit: it is a long and difficult lesson, and in many ways I am very dull. But creation is a patient teacher, just as Christ is a teacher of patience. Both creation and Christ address my rubbled-over heart; both, with infinite patience, teach me how my I-ish-ness interferes with compassion. Both of them use pedagogies of hospitality, forgiveness, and trust, forming a habit of belonging in which touch and love are as delicate and necessary as the liturgy of the moment — now moving from light to dusk to dark.

CHAPTER FOUR

A Covenant with Mystery

*I confess, of course, that it can be said reverently, provided that it
proceeds from a reverent mind, that nature is God; but because it
is a harsh and improper saying, since nature is rather the order
prescribed by God, it is harmful in such weighty matters, in which
special devotion is due, to involve God confusedly in the inferior
course of his works.*

John Calvin, *Institutes*[1]

"Nature is God." This "confession" of John Calvin will sound, well, just
odd to those who believe they know their Reformed theology. Admittedly,
he confesses this with some caution and warning: he must say it "reverently," and with "special devotion due." But there it is: "Nature is God."

To Calvin's credit, he has come as far as his theology will take him, and
he knows it and admits it. And to his credit and our edification, he wants
to be clear that what he is saying is not theology; rather, it is a confession
— a prayer. This is a confession that one would have to believe is grounded
in Calvin's own acute perceptions and experience of the surpassing beauty
and holiness of nature. His prayer is an act of devotion, a confession of
longing and desire. Nature captivates him as his God does. In this short

---

1. John Calvin, *Institutes of the Christian Religion*, I.V.5, ed. John T. McNeill, trans. Ford
Lewis Battles (Philadelphia: Westminster, 1960), 58. The translator, Battles, notes that "these
sentences reflect statements of Lactantius, who credits Seneca with being the best of the
Stoics, since he 'saw nature to be nothing else than God.'" But Battles notes that Lactantius
"also points to the confusion arising from this identification," the same confusion that Calvin, in his philosophical pursuit, is left with (see 58n22).

passage we catch a glimpse of Calvin facing nature. We see what he would no doubt refer to as "piety": in this case, "piety" as the power of creation to shape Christian formational identity.

Ursula Goodenough, a professor of biology, arrives at a similar point of transformative awareness: she reaches the limits of where biology alone will carry her, and in reaching that limit, she is honest and courageous, Prayer erupts, and molecular biology confesses wonder. Goodenough's experience leads her to find meaning at the heart of science, a meaning that she calls her "covenant with Mystery." In her book *The Sacred Depths of Nature*, Goodenough explains what are called "emergent functions" in nature. A simple example of an emergent function is that certain aspects of life can be explained by chemistry, but that the life that emerges from the chemistry of biomolecules (chemistry's most basic elements) is something more than the collection of molecules themselves. Whatever emerges from something more than the collection of its most basic parts is an emergent function. The origin of life itself is an emergent function. Self-awareness or consciousness is an emergent function. Emergent functions cannot be explained, even on the basis of their most elemental parts or physics.

Just as Calvin comes to an "end" of where reason and his theology can take him (his piety leads him to confess that "nature is God"), Goodenough encounters emergent functions: her response is a personal "covenant with Mystery," which she describes as her "response to the emergence of life not with a search for its Design or Purpose but instead with outrageous celebration that it occurred at all."[2]

Goodenough is shaped and formed by what she is and does: as a scientist, she has dedicated her life to ecological attentiveness; as a human being seeking answers to ultimate questions, she encounters sacramental wonder. John Calvin is little different: as a theologian and churchman, he has dedicated his life to "God's handiwork," giving that handiwork the ecological attentiveness available during his life; as an honest seeker, his piety leads to seeing nature as sacramental wonder. Both establish their own covenant with wonder: at the most fundamental level of mutual agreement between humanity, creation, and mystery, the sacred matters.

2. Ursula Goodenough, *The Sacred Depths of Nature* (Oxford: Oxford University Press, 1998), 27-30, 167-68.

Our Covenant of Mystery

INTENTION   The intention of this practice is to enter a covenant of mystery with creation.

PRACTICE   The practice in the *Field Guide,* "An Ecological Perception of Place," will help you focus on nature in ways that will make it easier to enter into a covenant of wonder with nature.

A covenant is an agreement, contract, promise, or pledge. There are two kinds of biblical covenants between God and humanity:[3]

1. Conditional: a covenant that guarantees God will do God's part when *humans meet the requirements* stipulated in that covenant.
2. Unconditional: distinguished from a conditional covenant by the fact that its *ultimate fulfillment* is promised by God and depends on God's power and sovereignty for its fulfillment.

- Allow yourself some time to seek and find an object or ecosystem with which you are familiar.
- Whether a professional ecologist or a novice with a field guide in hand, when you have found what you are looking for, give it as much ecological attention as you can. You might want to use your field guide as an aid to help you journal, photograph, draw, or simply contemplate or explore your surroundings.
- As you are ready, let your senses and awareness enfold your object up to — and perhaps beyond — the point at which your awareness comes up against something "more" in nature than the material/ecological, something you can call mystery or wonder. Allow the mystery to unfold in you. Notice where your consciousness rests: with attentiveness, with mystery, or somewhere in balance.
- Exchange the word "God" with the word "nature" in the definitions of covenant above. What are possible covenants of wonder that you can form between yourself and nature? What covenants is nature making with you? What covenants can you make with nature? Are they conditional or unconditional?

---

3. There are several instances in the Hebrew Bible where God makes a covenant with God's people (see Gen. 1:26-31; 3:16-19; 9:1-8; 12:1-4, 15:1-7; 17:1-8; Exod. 20:1-31; Deut. 30:1-10; 2 Sam. 7:4-16; Jer. 31:31-40).

- An example from Scripture that is a covenant not only with humanity but with the earth and all creatures of the earth is found in Genesis 9, where God sets an unconditional covenant with Noah and his descendents never again to destroy the earth with a flood. The sign of this covenant is also from nature, and it is itself a wonder: a rainbow.
- How is your covenant with nature related to your "covenants" or your relationship with God?

....

Mystery and the Face of Nature

> *How can one learn the truth by thinking? As one learns to see a face better if one draws it.*
>
> Ludwig Wittgenstein[4]

Contemporary philosophers who are focusing on ethics and aesthetics, and psychotherapists who are searching for a language by which to express our emotional connection to nature, have also looked to the "face" as a way of expressing the mystery of this relationship. As the human face both reveals and conceals, so does the "face" of nature reveal its ecological qualities to the attentive participant even as this face of nature conceals something of its sacramental qualities.

The philosopher Emmanuel Lévinas captures something of the mystery and ethical quality of the face when he says that "access to the face is straightway ethical."[5] For Lévinas, the simple act of "facing" is a not only a gesture of hospitality; it entails an ethical response that addresses the needs and desires of any face that is willing to show vulnerable accessibility. Another contemporary philosopher, George Steiner, articulates a similar vision of hospitality, ethic, and mystery based on connectedness, relationship, and forgiveness. He says: "A reflection on or a 'thinking of' meetings, of encounters, of communication, itself entails a morality. An analysis of enunciation and signification — that is, any form of signal to the other — entails an ethics."[6] Simply put, he, too, knows that access to

---

4. Cited without attribution in Jonah Lehrer, *Proust Was a Neuroscientist* (New York: Houghton Mifflin, 2007), 96.

5. Emmanuel Lévinas, *Ethics and Infinity,* trans. Richard A. Cohen (Pittsburgh: Duquesne University Press, 1985), 85.

6. George Steiner, *Real Presences* (Chicago: University of Chicago Press, 1989), 141.

the face is straightway ethical. Creation, too, is a system of meetings, signals, encounters, and communications. It is a "face" that offers relationship and entails an ethic, thus giving form and shape to our lives.

The psychoanalytic psychotherapist Shierry Weber Nicholsen, in her book *The Love of Nature and the End of the World*, explores dimensions of our emotional experience with the natural world that are sometimes courteous, though more often not. In order to find a language for emotional experience with nature, Nicholsen also turns to the face, where she finds the "intimacy of reciprocal perception":

> The experience of beauty epitomizes the intimacy of reciprocal perception. The beautiful is seen within a reverberating perceptual field that it shares with the Other. In other words, what we perceive as beautiful is experienced as having a face that returns our gaze . . . the prototypical form of aesthetic reciprocity is a mutual gazing into one another's eyes and at another's face.[7]

Nicholsen affirms the "thou" of nature in its face: "For the natural world to have a face in this sense would mean opening ourselves up to exploration and reshaping by it through the very act of responding to its invitation."[8] Simply responding to the invitation of nature is an exploration in "reshaping" and spiritual practice that is bounded, we may hope, by an ethic of kindness.

As with any face, however, we have the choice to respond to the invitation with care, or we can choose to ignore it, abandon it, refuse to see it, abuse it, or dissociate ourselves from it. This is Nicholsen's critique: faced with the invitation of creation, humanity and contemporary culture have chosen ignorance, abandonment, even denial. The cultural pathology of denial underlies many of today's ecological crises. Given this cultural pathology, Nicholsen asks a crucial question: How is it that we allow ourselves to live in denial of nature's diminishment at human hands while remaining aware of a simultaneous invitation by nature to reconnection and healing?

As a partial answer to this question, Nicholsen turns to the work of James Hillman, who also reminds us of that mostly forgotten but essential

---

7. Shierry Weber Nicholsen, *The Love of Nature and the End of the World: The Unspoken Dimensions of Environmental Concern* (Cambridge, MA: MIT Press, 2003), 95, 97.

8. Nicholsen, *Love of Nature,* 99, 101.

human capacity — wonder. Wonder transforms denial and loss as effectively as it elicits acceptance and recovery. Psychic and spiritual transformation, even "the transfiguration of matter," Hillman writes, "occurs through wonder."[9] According to Hillman, wonder is formational, even of matter; and thus, for Hillman, the sacred matters. We have seen that within Christian formational traditions wonder fosters attention. Attention — to self, others, God, and creation — in turn fosters compunction, contrition, confession, and forgiveness. Giving open attention to creation is something that as humans we can do; following attention, we can accept the invitation in the face of creation; accepting the invitation, we can see that our acceptance and our gaze is "straightway ethical": we return to wonder, from which covenant forms and an ethic of hope returns.

> **PRACTICE 4.2**

Wonder: Facing Nature, Facing Hope

INTENTION   Using the Christian theological or spiritual virtue of hope, the intention of this practice is to face nature with hope as a discipline of invitation, hospitality, participation, and gift.

Thinking Like Queen Anne's Lace

> *The question is not what you look at, but what you see.*
>   Henry David Thoreau, *Journals* (November 16, 1850)

Aldo Leopold was one of the first modern writers to recognize and write eloquently about creation's power to change our perceptions and alter our consciousness. One particularly striking example of this happened for Leopold as he looked into the face of a dying wolf. He describes an incident that was to alter him for the rest of his life in an essay in *A Sand County Almanac* (1949). Early one morning Leopold and a few friends spot a wolf and her pups. He tells what happens next:

---

9. Nicolsen, *Love of Nature*, 102.

> In those days we had never heard of passing up a chance to kill a wolf. In a
> second we were pumping lead into the pack, but with more excitement
> than accuracy. . . . When our rifles were empty, the old wolf was down,
> and a pup was dragging a leg into impassable slide-rocks. We reached the
> old wolf in time to watch a fierce green fire dying in her eyes. I realized
> then, and have known ever since, that there was something new to me in
> those eyes — something known only to her and to the mountain.[10]

Facing the dying wolf, he is drawn into an unexpected intuitive understanding, a point of consciousness-shifting connection. The implication of
this, as Leopold makes clear, is that he now shares something with vital elements of creation: wolf knowledge, mountain knowledge.

Indigenous peoples who have not been displaced from their land share
this kind of knowledge as well. Christians of all persuasions are called —
even invited — to share such intimate, nature-knowledge: from the mountains the Creator "make[s] springs gush forth in the valleys; they flow between the hills, giving drink to every wild animal; and the wild asses quench
their thirst" (Ps. 104:10-11); all "creation waits with eager longing for the revealing of the children of God . . . that creation itself will be set free from its
bondage to decay . . . that the whole creation has been groaning in labor
pains until now" (Rom. 8:19, 21, 22); that the air is filled with the sounds of
this knowledge as we listen. "Let the heavens be glad, and let the earth rejoice; let the sea roar, and all that fills it; let the field exult, and everything in
it. Then shall all the trees of the forest sing for joy before the Lord; for he is
coming, for he is coming to judge the earth" (Ps. 96:11-13).

In open dry fields, prairies, and along roadways — often growing in
friendly gatherings from mid-July through early September — is a wildflower that I invite you to bend down and look at carefully. It has very
small cream-white, lacy petals that are collectively formed in the shape of
an inverted umbrella (called an umbel). The umbel is rounded at the bottom and nearly flat at the top with a slightly bluish-green stem; the green
leaves are very finely cut, almost fern-like, and they smell of carrot when
crushed. Beneath the umbel of petals is a parachute pattern of stems that
together support hundreds of these tiny floweret-petals, each one no more
than one-eighth of an inch across. This wildflower is commonly called
Queen Anne's lace *(Daucus carota),* named for the lace-like patterns

---

10. Aldo Leopold, *A Sand County Almanac: And Sketches Here and There* (Oxford: Oxford
University Press, 1949; reprint, 1987), 130.

formed by the formal, intricate arrangement of these hundreds of small flowerets. But besides the beauty of the lacy patterns, Queen Ann's lace is a flower with a secret. Within the shared umbel, in the very center of the hundreds and hundreds of flowerets, is one — and only one — reddish to wine-purple floweret, also one-eighth of an inch across. Just one — no larger or smaller than any of its uncountable, creamy white brothers and sisters. Facing Queen Anne's lace — letting it be as attentive to and astonished by you as you are by it — you share with its wine-colored eye something only the flower and the prairie know, as Aldo Leopold might say. You know connection with flower and prairie, and you know this with certainty, reverence, and devotion. And the myriad creamy white and the single wine-red flowerets form the face of a lover. Thinking like Queen Anne's lace, like a lover, you kiss the face of God. You will never be the same. You have become like Saint Francis of Assisi, *seeing* creation as a kiss of praise:

> Praised be You, my Lord, with all your creatures
> Especially Sir Brother Sun. . . .
> Praised be You, my Lord, through Sister Moon and the stars. . . .
> Praised be You, my Lord, through Brother Wind. . . .
> Praised by You, my Lord, through Sister Water. . . .
> Praised be You, my Lord, through our Sister Mother Earth.[11]

PRACTICE 4.3

Praising Like Queen Anne's Lace

INTENTION The intention of this practice is to participate with nature in creation's constant doxology to the Creator. Saint Francis of Assisi observed and experienced nature as an intimate relationship. In Thoreau's words, only in such "intimate seeing," and not just "looking," was Saint Francis able to make the link between nature as family and nature as praise.

11. From St. Francis's famous poem of creation praise that is variously titled "Canticle of Brother Sun," "Brother Sun, Sister Moon," and "Canticle of Praise." The cited translation is from *Francis and Clare: Complete Works*, trans. and with intro. by Regis J. Armstrong and Ignatius C. Brady (New York: Paulist Press, 1982), 38-39. It is important to note that Francis uses the Umbrian "per": we praise God *through* the natural world, but not God *in* the natural world. The latter would represent panentheism, of which there were and are a number of advocates in the Christian tradition; but Francis was not one of them.

PRACTICE

- Creation teaches us to pray. Creation in prayer teaches us (1) to find a balance between being what we are created to be and doing what we are created to do; and (2) within that balance, to abide in God's delight.
- Creation finds its own delight in leading us into such prayer. Look, find, and see how being present and open to nature allows nature to guide you in her ways of prayerful praise.
- Know whenever you face nature with attention and wonder that you are praising God, just as creation does the same.
- The psalmist writes: "Let the floods clap their hands; let the hills sing together for joy at the presence of the Lord" (Ps. 98:8). Watch, smell, feel something in nature: a river emptying into the ocean, the hills, the wine-purple floweret in the midst of white in Queen Anne's lace. Stay a moment to observe them clapping their hands, singing together with joy at the presence of the Lord. With practice, you will notice that nature is constantly praising God in this way.
- If, as Chief Sealth claims, nature is a web and you are a part of that web, simply in being yourself you give praise to God. How does what you do in nature — in that web — affect your relationship with God?

Praising like Saint Francis or praising like Queen Anne's lace, we begin to understand something of what the prophet Isaiah knows: that the Lord delights in you, that the Lord delights in your praise, that your land once named "Desolate" will not only be renamed, but you and the earth will become as bride and groom:

You shall no more be named Forsaken,
    and your land shall no more be named Desolate;
but you shall be called My Delight Is in Her,
    and your land Married;
for the Lord delights in you,
    and your land shall be married.

Isaiah 62:4

"Delight" is a common word used in Scripture to describe the feelings of God for creation and creation for God. Often this delight is expressed in terms of the delight of bride and groom, one for the other, as in Isaiah.

Captured in this delight, there is always a sense in which "your land shall be married" to you.

Married to the land — essentially a covenantal relationship of interdependence — it would be hard to imagine *not* seeing the delighting, ethical face of nature as we grow in practice and formation as Christians. The image of marriage is an image implying stability as well as growth: wedded to the land, we stand on solid ground; wedded to the land, we share with nature in her dynamic transformations and simplicity in both spiritual and physical ways. Chief Sealth *(Ts'ial-la-kum),* an indigenous American of the Pacific Northwest, tells the story of this connection, its delight, and ways of knowing in his own beautiful way:

> We are part of the earth and it is part of us.
> The perfumed flowers are our sisters; the deer,
> The horse, the great eagle, these are our brothers.
> The rocky crests, the juices in the meadow, the body heat
> Of the pony and man — all belong to the same family.
> This we know. The earth does not belong to man; man belongs
> To the earth. This we know. All things are connected like
> The blood which unites one family. All things are connected.

As if in a deliberate echo of marriage to the land depicted in Isaiah, Chief Sealth ends his testament this way: "Man did not weave the web of life; he is merely a strand in it. Whatever he does to the web he does to himself."[12] Whatever we do to the marriage between the land and ourselves, we do to ourselves. Every leaf, bud, cloud, wolf, mountain, and wildflower is a call, a voice, a word, a story, an opportunity for matrimony and celebration within this web, in which God takes such great delight.

The wolf, the mountains, Queen Anne's lace, the web: wherever we direct our love, attention, and wonder toward the face of nature, to which "all things are connected," we find that community where, in Paul's language, "all things hold together" in Christ (Col. 1:17). Within this community, holy nuptials are being performed all across this "holding together in Christ." This is where we can say, "I do," and transformation abounds.

If we continue to turn our faces away from the face of creation, we turn away from the *adama* (earth) in Adam, the *humus* (soil) in human. If we

---

12. From "Chief Sealth's Testament," cited in Margaret Silf, *Roots and Wings: The Human Journey from a Speck of Stardust to a Spark of God* (Grand Rapids: Eerdmans, 2006), 18.

believe that the sacred matters not, we turn away from the beloved, who is leaping upon the mountains and bounding over the hills like a gazelle (see Song of Songs 2:8-9); we turn away from the lover's two breasts, which are like two fawns, twins of a gazelle that feeds among the lilies. If we see no praise in the face of Queen Anne's lace, we turn away from the beloved, whose eyes are doves (cf. Song of Solomon 4:1, 5); if we see no mystery, we covenant no lasting promise. But if we gaze with clear, attentive, receptive, hospitable eyes into the face of creation, we risk the possibility of delight; we risk surprise, fear, grief, illumination, reconciliation, death, renewal, participation, doxology, and union as well. But primarily, I think, we miss delight. Yes, it is a risk. But the "other" always entails risk until the stranger, through invitation and hospitality, becomes the friend, becomes an intimate, becomes a delight. We can become friends, intimates, communities in covenant with the mystery of nature, in which every invitation to the "stranger" secures another ineffable strand in the web of creation. Paul's invitation that "we together have the mind of Christ" (1 Cor. 2:16b) is an invitation to think like a mountain, like a wolf, like Queen Anne's lace.

PRACTICE 4.4

Belonging

INTENTION Knowing what the wolf knows, knowing what the mountain knows, sharing the wisdom and beauty of Queen Anne's lace, being named "My Delight Is in Her," and Chief Sealth's wisdom and his insight that "all things are connected" — all of these speak of one thing: belonging. The intention of this practice is to experience belonging in nature through the art of poetry.

I sit with my back now against an old shade-giving burr oak in July. The hot odor of drying grasses and prairie rises, and the rain in the distance begins to glow. The hard, roped, but comforting bark settles into my spine as I join the oak's roots seeking those wisps of moisture drying in the earth. A white moth flutters on my chest. My own roots share the new wings of my heart. What is not belonging?

Imprinted by Nature

INTENTION   From an early age we are "imprinted," shaped, and formed by the land, by geography, climate, and the seasons. This practice is a simple experiment with the intention of helping us notice the early impact of place and ecology on our formation. We will notice how, in the process of this formation, nature imprints herself within us with a particular landscape or ecology that stays with us into adulthood and calls us with a longing and a sense of home.

The Book of Nature

CHAPTER FIVE

The Grammar of Nature

I bequeath myself to the dirt to grow from the grass I love.

Walt Whitman[1]

Some people, in order to discover God, read books. But there is a great book: the very appearance of created things. . . . Why, heaven and earth shout to you: "God made me!"

Augustine of Hippo[2]

In the mid 1950s, our family lived in Northern California in a small house that opened into a large world. The house sat on the border of a coastal redwood forest. I have since learned that we lived at the edge of a narrow strip of temperate rain forest that was dominated by redwoods, running from southern Monterey County in the south to just across what is now the Oregon-California border to the north. The forests of redwoods begin a few miles from the Pacific coast, running up the western flanks of the Pacific Coastal Range. They thrive in this ecology of heavy rain and daily fog, growing to heights of over 300 feet, especially in deep and hidden valleys along narrow creeks that seem to ooze out of the sodden mountains.[3] This

1. Walt Whitman, "Song of Myself," 52.1339, in *Leaves of Grass*, ed. Harold W. Blodgett and Sculley Bradley (New York: Norton, 1995), 89.

2. The following quotations from Irenaeus, Origen, Athanasius, and Augustine compiled by Fred Krueger, "Opening the Book of Nature.Com": http://www.bookofnature.org/library/ngb.html (accessed April 2009).

3. For a fascinating account of searching for and climbing the few remaining old-growth

was still a time when we would drink from these clear creeks, when water from such creeks was "sweet."

It rained a lot. And more than rain, there was fog — almost daily. But a redwood forest thrives on this constant cooling moisture. Running through these forests, with the fragrance of a redwood forest sucking water from the fog, one experiences something like a sixth sense that clarifies and opens fresh possibilities of exploration and adventure.

Those times were no doubt intensified by the imagination and adventure in the books I was devouring at the time: Kipling and Twain and Melville and Thoreau and James Fenimore Cooper. I loved Emily Dickinson, too, though I wouldn't call her "adventurous." Emily knew things I knew in my heart, and she could speak what I only know in my body, such as "skies that could not keep secrets."

Then Walt Whitman came from out of nowhere and changed the way I read and rode my bike and ran through the redwoods. With Walt I found that I no longer even needed to separate things from words, or myself from trees, or — perhaps most wonderful of all — myself from words. The redwoods, myself, the words they spoke and I spoke to them — we were a forest together, a "song," as Walt would say, through which trees would stand and I would run and the words would flow like the creeks and drizzle with the fog, giving a good soak to all.

Walt Whitman once asked, "Have you reckon'd a thousand acres much? Have you reckon'd the earth much? Have you practis'd long to learn to read?"[4] Redwoods, I know, do not reckon a thousand acres much; they do not reckon the earth more or less than they; they have centuries piled on centuries to learn to read, to learn to find a form for their sermons. Walt turned my sixth sense back to the trees, where I learned to wait in the presence of thousands of years of slow growing, learned the arts of stilling, found that running on the earth was sacred dance, and practiced long to learn to read. How could I fail to learn to read with a teacher like this:

> The spotted hawk swoops by and accuses me, he complains of
>   my gab and my loitering. . . .

---

stands of the tallest of these magnificent trees (a search driven primarily by wonder and love of the trees) and of the discovery of an incredibly diverse ecosystem in the canopy of these redwood forests (an exploration driven primarily by science and love of the trees), see Richard Preston, *The Wild Trees: A Story of Passion and Daring* (New York: Random House, 2007). The book does not disclose the location of the tallest of these coastal redwoods.

4. Whitman, "Song of Myself," 2.29-31.

I depart as air, I shake my white locks at the runaway sun,
I effuse my flesh in eddies, and drift it in lacy jags.
I bequeath myself to the dirt to grow from the grass I love,
If you want me again look for me under your boot-soles.
You will hardly know who I am or what I mean,
But I shall be good health to you nevertheless,
And filter and fibre your blood.[5]

I thank Walt for filtering and fibering my blood. In a literal sense, I never found that "I" he speaks of; I was young when I first started looking, and I know now that he doesn't mean the simple, literal "I" anyway. He means something more along the lines of what I found: "Ever since the creation of the world God's eternal power and divine nature, invisible though they are, have been understood and seen through the things God has made" (Rom. 1:20).

Many years later I found an old redwood tree of a man, Saint Augustine of Hippo. I am sure that Augustine and Walt could have walked arm in arm, hour upon hour, companions who together "reckon'd the earth much." Augustine writes: "Some people, in order to discover God, read books. But there is a great book: the very appearance of created things. Look above you! Look below you! Note it. Read it. . . . Why, heaven and earth shout to you: 'God made me!'" Augustine wrote those lines, but Walt Whitman could have written them. "I bequeath myself to the dirt to grow from the grass I love." Walt Whitman wrote those lines, but Saint Augustine could have written them.

Today I still run for exercise, though more often I walk or wander or purposefully get lost. I am thankful that, since I have "practis'd long to learn to read," the trees and the waters and the skies somehow keep speaking. Sometimes I am too dumb to hear or too tired to read, but I nevertheless know in my footsteps that

This alphabet of "natural objects"
Spells out a story.
Once you learn how to read the land,
I have no fear of what you will do to it, or with it,
And I know many pleasant things it will do to you.[6]

---

5. Whitman, "Song of Myself," 52.1331, 1337-41.

6. Aldo Leopold, "Wherefore Wildlife Ecology?" in *The River of the Mother of God and Other Essays,* cited in Marybeth Lorbiecki, *Aldo Leopold: A Fierce Green Fire; An Illustrated Biography* (Helena, MT: Falcon Publishing Co., 1996), 181.

Nature is an "alphabet of natural objects," an alphabet and a story more ancient than the scriptures. But like the scriptures, nature is a book: it tells a story that will do many pleasant things to you.

PRACTICE 5.1[7]

An Alphabet of Sound, The Language of Creation

The heavens are declaring the glory of God;
  and the firmament proclaims God's handiwork.
Day to day pours forth speech,
  and night to night declares knowledge.
There is no speech, nor are there words;
  their voice is not heard;
yet their voice goes out through all the earth,
  and their words to the end of the world.

Psalm 19:1-4

INTENTION   From Psalm 19 we learn that creation has its own language, a "speech" uttered in a "voice [that] goes out throughout all the earth." Creation's "voice is not heard," yet her "words" reach the ends of the cosmos. This practice is an exercise in listening as a condition of reading the book of nature. In it we will concentrate only on sound (just one way of "reading"). The intention of the practice is to be a simple primer for beginning to learn the language of the book of nature. A few responses from others who practiced the exercise are included in order to help make this a collaborative listening project.

PRACTICE   Find a place in the natural world where you can listen uninterrupted for about thirty minutes.

• Listen to the environment for fifteen minutes or longer, but for a predetermined length of time. Use a timer, clock, or any adequate method to define this time length.
• Describe in detail the sounds you hear (heard) and how you feel (felt) about them (you may want to do this during the predetermined time or

7. This practice is based on an exercise, "The Poetics of Environmental Sound," developed by Pauline Oliveros in *The Book of Music and Nature*, ed. David Rothenberg and Marta Ulvaeus (Middletown, CT: Wesleyan University Press, 2001), 133-38.

after). Write them in a notebook for yourself or for later sharing with a group.

- You are a part of the environment: include internal sounds as well as external sounds.
- Explore the limits of audibility (sounds that are highest/lowest, loudest/softest, simplest/most complex, nearest/most distant, longest/shortest).

SAMPLE RESPONSES

- "One thing I noticed right away was the absence of silence. There is always some kind of sound in the air."
- "I have just been in concert: the continuing concert of environmental sounds. I can hear it still."
- "Only a couple of minutes have passed and things are getting really involved already."
- "Five minutes have passed — only five minutes! Such a complex of varied sounds in such a short time. Well, onward — the sounds aren't waiting for me but are going on."
- "Sounds are very complex now. It is all but impossible to get them down; there seem to be a thousand things going on at once. Twelve minutes have passed."
- "I also noticed that my disposition was affected by the type of sounds I heard."

Scripture: An Out-of-Doors Book

> *God gave Solomon very great wisdom, discernment, and breadth of understanding. . . . He would speak of trees, from the cedar that is in Lebanon to the hyssop that grows in the wall; he would speak of animals, and birds, and reptiles, and fish. People came from all nations to hear the wisdom of Solomon.*
>
> 1 Kings 4:29, 33-34

Scripture is an out-of-doors book both in the sense that it should literally be read outdoors, and in the sense that it is a story about the out-of-doors. Read outdoors, Scripture breathes; it leaps out of your hands and into the world. As a story about the out-of-doors, it infuses creation with words and, as Michel Foucault has written, "forces language to reside in the world, among the plants, the herbs, the stones, and the animals."[8]

As a story about the out-of-doors, Scripture gives language to plants and herbs, to stones and animals. Scripture penetrates and instills nature with wonder: it re-creates nature as an ecology of miracles. Riding gently down the Mississippi, the great American storyteller Mark Twain wrote about nature similarly infused with a voice. The river, he says, is "a wonderful book, which told its mind to me without reserve, delivering its most cherished secrets as clearly as if it uttered them with a voice." Twain adds that the Mississippi "was not a book to be read once and thrown aside, for it had a new story to tell every day."[9] Foucault and Twain may not have been avid Scripture readers. For this reason, their own careful reading of the book of nature directs us toward the apostle Paul's writing in Romans: "Ever since the creation of the world, God's eternal power and divine nature, invisible though they are, have been understood and seen through the things God has made" (Rom. 1:20). Yahweh is an out-of-doors God; Scripture is an out-of-doors book.

Nature, as it tells the story of an outdoor Creator and as it mirrors Scripture, is not limited to any particular denomination, church, or rite. In the Belgic Confession, for instance, nature is "a beautiful book in which all creatures, great and small, are as letters to make us ponder the invisible things of God" (Article 2). A recent "Pastoral Letter" from Roman Catholic Canadian bishops remarks that each Christian is called to deepen his or her capacity to appreciate the wonders of nature as an act of faith and love. Using a beatitude from Matthew's Gospel to draw together nature, virtue, and God, the letter continues: "[I]n the silence of contemplation, nature speaks of the beauty of the Creator. If you look at the world with a pure heart, you too will see the face of God" (see Matt. 5:8).[10]

Nature is not only ecumenical as it tells the stories of its Creator; it has been telling these stories across traditions and throughout the centuries from the beginning of Christian spiritual traditions. Centuries before the pastoral letter and even the Belgic Confession (though not as long ago as the birth of many redwood trees!), the seventh-century monk Maximus

8. Cited in Barbara Ann Kipfer, *The Order of Things* (New York: Workman Publishing Company, 2008), 35

9. Mark Twain, *Life on the Mississippi* (New York: Library of America, 1982).

10. Canadian Conference of Catholic Bishops, "A Pastoral Letter on the Christian Ecological Imperative," #15: www.cccb.ca/Files/pastoralenvironment.html (accessed April 2009).

the Confessor also spoke as a person steeped in the creation stories of nature and how these stories echo the stories of Scripture: "Creation is a bible whose letters and syllables are the particular aspects of all creatures. Conversely, Scripture is like a cosmos constituted of heaven and earth and things in between."[11] A beautiful example of how seriously and ecumenically Scripture was read in the past as an out-of-doors book comes from the great twelfth-century reformer, theologian, and mystic Bernard of Clairvaux. There was hardly another writer more immersed in Scripture than Bernard of Clairvaux. As he reflects on nature in this passage, he moves effortlessly between the two books that he loved, both "penned" by the same Author:

> The smiling countenance of the earth is painted with varying colors, the blooming verdure of spring satisfies the eyes, and its sweet odor salutes the nostrils. While I view the flowers, while I breathe their sweet scent, the meadows recall to me the histories of ancient times; for while I drink in the sweetness of the flowers, the thought occurs to my mind of the fragrance of the clothing of the Patriarch Jacob, which the Scripture compares to the odor which mounts from a fruitful field. . . . In this way, while I am charmed without by the sweet influence of the beauty of the country, I have not less delight within reflecting on the mysteries which are hidden beneath it.[12]

In Bernard of Clairvaux we find a natural, unhurried, but palpable familial relationship emerging between the books of nature and Scripture. The book of nature adds its own wisdom to the book of Scripture, while the book of Scripture sends us outdoors prepared for miracles, and with "not less delight within reflecting on the mysteries which are hidden beneath [the beauty of the country]."

11. Maximus, *Ambigua (Books of Difficulties)*, 10, in *Maximus the Confessor*, trans. Andrew Louth (New York: Routledge, 1996), 110.

12. Bernard of Clairvaux, *Life and Works of St. Bernard, Abbot of Clairvaux*, trans. Samuel Eales (London: John Hodges, 1889), 2:464.

PRACTICE 5.2

Scripture: An Out-of-Doors Book

INTENTION   The intention of this practice is to read Scripture, with Wendell Berry's help, as an out-of-doors book: it is the story of creation, and it is best read open to the sky. When we read Scripture in this way, the miraculous is not the extraordinary but the common mode of existence; the common mode of existence can become extraordinary.

Book of Nature: Spectacles of Scripture and Wisdom of Virtue

> *The creatures are like letters proclaiming in loud voices to their Divine Master and Creator the harmony and order of things.*
>
> Athanasius

Lovers of creation have long recognized that on earth as it is, reading the book of nature teaches, guides, and forms individuals and communities. And for nearly as long, acting in a kind of circular pattern of interpretation, these same lovers of creation have noticed that both Scripture and the way we live our lives within creation (i.e., virtue) deepen and give clarity to the ways we read and interpret the book of nature.

John Calvin uses two images to illustrate how the book of nature and the book of Scripture can be read together and how each can give a clearer image of God in the process. The first image is that of the book of nature as a mirror in which we can contemplate God: "God reveal[s] himself and daily discloses himself in the whole workmanship of the universe. . . . Upon his individual works he has engraved unmistakable marks of his glory. . . . The universe is a sort of mirror in which we can contemplate God, who is otherwise invisible."[13] In the second instance, Calvin uses the image of Scripture as a lens or pair of spectacles through which we can read the book of creation more clearly. He says:

---

13. Athanasius, "Oratio contra Gentes," quoted in Clarence J. Glacken, *Traces on the Rodian Shore: Nature and Culture in Western Thought from Ancient Times to the End of the Eighteenth Century* (Berkeley: University of California Press, 1967), 203.

Just as old or bleary-eyed men and those with weak vision, if you thrust before them a most beautiful volume, even if they recognize it to be some sort of writing, yet can scarcely construe two words, but with the aid of spectacles will begin to read distinctly; so Scripture, gathering up the otherwise confused knowledge in our minds [nature gives "knowledge," but not clear knowledge], having dispersed our dullness, clearly shows us the true God.[14]

John Calvin is clearly writing of a "reading" of nature that goes beyond simple understanding of nature itself. In each case, the key element is that the book of nature, read carefully, allows us to *contemplate a God who is otherwise invisible* and *clearly shows us the true God.* This is really quite astounding in Calvin: to contemplate the true God in nature. But it is his unmistakable conclusion that the book of nature mirrors God, and Scripture clarifies God in just these ways as we read the book of nature.

Calvin is an example of a Reformation father who uses Scripture as a lens to read nature and in the reading is guided into companionship with and contemplation of what he calls "the true God." Maximus the Confessor, from the Orthodox tradition, gives us an example of the more ancient tradition of reading the book of nature through the lens of virtue, and in the case of Maximus, through the lens of contemplation, which is inseparable from virtue in his writing.

Unlike John Calvin, Maximus the Confessor (ca. 580-662) is an example of the Orthodox emphasis on union with God, or *theosis,* as a way of reading creation through virtue. The clarifying virtues that lead to *theosis* are varied: depending on the writer they might include forgiveness, generosity, gentleness, hospitality, justice, simplicity, prayer, poverty, attention, watchfulness, contemplation, and compassion. For Maximus, the virtues provide the discipline necessary *to be with* nature in a centered, present way; nature moves us into companionship, the ability *to be with* the immanent, present God. For Maximus, as for Calvin, Scripture plays an important role in seeing creation clearly: "In this way [creation] is seen to be something like a book [the "book of law"]. For a book has letters and syllables; it also has words . . . the author of existence gives himself to be beheld through visible things [i.e., the "book of nature"].[15] But for Maximus,

14. John Calvin, *Institutes of the Christian Religion,* I.V.1, I.VI.1, ed. John T. McNeill, trans. Ford Lewis Battles (Philadelphia: Westminster, 1960), 52-53, 70.
15. Maximus, *Ambigua (Books of Difficulties),* 10.18, 1128A, p. 110.

reading the book of nature in the context of *virtue* elicits contemplation of God in a way that includes Calvin's emphasis on Scripture, but adds to it. Maximus says that virtue *and* Scripture help us read the book of nature: "[S]o the written law is potentially the natural and the natural law is habitually the written, so the same meaning is indicated and revealed."[16]

Also unlike Calvin, who teaches that nature (and therefore God) is most clearly seen through Scripture, Maximus places emphasis on the journey into God, theosis, once again in virtue and contemplation. Accordingly, he describes five modes of contemplative practice in the natural world that form contemplative practice in the kinds of virtue that lead ultimately to a contemplative "ascent" to or union *(theosis)* with God:

> [The first] three of them are intended to lead us to the knowledge of God. . . . The other two to educate us to virtue and to assimilation to God. The man who *forms* himself in accordance with these becomes God [i.e., deified], experiencing what God is from the things that are, as it were seeing with his mind the complete impression of God in accordance with goodness.[17]

God is seen through the virtue of "goodness," while contemplation of God through creation itself reveals the divine "Goodness." For Maximus the Confessor and his tradition, contemplation of the book of nature coupled with Scripture is the route to ascension to vision/union with God.

Thus, for Calvin, the lens of Scripture "clearly shows us the true God." For Maximus the Confessor, virtue and contemplation serve as another lens through which humanity "becomes God — experiencing God from the things that are [nature]." For both Calvin and Maximus, the book of nature is a route into the mystery of God, and nature is thus a complement to both of their approaches. Nature is the still point between the transcendent and the immanent God; the book of nature is the still point between virtue and contemplation.

---

16. Maximus, *Ambigua,* 10.18, 1129C, p. 112.
17. Maximus, *Ambigua* 10.19, 1133B-C, p. 119 (italics added).

The Beatitudes and Reading Nature

INTENTION   The intention of this practice is to use the Beatitudes as an example of reading nature through the "spectacles" of Scripture and virtue.

PRACTICE   The conclusion to *Nature as Spiritual Practice* is entitled "The Green Beatitudes." In that section we will look even more closely at the Beatitudes as model and guide for both contemplation of nature and virtue or earth-care in nature. As we work our way to the conclusion, begin to notice nature itself as an ideal point of balance between contemplation and virtue (or compassion). This point of balance between contemplation and virtue is a way of seeing God at the center of all things. The longer version of the Beatitudes, or the "Sermon on the Mount," is found in Matthew 5:3-11.

- Find a place in nature, settle in, notice your breath in order to become still, and read through Matthew's Beatitudes slowly several times. You may wish to use a practice that slows your reading to a meditative pace, such as *lectio divina.*

- As you are ready, read each Beatitude one at a time and pause after each, applying that saying to the natural world around you. It may help to imagine that Jesus' sermon is addressed to nature. This is not as odd as it may at first seem: Saint Francis of Assisi is famous for preaching to nature in just this way.

- Notice how each Beatitude can be applied to the natural world. Or, to put it another way, imagine the Beatitude as a special pair of glasses through which you observe nature. For example, the first Beatitude in Matthew 3:3 is: "Blessed are the poor in spirit, for theirs is the kingdom of heaven." Observe or walk through nature, watching for what you see or experience as "poor in spirit." This could be a dying or degraded part of nature; or "poor in spirit" can also mean "humble." What in nature is humble? One aspect of humility is simply being what one is created to be. How is a tree, for instance, being what it is created to be?

- How does what you see in nature as "poor in spirit" translate into a blessing?

- The Beatitudes are also virtues, ways of compassionate presence within the world. How do the Beatitudes translate into a compassionate way of being in the world? In the first Beatitude, for example, what would it mean for you to be "poor in spirit" in your interactions and connections with nature? How does behavior on your part that is "poor in spirit" bless nature?

- Go through each of the Beatitudes in the same way, pausing between each as long as you would like or are inspired to do so. You may wish to do each Beatitude on a different day or in a different location. Use a pace that is comfortable for you.

Nature as Book and Sermon

> *Some of the Pharisees in the crowd said to him, "Teacher, order your disciples to stop." He answered, "I tell you, if these were silent, the stones would shout out."*
>
> Luke 19:39-40

The apostle Luke writes that stones can and will shout out the gospel (good news) of Christ. Some writers in the Christian spiritual traditions write about hearing the "shout" of Luke's stones in ways that remind us of reading a book. Other writers seem to experience this same "shout" as though it were a kind of sermon. The distinctions are not hard and fast, nor — at least in most cases — does one actually read or even hear the "shout" of Luke's stone in the same ways we read a book or hear a sermon. But as this section illustrates, being attentive to creation both as "book" and "sermon" opens us to "hearing" Luke's stones "shout" in new ways.

Unlike most books and sermons, the "shouts" of stones are heard in ways that are fully embodied. The books and sermons of creation are "read" and "heard" in ways that involve all of who we are as human persons or communities: these would include all our senses and perceptions, our imaginations and memory, our hopes and dreams and aspirations, our intellect and mind and understanding, our will and our desire, our love, our attention, and our wonder. Luke's stones shout and are heard by some; to others they are silent. Closer, embodied listening helps us learn that silence itself is nature's sermon or book. I believe that, if you listen to the silence of stones, you will hear a sermon like nothing you have ever heard from a pulpit.

It is not important to make too strong a distinction between the "books" and "sermons" of nature. For our purposes we can say that (1) "reading" the book of nature is a way of talking about our own attention, wonder, and love given in a full, embodied way to interpreting nature, while (2) "hearing" the sermons of nature is a way of experiencing — again in a full, embodied way — nature's loving us in ways that promote a "clear remembrance of the Creator." The first has more to do with our experience of nature as a sacramental ecology, while the second has more to do with nature awakening us to the divine presence. Though creation, including humans, can go awry, and the intention of sermon or book may be lost in competing "shouts," both — when read clearly and heard accurately — have to do with the same, mutual attraction: love of the Creator.

PRACTICE 5.4

Ravens and Lilies: Care and Being Cared For

INTENTION   The intention of this practice is to read the book of nature as a way of attending to and loving nature and to listen to the sermons of nature as a way of being loved and cared for by nature in return.

It is clear that the nature writer Barry Lopez gives a musician's listening ear and an artist's seeing eye to nature, whether as a book or a sermon, and anticipates the perils of *not* hearing or seeing the stone — in this case the arctic seal: "To contemplate what people are doing out here and ignore the universe of the seal, to consider human quest and plight and not know the land, I thought, to not listen to it, seemed fatal."[18] Not to listen to or hear the land is "fatal." That is a blunt but accurate warning of what can happen if we ignore or disconnect ourselves from the "shouts of stones." In his book *Arctic Dreams*, Lopez travels to Saint Lawrence Island, above the Arctic Circle, where he encounters the Yup'ik people. The Yup'ik have met "outsiders" such as Lopez before, and they have a word for them that is translatable as "the people who change nature." Sadly, the people who change nature are not the people who encounter nature as practice. Above the Arctic Circle, the Yup'ik people hear sermons that are often harsh,

18. Barry Lopez, *Arctic Dreams: Imagination and Desire in a Northern Landscape* (New York: Vintage Books, 1986), 13.

deadly, and cruel. But they also hear sermons of remembrance; they hear sermons about not forgetting, about nature as provider, sustenance, and inspiration. Those from outside hear no such sermon: we are the people who do not hear sermons in the snow; rather, we are "the people who change nature." The Yup'ik participate in nature as practice; those from the "outside" do not.

"The people who change nature" respond with their own agenda, be it economic, political, social, or even religious. A companion to nature, one who practices nature-care, reads, listens, acknowledges — *then* responds. Lopez is an optimist: he believes that humanity's first wisdom was earth-wisdom, a wisdom that listened to stones and a few other well-chosen companions: "Our first wisdom as a species grew out of such an intimacy with the earth. . . . Whatever wisdom I would find, I knew, would grow out of the land. I trusted that, and that it would reveal itself in the presence of well-chosen companions."[19] This "intimacy with the earth" is an interpretive tool for reading what the book of nature has to teach us. It is also an interpretive tool for reading Scripture. The more one reads Hebrew Scripture, the more apparent it is that the Hebrew people had just such an intimacy with the earth: they read the book of nature and they drew wisdom from the land. In the Christian New Testament as well, Christ evinces a similar intimacy with the earth: his teachings spring from a profound and deep earth-knowledge that can only have taken root in the context of deep earth-wisdom. At one point, Christ himself listened to stones and chose not to "change the land" by turning the stones into bread (see Matthew 4:3).

It is impossible to say exactly what Jesus heard from the earth as he listened to deserts, hills, pastures, rivers, birds, olive groves, sheep, remote places, towns, and inland seas, the places where he grew up, practiced his ministry, and gave his life. But between the lines of his words in the Gospels is a profound listening of the most attentive kind, a listening so profound that he heard even stones speak the wisdom of God. Barry Lopez begins to describe the kind of listening Jesus must have practiced:

A man in Anaktuvuk Pass, in response to a question about what he did when he visited a new place, said to me, "I listen." That is all. "I listen," he meant, to what the land is saying. I walk around in it and strain my senses

19. For the Yup'ik people's concept of "people who change nature," see Lopez, *Arctic Dreams*, 39-40.

in appreciation of it for a long time before I myself ever speak a word. Entered in such a respectful manner, he believed, the land would open to him. . . . [American painters] came to conceive of the land as intrinsically powerful: beguiling and frightening, endlessly arresting and incomprehensibly rich, unknowable and wild. "The face of God," they said.[20]

Jesus Christ, the perfect host, was also a master translator: he translated fig trees and wine and stones: "I tell you, if these [disciples] were silent, the very stones would shout out" (Luke 19:40). Translating its sermons and books, a host of the land does not change the land, but such a companion joins the land. Such a companion of the land was Jesus: to this day all of nature bears the stamp of his companioning, not to be forgotten or changed but to be touched.

PRACTICE 5.5

Touched by a Tree

INTENTION   The intention of this practice is to "read" and "listen" to nature through the sense of touch. The sense of touch is unique. David Abram has written: "To touch the coarse skin of a tree is thus, at the same time, to experience one's own tactility, to feel oneself touched by the tree. And to see the world is also, at the same time, to experience oneself as visible, to feel oneself seen."[21]

PRACTICE   Read again the above quote about the Yup'ik hunter who listens and waits. We are not very good at listening to nature in this way. Find a place in creation to which you can give a fresh reading and where you can concentrate all your senses as you "touch" the sermon of creation in silence. Bring along something to eat.

- As Abram reminds us, to touch something with your hand provides a dual sensation: you will feel what you are touching and feel the feeling of being touched. Try it: rub your thumb and index finger together and you will feel each finger feeling and being felt. Feel nature. If, for example, you are touching a tree, notice that as you touch and feel the bark, at the

---

20. Lopez, *Arctic Dreams*, 257.
21. David Abram, *The Spell of the Sensuous: Perception and Language in a More-than-Human World* (New York: Pantheon Books, 1996), 68.

same time you sense yourself feeling the touch of the bark. Though we seldom notice, this is the case with everything we touch or feel.

- Try noticing touch and being touched at the same time. Do you move back and forth between being aware of touch and being touched, or do you sense both simultaneously?
- Taste is very much a tactile sense: touch is essential to taste. Take a bite of fruit or whatever you brought with you. As you taste an apple, for instance, notice how you taste the apple while at the same time you feel the apple in your mouth. Can you separate this tactile sense from the taste itself?
- Sight, if we grant that the "other" is also a subject and loved by God (Heb. 1:3), also sees and is seen. Look closely at something in nature. How is nature seeing *you* in return?
- Find a fragrance in nature and try shutting off your other senses and concentrating on the fragrance. As you inhale the fragrance, how do you experience yourself taking in the odor? Is it a dual sense as is touch?
- Finally, listening and hearing also lend themselves to Lopez's plea for renewed attention to the wisdom of the earth. Listen to yourself hearing nature.
- Spend time practicing different ways to experience these dual capacities of all your senses in nature.

Anne Whiston Spirn is a woman so attuned to the books and sermons of nature that she urges us to encounter nature as a primer for learning the forgotten language of divine presence. It is a forgotten language, is it not? Once known, now hardly spoken. Spirn teaches herself to read the almost forgotten book of nature and sermons of the landscape by tuning her body and mind and spirit to envisioning creation as a book "printed" in sound and taste and sight and touch:

Verbs, nouns, adverbs, adjectives, and their contexts . . . mirror landscape processes, products, and their modifiers. Just as a river combines water, flowing and eroded banks, sentences combine actions and actors, objects and modifiers. . . . A river's history, a tree's, is the sum of all its dialogues.[22]

22. Anne Whiston Spirn, *The Language of Landscape* (New Haven: Yale University Press, 1998), 15, 48.

For Spirn, the very stones do in fact "shout." She knows that we are imprinted with the landscape of our early childhood and that the language of that landscape is our native tongue, if we would only choose to give attention and memory to the world around us. Her "grammar" of nature teaches in proverbs and parables that are formulated, not from logic or reason alone, but through the enhancing wisdom of imagination, memory, and intuition. The language of landscape, as Spirn describes it, is complex in meaning, layered, ambiguous, never simple or linear. Yet in a landscape each rock, each river, each tree has its story of companioning and hosting to tell.

PRACTICE 5.6

Nature's Parts of Speech

INTENTION   The intention of this practice is to begin to (re)learn the language of creation at a grammatical level by noticing how nature can be seen and interpreted — metaphorically and literally — in terms of parts of speech, such as verbs, nouns, adverbs, and adjectives. This is a practice of listening, noticing, and granting nature its language.

CHAPTER SIX

The Sacred Idiom of Nature

> *More fragile than he would have thought. How much was gone already? The sacred idiom shorn of its referents and so of its reality.*
>
> Cormac McCarthy, *The Road*

The great fourth-century bishop Saint Basil of Caesarea once preached on the subject of the earth's own eloquent sermon:

> I want creation to penetrate you with so much admiration that everywhere, wherever you may be, the least plant may bring to you the clear remembrance of the Creator.[1]

What is the purpose of a sermon if not that it may "bring you the clear remembrance of the Creator"? When I was a young child running free through redwood forests, though I did not know it at the time, creation was penetrating me through and through. Not initially with "admiration" — that would come later — I was simply "penetrated," to use Saint Basil's word, by nature as nature is in itself. At the time, that was enough. Though I was unaware of it then, the penetration was preparation for "clear remembrance."

Barry Lopez reminded us in the preceding chapter that humans can become "those who change nature." In the following chapters we look at some of that "change" and what it means for humans and for the earth. This chap-

---

1. St. Basil, *Hexaemeron*, 5:2, trans. Blomfield Jackson, in *A Select Library of Nicene and Post-Nicene Fathers*, 2nd ser., vol. 8 (Grand Rapids: Eerdmans, 1952), 76.

ter serves as a transition between changing nature and the results of that change; and in this chapter we begin to look at the forgetting rather than the "clear remembrance" of Saint Basil. In a much bleaker vision of the earth than Saint Basil's, the contemporary novelist Cormac McCarthy depicts a global, apocalyptic "nuclear winter" in which the natural world is, in the words of this section's epigraph, "shorn of its referents and so of its reality." In McCarthy's felicitous phrase, nature was once a "sacred idiom."[2] In his novel *The Road,* he envisions creation as no longer either sacred or idiomatic: it does not bring God to remembrance, nor does it read or sermonize in a language, dialect, or style of speaking in any way particular to nature. For McCarthy, shorn of its referents — in this case, both the things themselves that have been destroyed and the names of those things that have been forgotten — creation falls into oblivion. It is not the case in McCarthy's book, but today much of the earth remembers us to our Creator. But what makes his book so chilling is the fact that also today some "referents" *are* missing or damaged or ill: the story does have gaps — gaps of oblivion.

From its inception, the Christian tradition has spoken of two books that remember us to God, in effect two books that help keep us this side of oblivion: the book of Scripture and the book of nature. When read with the eyes of faith, the book of Scripture reveals the fullness of the Creator. With or without the eyes of faith, the book of nature reveals, through its own sacred idiom, both ecological and sacramental wonders. With the eyes of faith, the book of nature is a much more interesting story. In fact, when it is read with the eyes of faith, a healthy and balanced book of nature is limitless in its power to shape, transform, revitalize, inspire, heal, and sanctify.

Lived in with care, prayed with care, and read with care, the sacred idiom of the natural world is a manual, a spiritual guide that forms us in remembrance of our true selves and of the Creator. We can "read" and understand the full reality of Colossians — that Christ is the image of the invisible God — by reading the book of nature with the aid of the book of Scripture. But Scripture itself becomes a vacuum of meaninglessness if we do not read it in the context of creation.[3] We bring full meaning to Scripture when we read it within the broader context of the Creator's own handiwork.

2. All McCarthy citations from Cormac McCarthy, *The Road* (New York: Knopf, 2006), 75.

3. This is not to imply that God is a meaningless vacuum without creation, only that without context *we* have no orientation for understanding God or Scripture or creation. However, a meditation on the attributes of God, if creation had not occurred, would be a valuable meditation.

The Sacred Idiom of Psalm 104

INTENTION The natural world is a sacred idiom that is formative of Christian identity. The intention of this practice is to read nature through Psalm 104, and then Psalm 104 through nature, noting what each reading helps us to remember about ourselves and about God.

Naming and the Oblivion of Names

> *The man gave names to all.*
>
> Genesis 2:20

Naming all creatures in Genesis 2 is a special privilege given to humanity. Though we have largely forgotten the process, naming infants was once considered a holy act. The same is true for Adam's naming of every living creature: it is an honor, an identity-bestowing act. In this act both creation and Scripture become the opposite of "oblivion," or forgetting. Instead of oblivion, Scripture and creation coalesce at the point of naming, each capable of bestowing power and meaning on the other. This is in part how we find our way — on this earth as it is — to God. Unfortunately, humans can also reverse this process. They can destroy the creation and they can take away the names.

In *The Road,* McCarthy presents an opening scenario in which humanity has done both: it has destroyed much of creation and stripped away names, letting them fall into oblivion. The book is fictional; nonetheless, it is a terrifying and disorienting account of nuclear winter. The book opens at the point of this winter where, along with many other species, humanity is about to become extinct. In the book an unnamed man and his unnamed son slowly find their way back to the sea. It is a journey that reverses evolution back to the point of its origin. Unfortunately, near the end of the book, as the two finally reach their destination, the sea itself is clearly dead. All this is bad enough, but adding to the dreadfulness, McCarthy also shows how the journey of the man and the boy along the "road" is also the slow journey of removing or forgetting names. The man and boy literally forget the names of things, mostly of created objects. In what is perhaps a greater loss, the names really no longer matter; nothing of the sacred matters. By the end of the novel it is unclear what has caused the most destruction and disintegration, the nuclear winter or the slow forgetting of names and their referents.

In McCarthy's story, the father and boy have a barely readable map, which they treasure. On this broken, fetid, ghastly road, the map is their only guide: it is guiding them to what they remember as "sea." But even the words "ocean" or "sea" are never spoken; they are only remembered by the father as a single, last hope. The father has never seen the sea, so even this primal ocean-memory is dim and ephemeral.

The Road is a dark journey into darkness. And though he never makes a direct connection in the book, McCarthy never strays far from Genesis 2:19-20: "The Lord God . . . brought them to man to see what he would call them; and whatever he called every living creature, that was its name. The man gave names to all the cattle, and to the birds of the air, and every animal of the field." In both Genesis and *The Road,* things (life itself) and names are interdependent on each other. In Genesis, naming gives status and meaning to life; in *The Road,* as "every living creature" falls into oblivion, so does its name.

> [The father had] had this feeling before, beyond the numbness and the dull despair. The world shrinking down about a raw core of parsible entities. The names of things slowly following those things into oblivion. Colors. The names of birds. Things to eat. Finally the names of things one believed to be true. More fragile than he would have thought. How much was gone already? The sacred idiom shorn of its referents and so of its reality. Drawing down like something trying to preserve heat. In time to wink out forever.[4]

By presenting a sacred idiom "shorn of its referents and so of its reality," McCarthy simultaneously warns of oblivion while awakening us to the sacred idiom we cannot afford to forget: the names, language, and meaning of creation.

---

4. McCarthy, *The Road,* 75.

The Oblivion of Names

INTENTION The intention of this practice is both to cherish names as they give reality to the things of creation and, on the other hand, to experience how the forgetting of names of things of creation is equivalent to forgetting the things themselves, as well as their Creator.

The Road is an apocalyptic nightmare. Yet oddly, in a similar way to how a meditation on death heightens awareness of the fragile miracle of life, McCarthy's work returns us to the natural world with a deeper sense of its own fragile mystery and the names, syntax, and idioms that constitute the voices of nature as creation seeks our ears and hearts and minds.

Ironically, for some indigenous peoples, there is an intuitive understanding of this same treasure of names. Some peoples sense the sacred power in "naming" so clearly that, in reverence, they refuse to speak the name of certain healing plants, feeling that if they did so they would diminish their power to heal. This is not some weird or perverted "magic"; rather, it is the same understanding of the power of naming exhibited by the writer of Genesis, only flipped: instead of bestowing power in naming as in Genesis, such peoples conserve power by not naming. These indigenous peoples read the letters and syllables of creation with integrity and skill, passing on the wisdom of recognizing, preparing, and administering plants and herbs that invigorate, calm, and heal.

An instance of one such group of people comes from the anthropologist Frances Densmore, who lived among the Ojibwa (or Chippewa) tribes in upper Minnesota and Ontario in the late nineteenth and early twentieth centuries. Among the Ojibwa, knowledge in the finding, harvesting, preparation, and use of medicinal plants and herbs was handed down from one generation to the next by members of the Midewiwin, or Mide, their society of healers. Early on, Densmore noticed that throughout all their training, diagnosis, and administration of medicinal plants (which Densmore was there to document), the Mide never once named a single plant. Their nature literacy and a deep reverence for the gift of the healing plant itself led the Mide to conclude that the healing quality of the plant resided not only in the plant and its ritualized administration, but also and equally in its name.

0008320763 8

Sell your books at
World of Books!
Go to sell.worldofbooks.com
and get an instant price
quote. We even pay the
shipping - see what your old
books are worth today!

Inspected By: rudy_sacrab

In the old days a person would not transmit any facts concerning medicines to even a member of his own family, one reason for this restriction seeming to be a fear that the information would not be treated with respect. So great was the secrecy surrounding these remedies that the names were never given of the plants, the person imparting the information showing the fresh plant.[5]

The Mide read the sacred idiom of nature and kept silent. In McCarthy's apocalyptic vision, the silence of names is oblivion. The grammar of creation can be a bit tricky: silence in one sense is sacred; in another sense, it is equivalent to death.

PRACTICE 6.3

Listening with Fresh Ears[6]

INTENTION   The intention of this practice is to bring fresh ears to the task of listening to the silence, the names, and the sonic language of nature.

PRACTICE   This practice can be done indoors or outdoors. The questions are helpful for learning, over time, to "hear" nature in every sense. Go over the following questions and allow them to open doors into new ways of perceiving (or reading) creation.

- Can you find the quiet place in your mind where there are no thoughts, no words, and no images?
- Can you remain in this quiet mind place by listening to all the sounds you can possibly hear, including the most distant sounds beyond the space you now occupy?
- Do you ever notice how your ears adjust inside when you move from one size space to another? Or from indoors to outdoors, or vice versa?

---

5. Frances Densmore, *How Indians Use Wild Plants for Food, Medicine and Crafts,* formerly titled "Uses of Plants by the Chippewa Indians," *Forty-fourth Annual Report of the Bureau of American Ethnology to the Secretary of the Smithsonian Institution,* 1926-1927 (New York: Dover Publications, 1974), 323. Densmore adds that, unfortunately, "the fact that persons were willing to impart their knowledge of these ancient remedies for publication indicates that the attitude of the Chippewa toward their old customs is passing away" (p. 325).

6. This practice is adapted from Pauline Oliveros, "Sonic Images," in *The Book of Music and Nature: Anthology of Sounds, Words, Thoughts,* ed. David Rothenberg and Marta Ulvaeus, copyright © Wesleyan University Press, 1995, 130-33. Used by permission of Wesleyan University Press.

- What is your favorite sound? Can you reproduce it in your mind? Would you communicate to someone else what your favorite sound is?
- Have you heard a sound lately that you could not identify? What were the circumstances? How did you feel?
- What do you sound like when you walk?
- Imagine the sound of a bird call. What kind of bird is it? When did you last hear it? What does it sound like? Can you imitate it?
- What is the most silent period you have ever experienced? Was it only a moment, or was it very long? What was its effect on you?
- What is the most complex sound you have ever experienced? What were the circumstances and how did you feel?

Postmodern, Indigenous Christians

> *You must be the thing you see. . . .*
>
> John Moffitt

In these chapters we have turned our faces toward the vast, infinite book of creation and have found in that book trustworthy guidance for spiritual practice that is formative of Christian faith and identity. Within the book of creation, as John Klassen, O.S.B., the abbot of St. John's Abbey in Collegeville, Minnesota, has written, the natural world becomes a stage, not for God's otherworldly sovereignty, but where a decidedly this-worldly reign is enacted:

> Jesus shows a wonderful attitude toward created things by using water, bread, fish, wine, light, creatures such as birds of the air, foxes, seed and mud. The parables show that Jesus assumed the worth of the created universe, the dependability of nature, the recurrence of the seasons, the normal pattern of sowing and harvesting, of planting a vineyard and caring for it, of seeing the clouds and counting on the rain. The natural world is the stage where the reign of God is enacted, the place where faith in God with all of its dimensions is lived out. The reign of God is not so otherworldly that we can treat the earth badly or with contempt.[7]

7. Abbot John Klassen, O.S.B., "Environmental Stewardship": http://www.saintjohnsabbey .org/abbot/041116.html (accessed Nov. 16, 2007).

Abbot Klassen reminds us how Jesus' own close reading of the book of nature exemplifies an engagement with the natural world that essentially allowed him to *become* the things he saw.

Unfortunately, Klassen's ability to read the book of nature with clarity is a rare gift today. Other powers capture our attention and stand in our way. Henry David Thoreau was perhaps the first to recognize that technology would likely overtake nature in terms of its ability to control and dominate human minds, culture, visions, bodies, and perceptions. He was correct: today our attention is drawn by a culture and technology that for the most part ignores creation. More recently, the philosopher Susan Sontag wrote in support of Thoreau's insight as she looked back to the nineteenth century as the crucial period during which culturally, psychologically, and philosophically, human consciousness was captured in the "predatory embrace" of the ecology of history, rather than the balanced ecology of nature.

> Ours is a time in which every intellectual or artistic or moral event gets absorbed by a predatory embrace of consciousness: historicizing. . . . We understand something by locating it in a multi-determined temporal continuum. . . . But the relation has been upset — permanently? — since the era climaxed by the French Revolution, when "history" pulled alongside "nature" and then took the lead.[8]

Sontag's point is that we find meaning in this "historicizing" process only according to a "predetermined temporal continuum." That is, our culture is captured by the "predatory embrace" of technology embedded only in culture and time. The effect of this shift from space, place, and thing to a determinist orientation toward history is a reorientation of priorities in which the objects of our desire move from sustainability to consumption, from connection and relationship to personal success, from life-giving relationships to virtual realities. Indigenous cultures, as we have seen, hint at the potential to reorient once more, away from the "virtual" alone toward the more life-giving systems of interdependence (community), reciprocal perception, and cumulative attentiveness found in time *and* space (place of nature).

Christianity has a perfect exemplar for such reorientation: the tree. As in other religions, trees are rich in meaning and symbolism in Christianity. The tree is an archetype: examples include the tree of knowledge, the tree

---

8. Susan Sontag, "Introduction," in E. M. Cioran, *The Temptation to Exist*, trans. Richard Howard, 2nd ed. (Chicago: University of Chicago Press, 1986), 7-9.

of life, the tree of the cross, the vineyard tree, the tree outside your window or under which you sit, a coastal redwood, an American beech, a tropical forest in Brazil. Trees in the Christian tradition call to each person or Christian community to become a "contemporary indigenous people" in our relationship to the planet. Postmodern, indigenous Christian people read Scripture and learn to "be what they see": they read Job 38 or Psalm 104 or Psalm 148 or the Song of Solomon or Colossians 1 or Revelation 22 or simply Psalm 95:1-4 — and they become brothers and sisters of plants and animals, rushing streams and mountains, meadows of lilies and constellations of galaxies. Or, flat out on the ground, arms outspread, they reorient to embracing the earth as an embrace of God.

Becoming what we see, embracing the earth in this way prepares us for the very advanced grammar of Matthew 5, the "Green Beatitudes." This advanced grammar is framed in the idiom of the poor in spirit, the mourning, those who hunger and thirst for righteousness, the merciful, the pure in heart, the peacemakers, or the persecuted. The grammar, when learned, turns out to be a simple return of us to ourselves and to creation: "Blessed are the meek, for they shall inherit [not "dominate" or even "steward"] the *earth.*"

Jesus lived a life of being what he saw: for the sake of the woman at the well, he *became* her. He *saw* and became the blind, the lepers, and the hungry; he saw and became the meek, he saw and became the pure at heart; he saw and became the geography from which he drew his teachings and his parables; he saw and became creation's suffering and creation's longing; and finally, he saw the need and became creation's redemption, reconciling all things to God by becoming creation's deepest need. The Anglican divine J. C. Ryle (1816-1900) sensed, as it pours from Scripture, the radical emergence of becoming what he saw in Christ's own indigenous teaching.

Hear what the Scripture says: "All things were made by Him, and without Him was not any thing made that was made." (John i. 3.) "By Him were all things created, that are in heaven and that are in earth." (Colos. i. 16.) "When He prepared the heavens, I was there: when He set a compass upon the face of the depth: when He established the clouds above: when He strengthened the foundations of the deep: when He gave to the sea His decree, that the water should not pass His commandment: when He appointed the foundations of the earth: then I was by Him, as one brought up with Him." (Prov. viii.27-30.) Can we wonder that the Lord Jesus, in His preaching, should continually draw lessons from the *book of nature?*

When He spoke of the sheep, the fish, the ravens, the corn, the lilies, the fig-tree, the vine — He spoke of things which He Himself had made.[9]

Shortly before he died, Pope John Paul II voiced a similar conviction. Pope John Paul spoke of the soul tuned to perceive the sacred book of nature as it reveals God's beauty and ultimately of becoming, in Ryle's words, "what [Christ] Himself had made." In a General Audience address, the Pope comments on the first portion of Psalm 19:1-5, which reads:

> The heavens are telling the glory of God;
>   and the firmament proclaims His handiwork.
> Day to day pours forth speech,
>   and night to night declares knowledge.
> There is no speech, nor are there words;
>   their voice is not heard.
> Yet their voice goes out through all the earth,
>   and their words to the end of the world.
> In the heavens he has set a tent for the sun,
>   which comes out like a bridegroom from his wedding canopy
>   and like a strong man runs its course with joy.

In response to Psalm 19, Pope John Paul's address reads in part:

> The wonderful Psalm 19 is not only a prayer in the form of a hymn of extraordinary intensity. . . . God illuminates the universe with the brilliance of the sun and illuminates humanity with the splendor of his Word contained in biblical Revelation. . . . They [the heavens] in fact "narrate," "announce" the wonders of the divine work. The day and night are also represented as messengers that transmit the great news of creation. This is a silent testimony. . . . But with the interior vision of the soul, with religious intuition not distracted by superficiality, man and woman can discover that the world is not dumb but speaks of the Creator.[10]

How we, as Christians, choose to hear and see the "narrations" and "announcements" of creation in the coming years depends, as Pope John

---

9. J. C. Ryle, "Christ is All": http://www.anglicanlibrary.org/donne/devotions/devotions09.html (accessed July 2008).

10. Pope John Paul II, "General Audience Address on Psalm 19," Vatican City, Jan. 30, 2002 (distributed by the Religious Campaign for Forest Conservation Information Service).

Paul II reminds us, on our ability to discover that the world is not dumb, but speaks of the Creator. It depends, I believe, on our ability to become postmodern indigenous Christians.

The Blind See

INTENTION The intention of this two-part practice is to experience "blindness" in order to "see" creation in new, often surprising ways that can help us become postmodern indigenous Christians.

Reading Christ in the Cosmos

> *The little flower of Jesus had to be and to remain always a drop of dew hidden in the divine corolla of her beautiful Lily of the valleys. A drop of dew, what is more simple and more pure?*
>
> St. Thérèse of Lisieux, "Letters"

Another way of encountering the book of nature is to recognize that often in reading this book, we read the "words" of God in nature, and they are, in effect, contemplation reversed: not a form of contemplation seeking God, as Maximus the Confessor taught and practiced himself, but rather God in contemplation seeking us, seeking our attention and our love. Saint Irenaeus of Lyons (died ca. 200) gives a succinct example of God seeking us through the craftsmanship of nature when he says: "Through creation itself the Word reveals God the Creator. Through the world he reveals the Lord who made the world. Through all that is fashioned he reveals the craftsman who fashioned it all."[11] Irenaeus speaks not only of God seeking us, but of the pattern or method by which we are sought — specifically, a Christic pattern. Each verb, every sentence and sermon, each mountain, river, and stone "shout," as Luke wrote, of the heart and good news of Christ beckoning us back into the sacred matters, through the matters of his creation.

One could hardly imagine a Christian saint more different in circum-

---

11. Irenaeus of Lyons, *Against Heresies*, in *Office of Readings* (Boston: St. Paul Editions, 1983), 164.

stances, culture, and times from Saint Irenaeus than Saint Thérèse of Lisieux (1873-1897). Yet Saint Thérèse, too, recognizes that in seeking the beauty in nature, she is in fact being wooed by God contemplating her through creation. In her profoundly simple way, a heartbreakingly unaffected way — what she called her "little way" of contemplating the world around her — we hear her as though she is experiencing this very phenomenon of God contemplating her:

> . . . the grass all whitened with simple daisies. . . . Well, I thought this morning near the Tabernacle that my Céline [her sister], the little flower of Jesus, had to be and to remain always a drop of dew hidden in the divine corolla of her beautiful Lily of the valleys.[12]

Saint Thérèse reads the book of creatures with purity of heart; she hears simple songs of praise; in these ways God is courting her. It is in this divine courtship, initiated by God, that she finds what she calls her own "little power." Her "littleness" serves to embolden her, much like Saint Francis, who is likewise emboldened by "poverty." Both — one in littleness, one in poverty — look upon creation as a river flowing with a perceptible song and as the palpable contemplation of Creator for creation, calling creation back to what Thérèse calls the "Divine Furnace of the Holy Trinity":

> I look upon myself as a weak little bird, with only a light down as covering. I am not an eagle, but I have only an eagle's EYES AND HEART. In spite of my extreme littleness I still dare to gaze upon the Divine Sun, the Sun of Love, and my heart feels within it all the aspirations of an Eagle. The little bird wills to fly towards the bright Sun which attracts its eye, imitating its brothers, the eagles, whom it sees climbing up towards the Divine Furnace of the Holy Trinity.[13]

Certainly we find our story in the narrative of Scripture and are formed by it. Just as certainly, we find God's story in books of nature and are formed by it. Thérèse, loved by and loving nature, faced by and facing creation, is formed by the book of nature as she herself becomes a living word. She is a bit of dew, a lily of the valley, a small bird with the aspira-

---

12. St. Thérèse of Lisieux, "Letters," 134, 141, in *St. Thérèse of Lisieux: Essential Writings*, ed. Mary Frohlich (Maryknoll, NY: Orbis, 2003), 65, 72.

13. St. Thérèse of Lisieux, *Story of a Soul*, in *Essential Writings*, 144.

tions of an eagle, surrendering herself wholly to the mantra of the Creator's holy contemplation.

To practice the book of nature as God's contemplation of us is to participate in Christic patterns. In rereading John Calvin or Maximus the Confessor, we can see that both, in their own ways, recognize a fiery, tangible, energized conversation between the book of nature and the book of Scripture that, if overheard, is a conversation about Jesus Christ calling us to become indigenous Christians again. Writers from outside the Christian tradition can also help us "relearn" how to listen in on this sacred conversation. The contemporary writer Freeman House describes a conversation between the book of nature and his own "book of experience," naming the conversation "reciprocal perception developed through a long practice of cumulative attentiveness."[14] Nature as practice opens our hearts to interrelationships between Christ, Scripture, others, our own experience, and nature that form just such "reciprocal perception developed through a long practice of cumulative attentiveness." Heard through our littleness, our poverty, our willingness to follow the Christic patterns of nature, reciprocal perception is nothing more or less than the fulfillment of the law: loving neighbor as we love ourselves. Nature teaches that to fulfill this single law is to allow God to woo us through the created things of the world so that we see our neighbor's love for us and receive that love as the gift it intends to be: loving nature loving us is much the same. We allow ourselves to be wooed.

The twelfth century in the Latin West is often referred to as an early Renaissance period, especially with respect to the intense attentive (almost scientific) and contemplative regard given to both nature and the human soul.[15] Attention, perception, and experience were, during that period, considered trustworthy teachers and guides of the human soul into God. A contemporary of Saint Bernard of Clairvaux, William of Saint Thierry (1085-1148), writes of Bernard: "Indeed, to this day he confesses that whatever competence he has in the Scriptures stems mainly from his meditating or praying in woodland or field. . . . [H]e has no other masters for such lessons but the oaks and the beeches."[16] In the sixteenth century, the Protestant reformer Martin Luther also focuses on Christ's incarnation and re-

14. Freeman House, *Totem Salmon: Life Lessons from Another Species* (Boston: Beacon, 1999), 99.

15. See Marie-Dominique Chenu, *Nature, Man, and Society in the Twelfth Century* (Chicago: University of Chicago Press, 1983).

16. *Bernard of Clairvaux: Early Biographies,* trans. Martinus Cawley, vol. 1 (Lafayette, IN: Guadalupe Translations, 1990), 31.

demptive work through which he brings humanity into a new and more vital connection with the natural world. Christ becoming human, for Luther, is the channel through which we apprehend beauty and the sacred quality of creation's own incarnate physicality:

> Now if I believe in God's Son and bear in mind that He became man, all creatures will appear a hundred times more beautiful to me than before. Then I will properly appreciate the sun, the moon, the stars, trees, apples, pears, as I reflect that He is Lord over and the center of all things.[17]

Coming from Luther, one of the great advocates of *sola scriptura,* this revealing confession of his experience of the flexible boundaries between Scripture and nature is intriguing, but not totally unexpected: with Christ, nature and Scripture share in a new and common redemptive bond.

Unfortunately, today many assume that scientific and religious models of nature and the cosmos must be at odds. This leaves people themselves detached and at odds from nature as well. John Hay says: "At the same time, the priesthood [i.e., scientists] that can take us beyond Jupiter to black holes and quarks seems to alter common nature into a detached state most people can't take in."[18] The "priesthood" of science shines a bright light into the book of the universe, but for many the result is a separation between the language of science and the language of the soul. This is a tragedy, both for the earth and for humanity, and it need not be. Diogenes Allen writes:

> Since the time of Kant, philosophers and theologians have all too often assumed that because we cannot conclusively prove God's existence from nature, the natural world itself cannot increase our understanding and love for God. But . . . the proof of God's creation from nature (natural theology) and contemplation of nature are not the same thing.[19]

Contemporary physics, which now factors in the phenomenon that observation itself affects that which is observed, actually helps affirm Allen's distinction between "proof" and "contemplation." It also affirms Freeman

17. Martin Luther, *Sermons on the Gospel of John* (chaps. 1-4), vol. 22, *Luther's Works,* ed. Jaroslav Pelikan (St. Louis: Concordia, 1957), 496.

18. John Hay, "The Nature Writer's Dilemma," in *On Nature: Nature, Landscape, and Natural History,* ed. Daniel Halpern (San Francisco: Northpoint Press, 1987), 8.

19. Diogenes Allen, *Spiritual Theology: The Theology of Yesterday for Spiritual Help Today* (Cambridge, MA: Cowley, 1997), 110.

House's experience of "reciprocal perception" between himself and those pink muscles of breeding salmon twisting themselves up the slimmest fingers of the Columbia River watershed. "Feeling with," sympathy, contemplation, reciprocal perception — these are the simple requisites of reading the book of nature, and they are becoming, I believe, the requisites of a new science that will find postmodern ways to find our way back to an indigenous relationship with the earth. Such a relationship need not preclude or exempt contemporary cosmologies or science. In fact, premodern guides may help show a postmodern way back to earth-connection, regardless of scientific persuasion. The Puritan divine Jonathan Edwards (1703-1758) reads the cosmos as contemplative spiritual practice:

> God's excellency, his wisdom, his purity and love, seemed to appear in everything; in the sun, moon, and stars; in the clouds, and blue sky; in the grass, flowers, trees; in the water, and all nature. . . . I often used to sit and view the moon for continuance; and in the day, spent much time in viewing the clouds and sky, to behold the sweet glory of God in these things.[20]

Everything of creation, including all that we are and will learn of the universe, is open to view "for continuance." Whether as scientists or laypeople, Christians dwell within that contemplative syntax and language that is the book of the universe. The book is alive and contains its own particular DNA: the DNA of Christ, split, and most wonderfully replicated and reformed within all things.

PRACTICE 6.5

Nature and Scripture Converse

INTENTION The intention of this practice is to sit in the midst of the conversation between nature and Scripture, and to begin to experience this conversation as Christ did.

PRACTICE You will need a Bible and an object of nature that has special meaning for you (shell, rock, feather, bird's nest, tree, etc.). It is best to do this with a companion.

---

20. Jonathan Edwards, *Personal Narrative*, in *The Protestant Mystics*, ed. Anne Fremantle (New York: New American Library, 1965), 126.

- Read the following from Saint Augustine aloud: "Some people, in order to discover God, read books. But the whole Trinity is revealed to us in creation. There is a great book: the very appearance of created things. Look above you! Look below you! Note it! Read it! God, whom you want to discover, never wrote that book with ink. Instead God set before your eyes the things that He had made. Can you ask for a louder voice than that? Why, heaven and earth shout to you: 'God made me!'"[21]

- Place your object from nature on the floor if you're inside, or on the ground if you're outside; or if it's large, such as a tree, sit some distance from it.

- If you are alone, journal; if you are with a companion, write or speak together about the object from nature. Say anything that comes to mind about what it is speaking to you of itself, of you, of your friend, and of God.

- Journal or talk with your companion also about what you each think is the still point, the center of your being as you sit, and what resides there.

- After some time, read Psalm 104, Psalm 148, a portion of the Song of Songs, or any other selection from Scripture that speaks to you in a particularly intense way about nature.

- When the reading is done, place the Bible, open to the passage you have read, on the floor or ground some distance from your object. Say aloud — or make conscious in some personal way — the fact that the object from nature and Scripture are in conversation. You may wish to pray that you become aware of, or part of, this conversation as it takes place.

- Sit quietly, imagining and listening to the conversation between this object from creation and the Scripture you have just read, and which is now present in the silence. From time to time you may wish to reread either Scripture or your object in order to keep current in the conversation.

- As you are ready, become aware of the space between the object from nature and the Bible, the space that is a circle of conversation, containing power and blessing and the fire of God. Recognize this space as Christ.

- Alone or with your companion, move into the space between the object and the Bible; hold hands together, pray whatever comes to your heart; and be present to the Spirit in Christ and in you as the sacred matters, here and now, in this conversation between Scripture and nature.

---

21. Augustine, from quotations compiled by Fred Krueger, "Opening the Book of Nature.Com": http://www.bookofnature.org/library/ngb.html (accessed April 2009).

Creation Contemplation

CHAPTER SEVEN

Nature as Liturgy and Prayer

Every time and place is a time and place of prayer.

Catherine of Siena, *The Dialogue*[1]

Earth prays! It gives praise: "Make a joyful noise to the Lord, all the earth; break forth into joyous song and sing praises" (Ps. 98:4). It prays lament: "We know that the whole creation has been groaning in labor pains until now" (Rom. 8:22). All creation prays and in doing so, as we listen, calls us into prayer. Creation is a sustained and sustaining prayer of God. Attending to creation, we attend to prayer; entering into creation, we participate in prayer; joining creation, we practice prayer; touching the petals of a rose, we touch prayer. The apostle Paul calls us to pray without ceasing (1 Thess. 5:17), and creation is certainly one form of constant prayer. If we were to join creation in this constant prayer, what a difference it would make for how we walk the earth. The early humanist Conrad von Gesner was aware of creation's constant prayer. He walked the earth praying like a mountain.

> I have determined, as long as God gives me life, to ascend one or more mountains every year when the plants are at their best — partly to study them, partly for exercise of the body and joy of mind. . . . I say then that he is no lover of nature who does not esteem high mountains very worthy of profound contemplation.[2]

1. *Catherine of Siena: The Dialogue,* trans. Suzanne Noffke, O.P. (New York: Paulist Press, 1980), 145.
2. Conrad Gesner, *On the Admiration of Mountains* (1555), cited in Paul Shepard, *Man in the Landscape: A Historic View of the Aesthetics of Nature* (New York: Knopf, 1967), 161.

On mountains von Gesner finds not only study, exercise, and joy (in themselves forms of prayer), but profound contemplation. Each leaf of grass, every breath of the raven, every lily of the field that neither spins nor toils, every groaning, every song, the whirlwind and the fig trees, mountains and leviathans — all these are prayer. The late physicist and astronomer Carl Sagan was fond of repeating that the universe is "star-stuff . . . billions and billions of stars." Perhaps we might say, more properly, that the universe is "prayer-stuff . . . billions and billions of prayers." An earthworm: prayer. The Grand Canyon: prayer.

Here is a prayer I witnessed: a great blue heron standing in water, still as stone, face and breast to the sun, its rippled shadow darkening the water behind. Fish are skittish of shadow: no shadow, they reason, no stork. Then, swifter than a yellow-shafted arrow, the heron's beak pierces the water. The head and beak tilt up with a jerk, and the long thin beak arches from the water with a small brown trout gut-speared at the end of it, writhing and squirming with droplets of lake tears splaying tiny fish scales in every direction. The bird gives a quick flip of the beak, and the fish — for just one moment — hangs free in the sky. Then it discovers the great heron swallow, the long-necked, relentless, great heron swallow into the darkness of neck and belly.

The Romanian philosopher E. M. Cioran writes: "There is a whole range of melancholy: it begins with a smile and a landscape and ends with the clang of a broken bell in the soul."[3] This whole range of melancholy — the smile, the landscape, the broken soul — is prayer. Not every prayer is a smile. The fish in the belly of the great blue heron is prayer.

Creation prays in several modes, none of which is independent of the other. All may be happening at once, like the prayer of deep calling to deep. *Ubuntu* is a South African term meaning "I am because we are." Creation prays forming interconnected "we are's" from the fecundity of innumerable humble "I am's." Using prayer in the widest possible sense, to include contemplation, here are five modes of creation prayer:[4]

1. Creation's Prayer to God
2. Humanity's prayer to God through creation

---

3. E. M. Cioran, *Tears and Saints*, trans. Ilinca Zarifopol-Johnston (Chicago: University of Chicago Press, 1995), 17.

4. On the relationship between prayer, meditation, and contemplation and the broader senses of prayer inclusive of meditation and contemplation, see Steven Chase, *The Tree of Life: Models of Christian Prayer* (Grand Rapids: Baker Academic, 2005).

3. God's own loving contemplation of creation
4. Creation as a manifestation of God's contemplation
5. Reciprocal prayer between creation and humanity as prayer to God

The practice below, "Creation Contemplation," gives practices and Scripture references that will aid in a lifelong practice of these forms of creation contemplation. Praise is certainly one mode of these forms of creation prayer. Prayer as divine presence is another mode of these forms of creation contemplation. John Calvin writes: "Lest anyone be excluded from access to happiness, [God] not only sowed in men's minds that seed of religion . . . but [also] revealed himself and daily discloses himself in the whole workmanship of the universe. As a consequence, men cannot open their eyes without being compelled to see him." Calvin adds that the whole universe is, in essence, one vast burning bush: "You cannot in one glance survey this most vast and beautiful system of the universe, in its wide expanse, without being completely overwhelmed by the boundless force of its brightness." For Calvin, creation is "engraved [with] unmistakable marks of God's glory."[5] Leaves of grass, the great blue heron and the brown trout, the whirlwind and the fig tree, mountain and leviathan, bush and bare feet on the earth — all of these are engulfed by the unmistakable marks of God's glory, aflame but not consumed.

PRACTICE 7.1

Creation Contemplation

INTENTION Prayer is a lifetime practice; creation contemplation is a way of life. The intention of this practice is to experience the five types of creation prayer or contemplation listed above.

Creation Prayer as Liturgy

And there was evening, and there was morning, the first day.

Genesis 1:5

Every Ash Wednesday we are reminded, as ash is applied to the forehead in the shape of a cross, that "dust you are and to dust you shall return." With this liturgical ritual we are called back to a remembrance of our mortality and the mortality of all created things. At the same time the ash reminds us of the glory of creation: as humans we are formed in dust and clay by the hand of God into which the breath of life is given. All of creation moves through the ritual of new life to death, from dust to dust. In this sense, as it moves through cycles and seasons, creation's vocation is prayer delicately entwined with its organic, creation liturgy.

The church's own liturgical calendar conforms and is informed by nature's liturgical seasons and rituals. Listening to creation as prayer is a meditative disposition rather than a category amplified by reason. We become assimilated to this "meditative disposition" through creation's own liturgy: the rising of the sun and its setting, morning, midday, afternoon, evening, night; the movement and phases of the moon; the rotation of the stars; the transformations of the seasons; the choreography of weather; tides and rivers, swimming, hunting, fires, the life-and-death cycles of birds and plants and fish, the dance of leaves across a lawn in fall, the decay of a mouse, the birth of suns. For centuries the church has practiced liturgy and sacrament as rituals keyed to the liturgy of creation. Today, very few make a connection between the church's liturgical cycles and creation's changing seasons. Yet attending to creation — its signs and miracles as well as its births and deaths — we can begin to join nature's own practices of ritual and worship and quite naturally bring them back into the church. At its basis, liturgy is transformation. Paul Shepard has written:

> Ancient peoples believed themselves to be participants in the rising of the sun and the change of seasons. . . . If modern culture is broken from its own primal nature, perhaps it has lost faith in those masters and interlocutors [other animal species] who give form to our understanding and reassure us of the wisdom of transformation.[6]

6. Paul Shepard, *The Others: How Animals Made Us Human* (Washington, DC: Island Press, 1996), 126.

The wisdom of transformation is in the liturgy of the seasons and the rising sun, just as the wisdom of transformation is in Lent, Good Friday, and Easter celebration. Believing that we are participants in Easter can help us once again believe that we are participants in the rising sun. Believing we are participants in the liturgy of the rising sun will help restore our belief that we are participants in the liturgy of Easter. There is God-lust in creation: believing ourselves to be participating in the liturgical prayers of creation, we become a part of creation's God-lust, as we are meant to be. It is time for Christians to again participate in the rising sun.

What are some of creation's liturgical rituals? There are many. For two to three weeks in the fall, for instance, burr-oak acorns drop from their trees with the sound of heavy rain; they fall randomly, but liturgically. The earth proclaims the Creator's craft, the nights whisper knowledge, the days overflow with the speeches of love (Ps. 19:1-4). Creation transforms as the Creator perfumes the valleys and hills; he quenches every thirst; he compels food to come out of soil, and shows in creation wisdom that is manifold, wise and full, satisfying every desire (see Ps. 104). "For there is hope for a tree, if it is cut down, that it will sprout again, and that its shoots will not cease" (Job 14:7). "For as the rain and the snow come down from heaven . . . so shall my word be that goes out from my mouth; it shall not return to me empty" (Isa. 55:10, 11).

We are guests in a creation liturgy of longing; more than guests, we are brides of Love. The bridegroom sings:

Ah, you are beautiful, my love;
  Ah, you are beautiful;
  Your eyes are doves.
Ah, you are beautiful, my Beloved,
  Truly lovely.
Our couch is green.

Song of Songs 1:15-16

And this bridegroom, this Christ of creation, sings his liturgy of constant prayer: thankful, howling, cringing, yawning, sleeping, dying, at peace, in joy, longing, asking, receiving, abandoned, grieving, sorrowful, giving, confessing, extolling, praising, waiting, silent, speaking, connecting, adoring, broken, melancholy, eating, dark, aflame, smoldering, confused, triumphant, lost, dejected, attacked, protected, complacent, conjoining, contemplative, transformed, participating, present, lost and found, light and dark, united, alive, dying.

We all know that there is a time to be born, and a time to die; a time to plant, and a time to pluck up what is planted; a time to kill, and a time to heal; a time to break down, and a time to build up; a time to weep, and a time to laugh; a time to mourn and a time to dance; a time to throw away stones, and a time to gather stones together (Eccles. 3:2-5). These times perform creation's liturgy of constant prayer.

PRACTICE 7.2

The Liturgy of Creation

INTENTION   This section suggests that the cycles, movements, and elements of nature are themselves ritual and liturgy. As with participation in any ritual or liturgy, participation with the liturgy of creation forms and transforms identity and consciousness. Over the centuries, the church's liturgical calendar has been marked off in "seasons." The intention of this practice is (1) to notice the many cycles of nature and to experience the formational qualities of the liturgy of creation; and (2) to witness and participate in the larger worship or liturgical practices of the church transposed to nature.

Prayer, Miracles, My Daughter, and Erasmus of Rotterdam

> *Jesus made the water wine. . .*
> *Now everything's a miracle.*
>
> Peter Mayer, "Holy Now"

In an earlier book I used the metaphor of a growing tree to trace different kinds of prayer, meditation, and contemplation through Christian history and in the lives of contemporary believers. In that book, *The Tree of Life: Models of Christian Prayer,* I describe five models of prayer and contemplation: prayer as conversation (roots of the tree), prayer as relationship (the trunk), prayer as journey (the branches), prayer as transformation (the leaves), and prayer as presence (the fruit). These can also serve as models or aspects of Christian formation and as five ways in which we participate with God in the practice of creation prayer.

We participate, for instance, in prayer with nature as partners in the syndetic web of *relationship* that unites all life and creation to God. As in any relationship, this mode of prayer *with* nature includes dimensions of friendship, affection, intimacy, shared interest, and love, as well as periods of enmity, anger, and separation. Relational prayer with nature is, at basis, deep longing summoning deep need; it is a response to the call of desire.

Prayer of the earth is also, like the branches of a tree, a many-dimensioned *journey*. Whether wandering, finding, searching, lost, or at home, we are placed within the natural world (we are never outside of it) on a journey into attention and wonder, into the soul, and through creation into God.

Whether nature is in stasis or in flux, praying and the liturgy of creation is a journey of *transformation*. Mindful, practicing the presence of God, aware of the sacrament of the present moment, we do not take one step on this earth that is not transformative. To smell pine is to be transformed. Each breath is a transformation.

The tree, the forest, the pathway, the clearing are placed. Every narrative, every story in Scripture is placed. God, humanity, and creation, while maintaining their identity, nonetheless are united through the formational phenomenon of *presence:* presence in the prayer of the earth is both our presence to God and God's presence to us. In a similar way, the earth is present to God, and God is present to the earth. Presence itself — the simple reality of dwelling on earth as it is — is a relational prayer participating in a constant journey of transformation.

Relationship, journey, transformation, and participative presence are formative gestures of prayer in nature. They are acquired over time and are mainly the basis on which spiritual practice with creation is built up organically. However, many people are more familiar with the various forms of *conversational* prayer as spiritual practice. In exploring conversational prayer in nature, in this book (in contrast with my earlier book) I save the "roots" of conversation for the last. In a sense I am turning the tree of life upside down. You may have seen the tree of life depicted in this way — "planted" crown down, its roots in the air — in various drawings and pictures. It is a statement of the comprehensive inclusiveness of the symbolic tree as a unifying image, regardless of perspective. Inverted in this way, the tree's image is also helpful in its oddity: a tree planted upside down recaptures our attention and rekindles wonder, the kind of attention and wonder that are often lacking in daily conversational prayer.

All prayer — all liturgy — open the heart and mind to the possibility of miracle. My sixteen-year-old daughter, Rachel, and I were recently wondering about miracles. She is at a stage where she is wondering about a lot of things. Childhood wonder is glorious, a perspective on the world that itself reconfigures adult perspectives and is something to be sought, cherished, and reentered as we can. Adolescent wonder is also glorious. It seems to spring from that sublime audacity and confusion of becoming a true self, a personality within a community of personalities. Rachel thought that changing water to wine was probably a miracle. I told her that I thought so, too, but that that was no more a miracle than a small seed setting tentative roots, nourished initially by its little seed case, eventually turning soil and air and water into a giant tree. There happened to be a large tree close to where we were sitting. I asked her if she thought the tree was a miracle. She said "no," but I could see that she was listening to the tree in a new way.

I suggested that perhaps whether or not the tree was a miracle depends on how we look at it: for some people who are asleep as they walk the earth, the tree is not much more than a dream; for others, who are awake with attentive wonder, it may perhaps be both a physical, material tree *and* a miracle. I think that Rachel will ponder that for a while. But then she said something that woke me up: "What about the leaves?" I had been asleep to those leaves. This is one of the consolations of community: to point and awaken what other individuals may miss on their own. After a while (I am slow) I answered: "Yes, I think each leaf is a miracle. Each leaf is certainly a prayer."

I left that conversation (in addition to yet again feeling a deeper love for my daughter) with the sense that sharing nature in conversation with another is another route into creation's own prayer and liturgy. The conversation with my daughter awakened me to the holy miracle of a few leaves, a few leaves that linger in my heart as prayer.

PRACTICE 7.3

Holy Now

INTENTION The intention of this practice is to awaken our consciousness to the miracles that surround us everywhere in nature.

PRACTICE   Online, go to URL http://www.petermayer.net/music/?id=4, where you will find the complete lyrics to Peter Mayer's song "Holy Now," from his album *Million Dollar Mind*. The song is also available for downloading from your favorite music website.

• Read the complete lyrics or, better, download Mayer's song; listen and enjoy. After reading or listening to the song several times, take a walk in the natural world with attentive wonder, focusing on the ordinary yet noting the extraordinary.
• Remember that you are in fact connecting to the prayer of nature. This prayer becomes your own prayer of wonder as you begin to see creation as God's miraculous, continuous prayer.
• Ask yourself whether a tree is a miracle. Are its leaves prayer? As a way of seeing that everything is a miracle, practice trying to find what in nature is not miracle or prayer. If you are truly open to nature prayer and your own prayer of the earth, you will find it difficult to find something in creation that is not prayer — even death. The possible exception to this is areas of creation degraded by humanity.
• After a time you will see that walking on the earth as prayer shapes attention, wonder, hope, and faith in a way that makes a stone no less miraculous than the birth of a fawn.

There is another way of entering into conversational prayer with nature. For instance, what exactly is the "joyful noise" of all the earth (in Psalm 95 and elsewhere)? One way to approach the question of nature's "joyful noise" is to look at the beginning of John's Gospel in a slightly different way than most of us are used to. Most people remember its opening: "In the beginning was the word." But there is another way. At the beginning of the sixteenth century, the early humanist scholar Desiderius Erasmus of Rotterdam was deeply engaged in a project of editing Greek manuscripts of the New Testament and creating from them a new and complete Latin translation. Arriving at the Gospel of John, Erasmus made an unconventional translation of its opening words, a translation, however, that can help us recognize and participate in conversational prayer with a creation that is in the habit of "making a joyful noise." Instead of the conventional translation of John's Greek into the Latin ("In principio erat Verbum" [*verbum* for the Greek λόγος]), Erasmus translated it as "In principio erat

Sermo."[7] Thus, according to Erasmus, John's Gospel opens, not with "In the beginning was the Word *(Verbum),*" but "In the beginning was the Conversation *(Sermo).*" The shift is subtle, yet it modifies and has profound implications for theology, prayer, and the very "coming into being" of creation:

> Erasmus's translation makes the act of creation not a unific spoken word, which in its singular and isolated way brings the universe into being, but rather a communitarian event based on a process of dialogue. The implication of Erasmus's translation is that the act of creation was, and in a real sense continues to be, an ongoing conversation. . . . Prayer [is] an essential partner in this creative conversation.[8]

At the level of "conversation," walking with the earth in prayer is a rich and textured exchange involving listening, hearing, words, resting, responding, and silence — that is, all the components of "conversation." "In the beginning was the Conversation" implies that not only God, Christ, the Spirit, and Wisdom, but also nature herself (including humanity) are participating in this ongoing creation-prayer.

The joyful noise we hear is, in fact, this *sermo,* the community conversation of creation-prayer. Do you hear it?

PRACTICE 7.4

No Sign but Everything That Is

> The Incarnate Word is with us,
> is still speaking — is present
> always, yet leaves no sign
> but everything that is.

> Wendell Berry, "Sabbaths, 1999," IX[9]

INTENTION In this practice we "go back to school," and the teacher will be creation herself. Intentions include learning to meditate on and listen

---

7. On editions and translations of Erasmus's work, see Steven Chase, *The Tree of Life,* 261n1.

8. Chase, *Tree of Life,* 58.

9. Wendell Berry, in *Given Poems* (Emeryville, CA: Shoemaker and Hoard, 2005), 78.

to the conversation of creation and to develop and exercise your own way of entering contemplative prayer with the natural world.

PRACTICE
- Begin this practice by praying that the divine will guide you as you begin to learn the language of creation. As you begin, remember to approach nature in ways that are most life-giving to you: sitting, walking, camping, canoeing, sitting in a city park, getting lost in the desert, journaling, photographing, or just wandering.
- Reflect on Erasmus's translation of John 1:1: "In the beginning was the conversation." How does the idea of creation coming into being through "conversation" rather than "word" affect your relationship to nature?
- Begin to imagine that all you perceive around you was born from holy conversation and is, in fact, a continuous conversation between creation and God. How does this affect your image of God? What does it mean for how you can participate in this conversation as prayer?
- Notice that Berry uses the image of the "Incarnate Word" in his poem. But Berry also implies that this incarnation, this enfleshment, is less a single word than an ongoing conversation. More than that, the "Incarnate Conversation" is ever present: Berry says that this conversation leaves no sign — except everything that exists. Consider, journal, photograph, paddle, or camp your way into how this might be a poetic way of speaking of the miraculous in the everyday for you.
- If the "Incarnate Conversation" speaks in signs through everything that is in creation, how does this affect your relationship with nature? Your contemplative prayer in and with nature? Your connection with God?

Mystery: Ephemeral and Enduring

> *The floods have lifted up, O Lord,*
> *the floods have lifted up their voice.*
>
> Psalm 93:3

Obviously creation — let's continue to use trees for an example — does not use language or words in the same sense that humans do. Likewise, listening and silence, which are the complements of words in our language, are not the same as the listening and silence of trees. We can evoke the listening and silence of nature or trees in writing, as good poets, nature writers, and Scripture have always done. But such writing is never the language of a tree or a forest itself. Nevertheless, we join the prayerful conversation of trees through attentive wonder, by listening to creation "make a joyful noise to the Lord."

Good conversation, whether with another person or with nature, requires careful attention, holy listening, and reverent response. A large oak partially overhanging a lake drops an acorn into the water with a sharp "plink," startling a toad on a nearby lily pad to leap with a "blurb" into the murky water with a sound like that of mud boiling. You don't see the frog; you just notice the ripples. This is a conversation of trees, a prayer of oak-ecology. All our senses tell us something about the prayer of trees. The prayer of trees is as much visual as auditory, as much fragrance as sound: we hear the prayer of trees in what we see, smell, taste, and feel. Climb a tree. You will find that it is moving and vibrating with the wind in ways you would never experience from the ground. Wrap your arms around its trunk and bury your face in its bark — its fragrance, its solidity, its mass, its companionship. All these are also the prayer of trees.

The Japanese Shinto tradition ritualizes its own prayerful conversation of trees. Shinto tradition parallels that of Western attentiveness and wonder: a Shinto forest is both enduring and ephemeral; there is mystery in both ecology and sacramentality. Individual trees, though some ancient specimens are over a thousand years old, are ephemeral: eventually they all die. On the other hand, from generation to generation to generation, the forest itself endures. But the Shinto tradition recognizes that, from another perspective, a single tree is solid, material, beautiful, and endures beyond a single human life. Yet, when measured against the cycles of creation or the mind of God, the forest is itself ephemeral, the mere blink of an eye. Anne Whiston Spirn writes of the ephemeral and enduring nature of these forests as a kind of ritualized and sacred "intention" that is focused on reverence and care for nature as much as reverence and care for the mystery of nature:

> The forest at Ise is ancient, dark, and dense. Most of the broad, towering cypress and cryptomeria trees are hundreds, some more than a thousand years old. . . . The trees germinate, grow, reproduce, and die, yet the forest endures. By ritual the huge forest of ordinary trees is transmuted into a sacred precinct. . . . Uncut for thirteen hundred years, except for a few

trees felled to construct the shrines, the forest embodies both endurance and the ephemeral.[10]

The enduring and ephemeral prayer of trees is something that careful listeners hear and participate in, regardless of tradition, culture, or religion. Trees and forests seem to transmit the mystery of nature directly to the ears of the heart. In his book *Forests: The Shadow of Civilization*, philosopher and cultural historian Robert Pogue Harrison actually traces the long journey of the human relationship with forests from stages of darkness, dread, violence, magic, myth, and extreme danger to stages of light, resource, adventure, spiritual awakening, recollection, solitude, introspection, and prayerful self-awareness.[11] Perhaps second only to the sun, the moon, and the stars — and equal to rivers, mountains, deserts, and the seas — trees and forests awaken the poetic imagination to both their enduring and ephemeral nature. The German poet Rainer Maria Rilke opens his *Sonnets to Orpheus* with a sonnet that sings, with an almost painfully beautiful voice, of the prayerful conversation of trees. "Oh tall tree in the ear!" sings Rilke, in a poem in which a tree is no less an organ of hearing than a temple of clarity where the sacred takes up its holy residence. Rilke presents all creatures as quiet, still, listening to the prayer with the ears of "a temple deep inside their hearing":

A tree ascended there. Oh pure transcendence!
Oh Orpheus sings! Oh tall tree in the ear!
And all things hushed. Yet even in that silence
a new beginning, beckoning, change appeared.

Creatures of stillness crowded from the bright
unbound forest, out of their lairs and nests;
and it was not from any dullness, not
from fear, that they were so quiet in themselves,

but from just listening. Bellow, roar, shriek
seemed small inside their hearts. And where there had been
at most a makeshift hut to receive the music,

10. Anne Whiston Spirn, *The Language of Landscape* (New Haven: Yale University Press, 1998), 55.

11. Robert Pogue Harrison, *Forests: The Shadow of Civilization* (Chicago: University of Chicago Press, 1992).

a shelter nailed up out of their darkest longing,
with an entryway that shuddered in the wind —
you built a temple deep inside their hearing.[12]

PRACTICE 7.5

Contemplative Prayer as Stalking Mystery

INTENTION   The intention of this practice is to enter into creation contemplation, paying very careful attention by "stalking" in nature — perhaps a deer, perhaps a wildflower — and then to notice the shift from stalking the object to stalking mystery, and the shift from stalking into an ephemeral and enduring prayer of creation.

Stillness, Listening, and Silence

> *But blessed are your eyes, for they see, and your ears, for they hear.*
>
> Matthew 13:16

Here in Matthew, the God of Abraham and Sarah, the God to whom all earth sings, erects temples of blessing. Our whole body becomes an eye and ear. In silence, listening, out of the stillness, as Rilke renders it, "within the temple of their hearing," we hear creation "making a joyful noise"; we hear the "day pour forth speech."

Entry into the temple of listening is a shift in consciousness, a simple one, yet as essential as that pause in breath between exhale and inhale. Entry comes from a whisper that, for no particular reason, we consent to follow. Reverence is a point of entry into that temple of our hearing. And creation itself is a point of entry: dwelling over time in forest and tree, the temple accumulates wisdom in the form of hints, cautions, prudence, perseverance, and attentive wonder, the precious keys to the temple of silence. Classic Christian writing and wisdom are themselves deeply sensitive and

---

12. "Sonnets to Orpheus," translated by Stephen Mitchell, copyright © 1982 by Stephen Mitchell, from *The Selected Poetry and Prose of Rainer Maria Rilke*, translated by Stephen Mitchell, p. 411. Used by permission of Random House, Inc.

practiced in the arts of stillness and listening to the silent song of God in that inner temple we call "soul." The arts from these Christian prayers and rituals intend to help us enter deep inside our longing, where silence blossoms into "a joyful noise." Silence also has a deep grammatical structure that has the potential to open as the voice of nature. Much of Christian contemplative teaching that directs us toward nature is initiated and sustained in silence, which fosters attentiveness to creation. In praise or in lament, silence in nature offers a temple deep within our hearing.

In his *Spiritual Canticle,* Saint John of the Cross speaks of a soul that begs her beloved to put an end to her longings and let her eyes behold him as the silent music of love:

Extinguish these miseries . . .
And may my eyes behold You,
Alone. . . .
The tranquil night
At the time of the rising dawn,
Silent music,
Sounding solitude,
The supper that refreshes, and deepens love.[13]

We read and listen to nature, and we hear "silent music,/sounding solitude" emerging from the tranquil night, the rising dawn. John implies that nature opens our eyes to the light of God and the "sound" of that light is "silent music." Substitute something from nature for the "You" of the poem — a mountain, a river — and nature itself becomes the "tranquil night," the "silent music," the "sounding solitude" that refreshes and deepens love. Nature seems willing and able, and she has been created to help us do just that. John is also inviting us to attend to that temple deep within our hearing. A temple — the etymological root of "contemplate" — abides within our hearing as a heightened perception of silence.

How is a tree or forest "silent music"? How is the river "sounding solitude"? How is a sunset "the supper that refreshes and deepens love"? These are angles of perceptional vision taught by the Christian contemplative traditions that streak the material mystery of creation with the glory of God.

13. St. John of the Cross, "Stanzas Between The Soul and The Bridegroom," in *The Spiritual Canticle,* 10, 15, *The Collected Works of St. John of the Cross,* trans. Kieran Kavanaugh and Otilio Rodriguez (Washington, DC: Institute of Carmelite Studies, 1979), 411, 412.

PRACTICE 7.6

The Sacrament of Silence

INTENTION The intention of this practice is to experience silence in creation as sacramental.

John Calvin teaches that listening, attention, silence, and wonder are — all of them — prayer. In fact, in a memorable phrase he says that "the tongue is not even necessary for prayer":

> We should hold that the tongue is not even necessary for private prayer. . . . [Yet] even though the best prayers are sometimes unspoken, it often happens in practice that, when feelings of mind are aroused, unostentatiously the tongue breaks forth into speech, and the other members into gesture.[14]

Reading Calvin, one can imagine a field of yellow-golden poppies where "the tongue is not necessary for prayer," where the field of poppies gestures reverently, bowing in the wind, a ritual of yellows and golds, a temple of joy and bloom. Complementing Calvin in our time, Margaret Guenther writes: "Dreams, angels, prophets — and silence. Our multidimensional God speaks in many voices."[15]

Barbara Brown Taylor also speaks to the paradox of the intimate and connective relationship between word, on the one hand, and silence, on the other. She asks: "[H]ow shall I break the silence? What word is more eloquent than the silence itself?"[16] There is no answer really, except perhaps the Author of silence. Taylor adds: "Silence and speech define each other. One is the inhale. The other the exhale."[17] Our conversation with creation could hardly be more succinctly stated: in silence and speech, our breath draws us closer to creation than we often are to ourselves.

As is true of nature, love can be both fragile and disorienting. Renita Weems reminds us that formation in love often takes us through pain-filled

---

14. Calvin, *Institutes of the Christian Religion*, III.XX.33, pp. 896-97.
15. Margaret Guenther, *The Practice of Prayer* (Cambridge, MA: Cowley, 1998), 39.
16. Barbara Brown Taylor, *When God Is Silent* (Cambridge, MA: Cowley, 1998), 3.
17. Taylor, *When God Is Silent*, 96.

and purgative silences, but "no matter how lonely, quiet, and unpredictable the journey, with patient listening holy silence can become music."[18] Nature, like love, is a formation-crucible for that temple within our hearing, a temple in which silent music finds community in sounds of solitude.

18. Renita J. Weems, *Listening for God: A Minister's Journey through Silence and Doubt* (New York: Simon and Schuster, 1999), 17.

CHAPTER EIGHT

Hovering and Hazelnuts
as Contemplative Prayer

Everything in nature invites us constantly to be what we are.

Gretel Ehrlich, "On Water"[1]

By the twelfth century in the Latin West, Christian forms of contemplation and prayer had become manifold in their diversity, nuanced in ways intended to appeal to intellect as well as heart and soul, and intended to evoke both wonder and awe. Along with contemplation of God, Scripture, holy writings or images, and personal experience, the contemplation of nature was practiced under the theological assumption that creation was itself imprinted with visible and invisible vestiges, images, and likenesses of the Creator. Divinity was understood as uncreated and in that sense completely other than creation. But at the same time, Christian contemplative consciousness encountered a cosmos in which, as Augustine had taught, "God is poured forth in all things and God is Himself everywhere, wholly."

Richard of Saint Victor (d. 1173) was one such contemplative theologian who provided the Christian tradition with a variety of forms of prayer, meditation, and contemplation. In his most nuanced account of contemplation, *Mystical Ark* (or the *Benjamin Minor*), Richard focuses on six refined forms of contemplation, four of which focus on contemplation of creation. In this work Richard gives two preliminary and concise definitions of the art of contemplation. He writes that contemplation "is an insightful and free consideration of the soul extended in all directions in per-

---

1. Gretel Ehrlich, "On Water," in *Words from the Land,* ed. Stephen Trimble (Las Vegas: University of Las Vegas Press, 1995), 205.

ceiving all things." His second way of speaking about contemplation is as "the free, sharp-sighted gaze of the soul hovering with awe in the visible showings of [divine] wisdom."[2]

"Hovering" is an important image of contemplation in Richard's writings. It is an image drawn from nature — from his apparent love of watching birds. In fact, he links a variety of patterns of bird flight to various forms of meditation and contemplation. For instance, Richard notices that birds can fly back and forth between various points, but they do so while maintaining a basic, linear pattern of flight. He uses this pattern of flight drawn from nature to illustrate a form of contemplation in which one is able to move fluidly in and out of contemplation without effort. In this form of contemplation, the imagination is able to move intentionally throughout the day, mindful of divine presence throughout creation.

A second way Richard teaches the arts of contemplation is through the image of birds flying in circular patterns. Some birds, Richard notes, actually soar in patterned circles while others move toward or away from a center forming spirals as they fly. For Richard, these patterns illustrate various forms of contemplation using intellect or reason (rather than imagination) by which we may contemplate nature in a more focused and concentrated way. Today, this spiritual path or form of contemplation is very close to what we would call science, or the empirical method coupled with mindfulness. Those who have worked in the sciences are aware that the kind of attention they often need to give, far from separating the object from the worker, actually seems to suspend the worker in a kind of relational connection. Richard is also very clear that this contemplative form of circling or spiraling around some object or thought is self-implicating: it implicates the contemplative in a subject-to-subject relationship. Self-implication, in turn, forms and shapes according to the subject of nature on which attention is focused.

"Hovering" is, for Richard of Saint Victor, a pattern of flight representing the highest forms of contemplation. He uses it in his most concise definition of contemplation, which is a "hovering with awe in the visible showings of [divine] wisdom." "Hovering" in Richard's writing on contemplation is beyond imagination, reason, or mind — as a hovering bird is both still and in motion. "Hovering with awe in the visible showings of wisdom" contains the paradox of maintaining an alert and restful con-

---

2. Richard of St. Victor, *De arca mystica: De gratia contemplationis, seu Benjamin Maior* (*The Mystical Ark*), in *Patrologiae Latinae*, 196, ed. J.-P. Migne (Paris, 1855) (my translation).

sciousness to the present. "Hovering" allows qualities of the paradox of nature to be suspended in a moment of insight: the visible and invisible, for instance, become mutually enhancing, or the material and the spiritual inform one another. In hovering, the ecological and the sacramental converge without dissolving. As with the stillness in motion of the hovering bird, the ecological and sacramental features of nature are highlighted together in the contemplative, hovering gaze.

God participates in this paradox as well: being the wholly Other, God is still everywhere wholly; being of one substance, God hovers as three persons; Christ is the eagle of hovering — fully human and fully divine. "Hovering" is Richard of Saint Victor's image, drawn from creation, to illuminate an awareness of and participation in the sacred matters at the precise point where language falters in the face of divine incomprehensibility. It is just at this vulnerable point of incomprehensibility that the holy crystallizes as "bird," "bee," "locust," "fly" — as a new kind of temple.

Richard of Saint Victor is not unique in this way of describing Christian formation practice through contemplation of creation. His way, in fact, is the way of many masters of Christian prayer. The cultural, philosophical, and theological distance between Richard of Saint Victor and Francis de Sales (1567-1622), for example, is wide. But both move easily between contemplation of nature as a means of the soul's journey to God and the use of images, objects, and systems drawn from nature to describe contemplation and true prayer.

Commenting on Francis de Sales's *Treatise on the Love of God,* Wendy Wright notes that, for Francis, "the world is a world of hearts and of desire, divine desire graciously inclining toward creation and human desire reaching to God."[3] Indeed, for de Sales, the language of creation is desire and love. Of creation he writes: "Love speaks not only by the tongue, but by the eyes, by sighs, and play of features; yea, silence and dumbness are words for it." Words fail, yet love speaks. Where human words fail, de Sales listens to the words of God, and what he hears is a form of meditation described in terms, "not of a fly for simple amusement, nor as a locust to eat and be filled, but as a sacred bee moves over the flowers of holy mysteries, to extract from them the honey of divine love." Through the hovering of the honeybee, De Sales instinctively hears the mystery at the heart of creation, the honey of divine love:

---

3. *Francis de Sales: Introduction to the Devout Life and Treatise on the Love of God,* trans. Wendy M. Wright (New York: Crossroad, 1993), 141.

The bee flies from flower to flower in the spring time, not at hazard but of set purpose, not only to be recreated in the verdant meadows, but to gather honey. . . . Such a soul is in meditation. She passes from mystery to mystery, not at random . . . but deliberately and of set purpose to find out motives of love or of some heavenly affection. . . . [I]n the Canticle of Canticles the heavenly spouse, as a mystical bee, settles now on the eyes, now on the lips, on the cheeks, on the hair of her beloved, to draw thence the sweetness of a thousand passions of love . . . inflamed with holy love she speaks with him.[4]

This mystical bee of contemplation works as a kind of heavenly enhancer in created form. Alighting on various parts of her beloved's face, the bee enhances and transforms the physical and sensual quality of love, not into the spiritual only, but into a thousandfold increase of passion manifested in physical form.

In the prayerful conversation of creation, there is no split, no dichotomy, no hierarchy between material and spiritual, body and soul; there is only what we might call "hovering" — stillness in motion. The material is as true and beautiful as the spiritual is. Spiritual formation in nature "hovers" at the contact boundary between these material and spiritual realities. These contact boundaries are the "various manifestations of divine wisdom" of Richard of Saint Victor.

PRACTICE 8.1

Hovering: Birds, Bees, Locusts, and a Fly

INTENTION   The intention of this practice is to attend to creatures that hover, noting their flight pattern as an aid to contemplation of nature.

Hazelnuts and Other Small Things

Have you ever held a hazelnut in your hand? The fourteenth-century anchoress Julian of Norwich has. In fact, she has lovingly and carefully spent

---

4. Francis de Sales, *Treatise on the Love of God,* 5.1, trans. Henry Benedict Mackey, O.S.B. (Westminster, MD: Newman Bookshop, 1949), 234-36.

time hovering over a hazelnut as a blessed manifestation of divine wisdom. In what she calls a "showing" (which she later wrote out as *Showings of Divine Love*), she sees the hazelnut encased in a shell and compares it to how we are encased in a body and in clothing. The nut itself, the soul, is "naked" — as we all are before God. Yet there is no dichotomy, no hierarchy between what she sees as shell and nut, or how she sees body and soul. For Julian, the hazelnut in the palm of her hand is a microcosm of creation: the ecological shell housing the sacramental nut. With the eye of her understanding she looks at the small nut and asks, "What may this be?" meaning, How is it that this single hazelnut exists at all? Why does it not rather melt completely away? Why does it not, as she puts it, simply "fall to nought." In the miracle and audacity of that little hazelnut she finds her answer: love of God:

> I marveled how it might last, for I thought it might suddenly have fallen to nought for littleness. And I was answered in my understanding, "It lasts and ever shall, for God loves it." And so all things have their being by the love of God. In this little thing I saw three properties: The first is that God made it; The second that God loves it; The third that God keeps it.[5]

The hazelnut *is* because God loves it. "And after this," Julian adds, "I saw God in a point. That is to say in my understanding. By which sight I saw that he is in all things. . . . For he is the midpoint of all things and all that he does."[6] God is that "midpoint" where creation takes place through divine making, loving, and keeping. One's cosmology makes no difference. Wonder matters, and God is the midpoint of all that matters.

PRACTICE 8.2

Shells, Burrows, Nuts — Small Prayers and Large

If your heart is straight with God, then every creature will be to you a mirror of life and a book of holy doctrine. No creature is so little or so mean as not to show forth and represent the goodness of God.

Thomas à Kempis, *Imitation of Christ*[7]

---

5. Julian of Norwich, *Showing of Love*, 5th chapter, trans. Julia Bolton Holloway (Collegeville, MN: Liturgical Press, 2003), 9.

6. Julian of Norwich, *Showing of Love*, 11th chapter, 19.

7. Thomas à Kempis, *The Imitation of Christ*, ed. Harold Gardiner (Garden City, NY: Image, 1955), 80.

INTENTION Following Julian of Norwich and Thomas à Kempis, the intention of this practice is to embrace littleness in creation, and in doing so to embrace all that God is.

PRACTICE People love to collect objects from nature (and should, as long as collecting them will not harm or deplete the earth): shells, feathers, rocks and stones, coniferous cones, grasses, wildflowers, fragrant evergreen branches, sticks with interesting shapes, berries and leaves and flowers for arranging, plants for medicinal purposes. This is a finding, wondering, and perhaps even collecting practice.

- Find something — from some suggestions above — that draws your attention immediately. In creation, searching and finding are akin to attention and wonder.
- Hold this object: ideally, you will be able to cup it in the palm of your hand, as Julian does, but this is not essential. Meditate on this object. Explore it with all your senses, imagination, intellect, heart, and soul. How does it, as Thomas à Kempis says, "show forth and represent the goodness of God"?
- Ask yourself why it exists, and why it exists with the particular characteristics it has. Ask yourself why it "is" rather than why it is "nought," as Julian says.
- Julian's answer is that God made, keeps, and loves it. Ask yourself the above question — why it "is" rather than why it is "nought" — in light of God's making, keeping, and loving it.
- Slowly let the object itself draw you to God.
- Julian marvels that a little thing, the hazelnut, is also in its own way "all that is made." That is, it is in microcosm representing the whole of all that is made — the macrocosm. Allow this "found" object to become a part of you and you a part of it. How are the two of you, together, a microcosm of "all that is made"?
- Take it home with you and live with it and it with you. What does it add to your prayer?

··

Place as Creation Contemplation

> *God's excellency, his wisdom, his purity and love, seemed to appear in everything; in the sun, moon, and stars; in the clouds, and*

blue sky; in the grass, flowers, trees; in the water, and all nature;
which used greatly to fix my mind.

Jonathan Edwards[8]

The stories of the people of God have one thing absolutely in common (in addition to God and people): they are placed — placed in the created world. Christian spiritual formation is replenished and refreshed as much by place and nature as it is by experience, architecture, and culture.

Christianity is an outdoors religion, outdoors in a place. One example of this, from a spiritual tradition that is not generally thought of as rich in imagination and wonder, nor overtly concerned with place, is that of Puritan piety. The Puritan meditative technique known as "spiritualizing the creatures" uses allegorical imagination and prayer to clarify scriptural or theological doctrine. Even in this allegorical, "spiritualizing" technique, place and creation play a key role. In John Bunyan's *Pilgrim's Progress,* for example, Prudence and Matthew engage in prayerful conversation using sun and fire to refer respectively to God's movement into creation (sun) and creation's return to its Source (fire).

> Matthew: What should we learn by seeing the Flame of our Fire go upwards? and by seeing the Beams, and sweet Influences of the Sun strike downwards?
>
> Prudence: By the going up of the Fire, we are taught to ascend to Heaven, by fervent and hot desires. And by the Sun sending his Heat, Beams, and sweet Influences downwards, we are taught, that the Savior of the World, tho' high, reaches down with his Grace and Love to us below.[9]

Bunyan formulates his meditation that "spiritualizes the creatures" of fire, flame, sunlight, sun, and earth — even as an allegory — using these elements also in a tactile, visual, and physical sense to illustrate what is otherwise unnoticed and unseen: our longing for God and God's longing for us. The "sweet Influences" of divine descent and human ascent can in fact happen only in *a place,* on the earth, a place where the sun sends down its light and where fire and its flame rise upward.

8. Jonathan Edwards, *Personal Narrative,* in *The Works of Jonathan Edwards,* vol. 16, *Letters and Personal Writings,* ed. George S. Claghorn (New Haven: Yale University Press, 1998), 794.

9. John Bunyan, *The Pilgrim's Progress from This World to That Which Is to Come,* ed. James Blanton Warey and Roger Sharrock, 2nd ed. (Oxford: Oxford University Press, 1960), 231.

Nearly a century after Bunyan's death, the theologian, preacher, and university president Jonathan Edwards was developing into one of the most eloquent and inspiring Protestant writers on nature. In much of his writing, but especially in his autobiographical *Personal Narrative,* Edwards tells not of practice only, but of being formed, ravished, and intoxicated by the beauty of the natural world. Nature practice arouses desire and a canticle of love so strong in him that he is often transported directly into conversation with Christ and to an overwhelming sense of the divine in all things, in all places.

> This I know not how to express otherwise . . . of being alone in the mountains, or some solitary wilderness, far from all mankind, sweetly conversing with Christ, and rapt and swallowed up in God. The sense I had of divine things, would often of a sudden kindle up, as it were, a sweet burning in my heart; an ardor of soul, that I know not how to express.[10]

Like Bunyan, Edwards continually "places" his nature prayer — in this case on a mountain and alone in the wilderness — whereas he says elsewhere that he often goes to "sing forth my contemplations."[11] Meditating on the human soul in relation to God, Edwards is also most moving when he compares the soul to a creature and how it occupies its place. In this case the soul is simply "a little white flower."

> The soul of the true Christian, as I then wrote my meditations, appeared like such a little white flower as we see in the spring of the year; low and humble on the ground, opening its bosom to receive the pleasant beams of the sun's glory; rejoicing as it were in a calm rapture; diffusing around a sweet fragrancy; standing peacefully and lovingly, in the midst of other flowers round about; all in like manner opening their bosom, to drink in the light of the sun. For no part of creature holiness had I so great a sense of loveliness, humility, brokenness of heart and poverty of spirit; and there was nothing that I so earnestly longed for. My heart panted after this, to lie low before God, as in the dust; that I might be nothing, and that God might be ALL, that I might become as a little child.[12]

---

10. Jonathan Edwards, *Personal Narrative,* in *Light from Light: An Anthology of Christian Mysticism,* ed. Louis Dupré and James A. Wiseman, 2nd ed. (New York: Paulist, 2001), 391.

11. Edwards, *Personal Narrative,* 392.

12. Edwards, *Personal Narrative,* 394.

With these examples — and there are so many more — we have to ask ourselves why it is that today we so often fail to experience place in nature as a guide, as prayer, as a path to conversation with Christ or an avenue into God? Edwards's reflection above is entirely prayer; and it is prayer in which body and soul dwell, irrevocably, in *place* within creation. Edwards's simple final prayer, "that God might be ALL," would not have occurred to him if God where not already ALL in the places of creation.

PRACTICE 8.3

Lessons in Prayer from a Small White Flower

INTENTION The intention of this practice is to place ourselves before nature with reverence, stillness, and openness in such a way that we absorb lessons from nature concerning our life of prayer and contemplation. These lessons may serve to reinforce and expand a current practice of prayer, or they may open completely new possibilities for prayer. We are going to attend to nature in a way similar to Edwards's way in the above quotation. We will also be paying attention to how nature herself prays.

PRACTICE Reread the Jonathan Edwards meditation on the small white flower.

• Before beginning to observe nature, after you have reread the passage, spend some quiet time noting how Edwards uses the small white flower as a point of departure for distilling a host of formational spiritual practices. Some of these he was no doubt already familiar with; some the small white flower may have reframed in helpful ways; still others, we can only imagine, came to him as new ideas, perhaps even surprises in his prayerful conversation with the flower.
• In creation, begin "reading in nature" as a prayer in this way; observe, be watchful for a comfortable place or a fine view or a single plant or animal that draws your attention.
• Notice all the ways in which the small white flower opens Edwards's heart and soul:
  – he says that he would like his soul to be like such a small white flower: low, humble, opening its bosom (his soul) to the intensity of the sun (God's love)
  – the small white flower is rejoicing

- it is diffusing a sweet fragrance (for the Lord)
- it is standing peacefully and lovingly in the midst of other small white flowers (faith community of souls)
- as a creature, it is not in itself holy
- it is calmly enraptured, lovely, humble, brokenhearted, with poverty of spirit
- Edwards, as he meditates on the "stance" of the small white flower before God, wishes only that, in imitation of the flower, he might in the same way lie in the dust before God, with a panting heart, becoming as a small child.

• Remaining in place and with your object or group of objects, begin to apply all senses (perhaps just one to begin, then begin adding as you feel the need). You may want to stand or sit close or at a distance. In whatever way you meditate, open your bosom (as Edwards would say) to whatever is calling you to be present.

• Begin to notice how what you've focused on maintains its relationship to the natural world around it. Is it small, large, colorful, broken, young, alone, supporting others, in a group, moving, at home on the earth, or at home in the sky, or on plants or trees? Give notice to anything that awakens your attention.

• It is obvious from Edwards's description that he is moving back and forth between the small white flower and what he knows as practice: the flower is small, low to the ground, humble; he has attempted the practice of humility before in a similar way, with mixed results. The flower seems to do it so gracefully and perfectly that nothing need be added or changed. The flower, in its way, is pure humility.

• Begin to associate what you notice in creation with a "posture" before God. As the associations come, at your own pace begin to associate these "postures" with spiritual-formation practices that you may already be familiar with but that the creation makes clear and explicit for you. Practice this posture; imitate it, consciously incorporating the posture into prayer. For instance, Edwards is put in mind of meekness, humility, broken-heartedness, and openness simply on the basis of observing a small white flower. What does nature put you in mind of in terms of reverence, prayer, or contemplation? Awakening to the spiritual and prayerful nature of creation in this way, imitate creation contemplation.

• The movement back and forth between Edwards and the small white flower involves a third: the Creator. The flower puts Edwards in mind of his own status measured alongside the Creator. The comparison leaves

him wishing he could "lie down in the dust" before God, who is ALL. Take a bodily posture that represents your sense of God in the midst of this encounter with nature. If your meditation leads you to a desire to place all before the God of ALL by lying face-down flat on the ground, do so, because that is prayer. If your urge is to touch or draw closer to the creation in acknowledgment of drawing closer to God, do so: it is prayer. Running, singing, twirling with arms in the air: it is prayer. Rage, tears, anger at what we do to this delicate but sustaining creation: it is prayer. Let your body pray as creation prays.
- Afterwards, you will want to spend some quiet time with this object or in this spot when you are done, reflecting on what has transpired.
- As you leave, know that you are leaving with a greater sense of the possibilities of prayer and a greater appreciation for nature both as a teacher of prayer and as itself a prayer.
- Leave with thanksgiving.

Nature, more than any other aspect of Christian identity formation, makes us aware that spiritual practice is a lifelong process, that it is both ephemeral and eternal. The story of God's people as told in Scripture is a story of continuous "placed-ness" within creation. Attention, wonder, and grace open the possibility for us to experience the places of creation as continual prayer. Unfortunately, as we will see in the next chapters, today much of the creation prayer is lament. The discord between the prayers of creation in Scripture, mostly of praise, and the prayers of creation we experience directly today, much of it lament, is exacerbated by humanity's own culpable disregard for the sacred places of creation.

Nature is sometimes static, sometimes in flux; it is sometimes healthy by being in harmony, sometimes healthy by being in conflict. It is seldom healthy in being ignored. As in any relationship, ignoring, isolating, or controlling someone or something are forms of abuse. We are in relationship with creation, but today much of that relationship is abusive. Given the fact that true hearing, receiving, responding, and relationship *are* Christian practice, the contemporary tendency to choose to plug into technology rather than ecological place is unfortunate. Technology is not evil in itself, but to the extent that it serves to cut us off from hearing, receiving, and responding to place in creation, it can be sinister.

On the other hand, where the sacred matters and where the relationship between nature and humanity is one of mutual prospering, creation contemplation is catechetical prayer that forms us organically. Ecclesial formation is often constrictive; it does not form us organically. Often it has as its goal conformity to certain creeds, rites, theologies, and standards. Creation practice has no such underhanded intentionality, at least none that humanity can name. Therefore, it is antithetical to ecclesial formation when that formation is constrictive. Nature, as practice less similar to this kind of constriction and more similar to catechetical prayer, moves honestly with the intentions of trust, hope, faith, love, openness, and compassion. Christian practice that is not done in this open, organic way brings us sermons that are like dead branches, worship as dry as desert sand, and prayer wearied by watering only with the salty rains of "shoulds" and "oughts," guilts and blames. Creation is not about "should" or "ought" or "blame." These are not in the vocabulary of nature as Christian spiritual practice.

Any relationship — companionship with nature included — is complex and messy. Yet somehow earth binds us loosely, tenderly, and insistently into an intricate web of belonging, even within the complexity and the mess. Simply to walk this place of earth is to do a walk of formation practice: the earth awakens, purifies, illuminates, delights and sometimes horrifies us. Creation, if we are willing to listen, shares her prayer with us: her grief, sorrow, and mourning as well as her joy, gladness, and hope. It is complex and messy. But it is also an adventure and, as Jonathan Edwards implies, one small white flower can serve up an adventure whose itinerary includes glory and pain, virtue and sadness, beauty and hope, all of which refashion body and mind and spirit into severe likenesses of Christ.

All this is risky business. The biggest risk of all is that nature will *place* us in the presence of God.

PRACTICE 8.4

Visio Divina *(Sacred Seeing)*

INTENTION Based on the ancient practice of *lectio divina* (sacred reading), the intention of this practice is to select an image in nature that captures your gaze and to engage it in the prayer process of *visio divina* (sacred seeing).

The Dark Night of the Planet

CHAPTER NINE

The Dark Night: Miseries and Signs

Why do men persist in destroying their habitat?

Paul Shepard, *Nature and Madness*

The earth dries up and withers, the world languishes and withers; the heavens languish together with the earth. The earth lies polluted under its inhabitants; for they have transgressed laws, violated statutes, broken the everlasting covenant.

Isaiah 24:4-5

It's inevitable: pay careful attention to the earth, walk the earth in wonder, marvel at the ecological beauty, pattern, and community of creation, develop the capacity to participate in the sacramental liturgy of the planet, and sooner or later you will notice places where the earth dries up and withers, the world languishes and lies polluted. In the chapters of this section, I will draw on Saint John of the Cross's most famous insight and apply it to our planet: that is, the "dark night," that dark period of the spiritual journey in which one painfully feels the absence of God, but a period that is normally a transforming process immediately preceding union with God. The dry earth, the withering world, the polluted planet are signs of the miseries of today's dark night of the planet. From natural causes — and increasingly from human causes — we find the earth to be in the midst of a dark night that might be compared to Dante's pilgrim at the beginning of the *Divine Comedy,* who, as he is about to enter the inferno of hell in the middle of his life's journey, "came to [himself] within a dark wood where the straight way was lost" (*Inferno* 1.2-3).

In the sixteenth century, theologian and mystic Saint John of the Cross experienced a series of lengthy disquieting and painful periods during which he felt himself estranged from God and life. John endured and then passed through each of these periods, which he later called "dark nights." In every case he was struck by the fact that the dark nights, though real, were also transformative. In *The Dark Night of the Soul*, Saint John describes the degrees of pain and loss as the soul journeys through a series of dark nights, before divine union in his work *The Living Flame of Love*, which considers the divine illumination that follows the dark night and describes the happiness and peace experienced by a soul devoted to God. Deeply aware of the sensual, psychological, and spiritual dynamics of these dark nights, Saint John speaks of his own transforming experiences in ways that today continue to serve as guidelines and even maps for a soul that is in pain and yet searching for God.

We can use the work of Saint John of the Cross and others like him to help us see more clearly the signs and miseries and pains of the dark night of the *planet* and to begin to work to console, even heal, some of the planet's pain. But, looking at the dark night of the soul described by Saint John and the dark night of the planet that we experience today, we are faced with a huge critical difference. The crucial differences are not the obvious ones of substance, physicality, or consciousness. The real difference is that, with the dark night of the planet, we are co-travelers, but there is no person who has passed through the dark night of the planet who can guide or illuminate our way from the other side. In other words, someone could write "The Dark Night of the Planet," but no one is in the position to write the planet's "The Living Flame of Love." As co-travelers we notice, participate in, and experience the miseries and signs of the planet's dark night, and we can even care for it and alleviate some misery. But as equal participants in the dark night of the planet, we have no one who has passed through this particular dark night to know if, in fact, this is a dark night preceding transformation or a dark night that will only grow more dark. There is no Saint John of the Cross to assure us of happiness and peace on the other side of the dark night of the planet.

It would be naïve to claim that the planet has never experienced a dark night. While earth has always had its own kind of beauty, it has also always had its violent and hostile shadow side. All living things die, often grotesquely, with no apparent justification or moral code other than survival.

Mountains erode and are washed back to the seas; continents break up and drift apart; asteroids decimate ancient species and planetwide ecologies; harsh storms change landforms in a matter of hours; glaciers of mile-thick milky ice alter continents in slow, imperceptible, creeping movements that last tens of thousands of years. In today's world, however, imbalance, depletion, and extinction are accelerated by human negligence, greed, and technology. "Natural" mechanisms of healing the delicate cycles between order and chaos in creation have been depleted or short-circuited. Even disregarding this power of self-destruction, human activity on earth as it is today has taken the planet on a journey that can be described as Dante describes his own "wood" at the edge of darkness: "savage and harsh and dense" (1.5)

Of course, life *is* savage and harsh and dense. And as Saint John of the Cross experienced and taught, this darkness is often a necessary phase of growth, transformation, illumination, even union with God. The planet longs for union with God; you and I long for God. Yet many of us remain in denial not only of the earth's longing, which is a spiritual reality, but of our own longing as well. Even worse, we remain in denial concerning the visible, material reality of the planet's current ecological darkness, which is a visible, material reality. In this chapter I will explore just a few of the many contributors to the current dark night of the planet, both spiritual contributions and material contributions. Many are "natural"; many more are not. In the next chapter I will also look more closely at some of the work of Saint John of the Cross. In examining some of the mechanisms and structures of the dark night of the soul as detailed by John, we may perhaps be in a position to discern more carefully the planet's ills and to develop more intentionally the capacity to shine some light into the depths of the planet's darkness. This we can do, again, if we realize that neither Saint John of the Cross nor anyone else can assure us that this darkness is, in the end, any kind of illumination.

These chapters are not joyful reading. Nor is "reading" the dark night of the planet a joyful thing. As a result of careful reading and response to the dark night of the planet, in fact, many begin to lose the ability to participate in nature as practice at all. They begin to lose the ability to pray with and through nature. One example of the dark night of the planet is that the Psalms seem to be speaking to a different earth entirely. Here, for instance, is a portion of Psalm 65:

> You visit the earth and water it,
>   you greatly enrich it;

the river of God is full of water;
>you provide the people with grain,
>for so you have prepared it. . . .
You crown the year with your bounty;
>your wagon tracks overflow with richness.
The pastures of the wilderness overflow,
>the hills gird themselves with joy.
The meadows clothe themselves with flocks,
>the valleys deck themselves with grain,
>they shout and sing together for joy.

(Ps. 65:9, 11-13)

How, some say, except perhaps as confession, can you with honesty pray this psalm today, in the midst of our earth's dark night?

PRACTICE 9.1

In the Dark Night of the Planet

INTENTION The intention of this practice is to join the earth in darkness, in mourning.

PRACTICE
- What, in nature, have been your saddest experiences?
- What were the "natural" causes (i.e., causes from nature) of your anger, mourning, fear, or sadness?
- What have been human causes in nature of your personal despair or hopelessness or sadness?
- Reflect on the fact that Adam and Eve alone ate forbidden fruit, yet all creation suffers. What is most likely to arouse sorrow or mourning or loss in you as you experience or recall nature today?

Ice, Heat, Feedback Loops, and Global Warming

> *"What do we do to save our world?" His questioners expected some-*
> *thing strategic; his answer was: "What we most need to do is to hear*
> *within us the sounds of the earth crying."*
>
> Question to and answer from Thich Nhat Hanh

Bill McKibben, in a recently popular and sadly prescient book, *The End of Nature* (which he wrote in the late 1980s), focuses his concern on the problem of global warming. As he writes in an introduction to the tenth anniversary edition of his book, he first began with two observations: one observation overturns our habits of thinking about how the earth evolves and changes; the second observation, similar to that of Henry David Thoreau more than a century earlier, recognizes that the supremacy of the "power" of nature has succumbed to the "power" of humanity. Today, humanity "rules" the ecology of the planet. Of the first observation, McKibben says: "We tell time badly — we're used to thinking of the Earth as changing with infinite slowness, but in fact it is now speeding up, changing in rapid, dangerous, and profound ways as a result of our alterations."

McKibben's second observation gets at the heart of what he means by "the end of nature": "We are no longer able to think of ourselves as a species tossed about by larger forces — now we are those larger forces. Hurricanes and thunderstorms and tornadoes become not acts of God but acts of man. That was what I meant by the 'end of nature.'" At the time he wrote that in the first edition of his book, McKibben says, "those of us who were convinced that the climate was warming fast were out on a limb. A sturdy limb . . . but a limb nonetheless." By the time he wrote the introduction to that second edition in 1999, the sturdy limb had turned into a solid rock. In 1995, the International Panel on Climate Change, a collection of 1,500 scientist assembled by the United Nations, concluded in a "dry but historic understatement" that "[t]he balance of evidence suggests that there is a discernible human influence on global climate." In that second-edition introduction, McKibben mentions, in passing, something rather ominous: the chemistry of global warming also involves "feedback loops," meaning that the rising temperature of the earth will itself feed back upon itself, speeding the rate of temperature increase even more.[1]

---

1. Bill McKibben, *The End of Nature*, 2nd ed. (New York: Anchor Books, 1999), xv, xvi, xvii-xviii, xxiv.

Fast-forward to the current decade. Whereas McKibben preached in an apocalyptic but still (barely) hopeful tone, Thomas Homer-Dixon, in an op-ed piece entitled "A Swiftly Melting Planet" in *The New York Times* of October 4, 2007, no longer bothers to take the measure of his science with caution. Dr. Homer-Dixon, a professor of peace and conflict studies at the University of Toronto, accompanies his article with a suitably apocalyptic black-and-white drawing by Jon Han. The editorial opens with these words: "The Arctic ice cap melted this summer at a shocking pace, disappearing at a far higher rate than predicted even by the most pessimistic experts in global warming. A big reason such change happens is feedback." Each year the arctic ice pack reaches its lowest point sometime in September, and over the last six years the trimming of the ice pack has increased each year, and each year its winter buildup has been less and less robust. These trends were alarming, but, as Homer-Dixon says, "most [scientists] thought the sea ice wouldn't disappear completely in the Arctic summer before 2040 at the earliest." But this summer has had "scientists scrambling to redo their estimates." Week by week, the Ice Data Center in Boulder, Colorado, reported an accelerating trend: "From 2.23 million square miles of ice remaining on Aug. 8 to 1.6 million square miles on Sept. 16, an astonishing drop from the previous low of 2.05 million square miles." On the basis of this data, Homer-Dixon writes, "one of the climate's most destabilizing feedbacks involves Arctic ice." Melting ice leaves more open ocean water, which absorbs about 80 percent more solar radiation than ice does (called the ice-albedo feedback), thus raising the temperature of the oceans, which only adds to the ice melt already underway as a result of global warming.

Dr. Homer-Dixon describes a series of other disastrous feedback loop effects, ending with a warning so dire that he chooses to illustrate his conclusion in terms of our most primordial relational bond: that of a mother and child.

> In the 1960s, mothers learned that the milk they were feeding their children was laced with radioactive material from atmospheric tests of nuclear weapons and that this contamination could increase the risk of childhood leukemia. Soon women organized themselves in the tens of thousands to demand that nuclear powers ban atmospheric testing. Their campaign largely succeeded.
>
> In response to the new dangers of climate change, we need a similar

mobilization — of mothers, of students and of everyone with a stake in the future — now.[2]

Knowledge Is Change

INTENTION The intention of this practice is simply stated but a lifelong endeavor. It is to find out all you can about one ecological problem, imbalance, or crisis and respond to it.

Tearing the Last Pages from the Last Bible on Earth

> *"Our children ought to be out there on the water," said Kennedy. "This is what connects us, this is what connects humanity, this is what we have in common. It's not the Internet, it's the oceans."*
> Robert F. Kennedy, Jr.[3]

In a recent book, compellingly written and researched, Richard Louv argues that we are disconnected from the natural world, and that disconnect has a significant negative impact on the development of both personality and intelligence, especially in children. He shows that the deficit is demonstrated in children as a severe decline in curiosity, object discrimination, and wonder. Louv draws on the work of the psychologist Howard Gardner as he goes on to describe seven kinds of "multiple intelligences." Several years after describing his theory of multiple intelligences, Gardner realized the need to add a new, eighth type of intelligence — "naturalist intelligence" (nature smarts) — which he describes in the following way:

> The core of the naturalist intelligence is the human ability to recognize plants, animals, and other parts of the natural environment, such as clouds or rocks. All of us can do this; some kids (experts on dinosaurs)

---

2. Thomas Homer-Dixon, "A Swiftly Melting Planet," *The New York Times,* October 4, 2007, A29.

3. Cited in Richard Louv, *Last Child in the Woods: Saving Our Children from Nature-Deficit Disorder* (Chapel Hill, NC: Algonquin Books, 2005), 198.

and many adults (hunters, botanists, anatomists) excel at this pursuit. While the ability doubtless evolved to deal with natural kinds of elements, I believe that it has been hijacked to deal with the world of man-made objects. We are good at distinguishing among cars, sneakers, and jewelry, while our ancestors needed to be able to recognize carnivorous animals, poisonous snakes, and flavorful mushrooms.[4]

Robert F. Kennedy, Jr., has made his name as an environmental lawyer for Riverkeeper, an organization that has helped bring the Hudson River watershed back to life. In researching his book, Louv had an opportunity to go fishing with Kennedy off the California coast. Kennedy told him of the many hours he spent as a child in the natural world and of what crucial importance it was for his own children to share in a similar connection with nature. Kennedy is sensitive to how the beauty or mystery of nature communicates God. But he is also aware that God is communicated through nature only to the extent that we are emotionally and intellectually capable of attending to nature. Louv shares some of Kennedy's reflections:

"God communicates to us through each other and through organized religion, through wise people and the great books, through music and art," but nowhere "with such texture and forcefulness in detail and grace and joy, as through creation," he said. "And when we destroy large resources, or when we cut off our access by putting railroads along river banks, by polluting so that people can't fish, or by making so many rules that people can't get out on the water, it's the moral equivalent of tearing the last pages out of the last Bible on Earth. . . . Our children ought to be out there on the water," said Kennedy.[5]

What Kennedy recognizes is that, with regard to community and connection — to paraphrase Bill Clinton — it's not the Internet, stupid, it's the oceans.

---

4. Louv, *Last Child in the Woods*, 71. The initial seven intelligences included: linguistic intelligence (word smart), logical-mathematical intelligence (numbers/reasoning smart), spatial intelligence (picture smart), bodily-kinesthetic intelligence (body smart), musical intelligence (music smart), interpersonal intelligence (people smart), intrapersonal intelligence (self smart).

5. Louv, *Last Child in the Woods*, 198.

PRACTICE 9.3

Nature Smart

INTENTION   The intention of this practice is to add and apply "nature smarts," or naturalist intelligence, as suggested by Richard Louv, to Howard Gardner's original seven "smarts," or modes of intelligence. The intent is to apply this intelligence to nature (rather than human-made objects) and to affirm wonder as a crucial part of this intelligence.

. . . .

Nature, Pathology, and Denial

> *"It's sad."*
>
> Jim Litchatowitch, biologist,
> quoted in the *Seattle Times* as officials declared
> the lower Columbia watershed coho salmon extinct

It *is* sad: the true pain of the earth today is our denial of its pain.

New work from interdisciplinary perspectives is beginning to address the issues of health and belonging in creation. The fields variously described as ecopsychology, ecotherapy, or green psychology usually take it for granted that Euro-American consciousness has long since broken connections with the natural world, resulting in a set of various pathologies, including denial.[6]

Paul Shepard was one of the earliest voices to identify nature-human relationships as pathological. In humanity's destructive exploitative treatment of the natural world, Shepard saw in Western civilization itself a pathology that he labeled "arrested psychic development." Psychic develop-

---

6. Most of those working in this field are not advocating neo-romanticism. Their writing has the tone rather of a plea to humanity to reconnect with the natural world in an organic way before the various pathologies they describe become untreatable and before the earth itself passes beyond a critical stage of ecological recovery. Ralph Metzner has been a leader in identifying and naming various psychopathologies of the nature-human relationship. Early on, Metzner outlined the growth of this interdisciplinary effort to articulate and address the dynamics of pathological connections between humanity and nature. See Ralph Metzner, "The Psychopathology of the Human-Nature Relationship," in *Ecopsychology: Restoring the Earth, Healing the World,* ed. Theodore Roszak, Mary E. Gomes, and Allen D. Kanner (San Francisco: Sierra Club Books, 1995), 55-67.

ment, both at the biological and psychic levels, involves the history of structural and psychological change within cells, organisms, or a society of organisms — without the loss of the organization that allows that unity to exist. Biologically, this is the process of events that allows an organism or a society of organisms to change gradually from a simple to a more complex level. For Shepard, contemporary humanity's treatment of nature represents a psychic development that is severely crippled: "[M]en may now be the possessors of the world's flimsiest identity structure — by Paleolithic standards, we are childish adults. . . . [We are suffering] from an epidemic of psychopathic mutilation."[7]

Another way of viewing this same phenomenon comes from Wendell Berry, who labels humanity's current psychopathological relationships to nature as "autistic." The current version of the manual of the American Psychiatric Association defines autistic as "pervasive development disorder [characterized by] qualitative impairment in reciprocal social interaction . . . qualitative impairment in verbal and nonverbal communication and in imaginative activity (such as role-playing, fantasy) . . . and markedly restricted repertoire of activities and interests."[8] This could be used equally well as a classic description of the consequences of dissociation from nature: impairment in reciprocal interaction, impairment in verbal and nonverbal communicative and imaginative activity, and marked restriction of activities and interests by humans in and concerning creation. Theodore Roszak, one of the leading voices in the ecopsychology movement, proposes other pathologies formerly considered solely from the perspective of human personality disorders that now, hauntingly, serve equally well to describe contemporary dysfunctional relationships with nature. These include addiction, collective amnesia, traumatic amnesia, repression of the ecological unconscious (ecological unconscious is the path to sanity), and dissociation.[9]

Drawing from the fields of environmental philosophy, ecopsychology, aesthetic theory, and social psychoanalysis, Shierry Weber Nicholsen is one

7. Paul Shepard, *Nature and Madness* (San Francisco: Sierra Club, 1982), 124, cited in Metzner, "Psychopathology of the Human-Nature Relationship," 58.

8. Generous thanks to Michael N. Thomson for pointing out that people who are differently abled do see things that others do not. Michael's own autistic son, for instance, "can spend endless hours looking at the stars . . . he knows their names and seasons." Michael has taught me that autism is best used as a negative trope for blindness toward the natural world *and* as a positive way of looking at the universe in new and unique ways.

9. Theodore Roszak, *The Voice of the Earth* (New York: Simon and Schuster, 1992), 320.

of the most cogent and integrative thinkers in this developing interdisciplinary field. In her book *The Love of Nature and the End of the World*, Nicholsen focuses on a curious and disturbing phenomenon: on the one hand, while there are psychic, spiritual, and emotional forces that drive our almost universal appreciation — even love — of the natural world, on the other hand, certain mechanisms allow our culture as a whole to "relegate matters of the environment to the periphery of their concern." Individually, many people love nature; yet oddly, we are a society that is culturally in denial of nature's dark night.

> My intention here has been to bring together our sense of connection with the nonhuman environment — its beauty, its mystery, its provision of a sheltering home for us — with the psychological forces that allow the destruction to continue. I think each of us knows both, and it is important to acknowledge their conjunction in us.[10]

Nicholsen's creative insight is to shift the psychological mechanism that allows human shame to induce silence concerning abuse and neglect to a cultural conspiracy of silence concerning the realities of abuse and neglect of nature. By degrading nature, we in effect violate love. Violating love of any kind leads to the same result: collective amnesia, shame, and the silence of denial.[11]

Our collective silence about abuse of both the ecological and the sacred qualities of nature can be frightening, even appalling. One of Nicholsen's most troubling examples of denial comes from the realm of the sciences. She gives the example of experimental vivisection on animals: "Some [physiologists] adapted a routine precaution: at the outset of an experiment they would sever the vocal cords of the animal on the table, so that it could not bark or cry out during the operation." This is cruel beyond a doubt. But Nicholsen cites Neil Evernden, who sees in this "experiment" something else happening that is even more chilling: the vivisectionist

10. Shierry Weber Nicholsen, *The Love of Nature and the End of the Word: The Unspoken Dimensions of Environmental Concern* (Cambridge, MA: The MIT Press, 2003), 1. On the psychological and socioeconomic sources of repression of pain for the world and the consequences of that repression, see Joanna Macy and Molly Young Brown, *Coming Back to Life: Practices to Reconnect Our Lives, Our World* (Gabriola Island, BC: New Society Publishers, 1998), 25-38.

11. On the relationship of love, shaming, and silencing, see Nicholsen, *Love of Nature*, esp. chap. 1.

who cuts the vocal cords of the animal simultaneously affirms and denies his *own* humanity:

> He was denying it in that he was able to cut the vocal cords and then pretend that the animal could feel no pain, that it was merely the machine Descartes had claimed it to be. But he was also affirming his humanity in that, had he not cut the cords, the desperate cries of the animal would have told him what he already knew, that it was a sentient, feeling being and not a machine at all.[12]

Nicholsen comments: "To feel the desperate suffering of any creature is terrifying. It can be so terrifying that we want to shut it out of our awareness. . . . Fears of wholesale environmental destruction are of precisely this kind — states of terror combined with utter helplessness and despondency."[13] Faced with terror, helplessness, and despondency, so many people — tragically but perhaps not surprisingly — choose to cut the vocal cords and turn away.

PRACTICE 9.4

The Sounds of the Earth Crying

INTENTION The intention of this practice is to "hear the sounds of the earth crying," as Zen Buddhist monk Thich Nhat Hanh put it. In the process we allow our own pain for the earth to surface. Allowing our pain for the earth to surface is the healthy, nondenying response to ecological crisis.

PRACTICE This practice is best accomplished through small-group sharing, and I will describe it as a practice for a group. If you are not with a group, journal your responses and feelings. Do not be reluctant to acknowledge distress about the situation the planet is in; it is important in these exercises to express this uneasiness and distress. We are trying to encourage rather than discourage appropriate expression of feelings.[14]

12. Neil Evernden, *The Natural Alien: Humankind and Environment*, 2nd ed. (Toronto: University of Toronto Press, 1993), 16-17, cited in Nicholsen, *Love of Nature*, 10.

13. Nicholsen, *Love of Nature*, 10.

14. Macy and Brown, *Coming Back to Life*, 27. The outline for this practice is found on pp. 91-94.

- If the group is new, make introductions. Let each participant have a period of time to explore thoughts and feelings about the environment without interruption.
- Have people gather in groups of about four (no fewer than three, no more than five). For this practice, allow each person his or her own period of time to speak, during which the others listen without response. The time should be the same for all members (5-10 minutes), with the facilitator keeping track of time.
- If the speaker finishes early or pauses, the group should sit in silence until the period is up. Out of the silence, the speaker will often find more to say.
- Themes for sharing (limit the number to four or five) are open ended and general, focused on participants' pain for the earth (or how they "hear the earth crying"). It is helpful to post themes on PowerPoint or in a handout. Possible themes for discussion might include:
  – A recent experience of the condition of the planet
  – When earth-suffering or uncertainty has impinged on your life
  – Time you felt pain for creation particularly acutely
  – When you first noticed you felt pain for the earth
  – How your feelings of pain for the earth have evolved
  – What concerns you most about the earth today is . . .
  – You think that the condition of our environment is becoming . . .
  – Ways you avoid these feelings are . . .
- After all have had a chance to speak without interruption, let the small groups as a whole share experiences and feelings for fifteen minutes. This portion of small-group discussion can center on issues that arose during the uninterrupted time, or any issues the group would like to explore.
- Reconvene the entire group and discuss themes and experiences that arose. Though solutions or inclinations toward action may be a part of the discussion, try to stay with earth sadness, the "earth crying," for this practice.
- If you are journaling, do the same. If it is easier for you to write your feelings as a letter to a friend, or as a letter to God, do so. Again, honor your feelings of pain for the planet and give yourself permission to express them.

Natural Causes: Violence, Decay, Death

The sensitive onlooker is shocked and distressed by the sight of a hawk seizing a piteously crying bird or a cheetah tearing the vitals from a living antelope.

Alexander Skutch[15]

In the midst of formative attention, wonder, awe, and beauty in nature, there has always been death. Hanging there at the end of a sentence that opens with wonder, awe, and beauty, "death" seems something of a stranger — yet it is always alive and well. Death forms identity, and meditation on death is spiritual practice as much as beauty is — perhaps more so. The incarnational, ecological reality of creation survives and is dependent on death: flesh and bones, leaves and limbs, forests and rivers die, decompose, and return to the earth to become components of new organisms and systems. Your great, great, great grandfather has long since become fertilizer for plants or grass that release oxygen into the air you breath. Death, decomposition, decay, and recomposition are "native" to the cycles of life and creation. In themselves, death, decomposition, and decay do not necessarily tilt the planet toward a dark night; but they do when they are accompanied by human causes, and thus they must be considered signs of the dark night.

Death as we usually think of it does not truly reflect the real, integrative relationship between death and the vital energy of nature's life-seeking orientation. On earth as it is, "Christ's victory over death" does not extinguish death. The order of death in creation remains; ironically, it is a "vital" part of the earth's passion for life. As St. Francis of Assisi implies in his famous "Canticle of Creatures," death is an intimate sister to life. Human death, in fact, actually affects the earth in a transformative way. Robert Pogue Harrison says that "humans bury not simply to achieve closure and effect a separation from the dead but also and above all to humanize the ground on which they build their worlds and found their histories."[16] Death thus humanizes the earth as the earth gives life to the human.

Death in itself is not a true "dark night." But death is a contributor to the

---

15. Alexander Skutch, *Harmony and Conflict in the Living World* (Norman: University of Oklahoma Press, 2000), 14.

16. Robert Pogue Harrison, *The Dominion of the Dead* (Chicago: University of Chicago Press, 2003), xi.

dark night, and more often than not it is a contributor that we are not even aware of. Outside of a little squeamishness that they engender in humans, for instance, most insects and spiders seem fairly harmless. In fact, many of them are tiny "death traps," as a recent Smithsonian report makes clear. Insects and other arthropods can cause injury and even death by their bites or stings: more people die each year in the United States from bee and wasp stings than do from snake bites. During every major war in history, more people have been injured or killed by diseases transmitted by insects than have been injured or killed by bullets and bombs. The bubonic plague was caused by bacteria carried by fleas that lived on rats and other rodents; an epidemic of this disease in Europe during the fourteenth century claimed 25 million lives, one-fourth of the population of the continent.[17]

The natural world can be cruel. A friend tells the story of watching an encounter between a bald eagle and a pied-billed grebe. My friend had spotted the bald eagle soaring above a bay on Flathead Lake in Montana while watching a group of pied-billed grebes. Grebes, with six genuses and over twenty species, are unusual birds. They are not ducks, nor are they related to loons, as once thought. Their unique feathers allow them to swim partially submerged with their head and beak just out of the water. They are ungainly on land and leave the water only to nest; they have narrow wings, and some grebes are reluctant to fly (in fact, two South American species are completely flightless).

In my friend's story, the bald eagle began soaring lower and lower over the group of grebes. Then, all at once, it swooped into the midst of a small flock of grebes — having spotted an injured bird. In a quick rush the eagle separated this one grebe from the rest of the group. Less wary than most ducks, grebes respond to danger by diving rather than flying. This grebe did the same. It was her last dive. With perfect timing, the eagle managed to hook its talons into the back of the grebe before she was able to dive deep enough to escape its reach. The eagle's talons alone were not enough to kill the bird, and a wet, squawking, and flapping grebe would be too much for even a bald eagle to lift from the lake and fly away with. So the mighty eagle simply used its weight and size to keep the grebe submerged underwater. Trapped by the weight of the eagle beneath the water, the grebe could neither dive deeper nor reach the surface for air.

---

17. National Museum of Natural History, Smithsonian Institute, "Basic Facts: Harm Done by Insects and Spiders": http://insectzoo.msstate.edu/Students/basic.harm.html (accessed Oct. 7, 2007).

For the first minute the water around the scene was a spew of wave and foam formed from the grebe's underwater struggle. The struggle continued for two minutes, then into three minutes, as the water grew slowly calmer, then stilled, the grebe asphyxiated. The drowned grebe was now simply heavy and waterlogged, still a dead weight for the bald eagle; but it was lifeless and still, an object the eagle could, with effort, lift from the lake. The eagle was obviously exhausted by the time it reached the shore with its catch. My friend watched as the raptor took time to recover her own strength, then slowly defeathered the grebe, and began her meal, stripping the meat in long segments from the bones.

Similar to the balance between death and life is the balance in nature between conflict and harmony. Billions of times a day, in different ways, similar stories of death and life are played out on the planet. Focusing on the balance between conflict and harmony, Alexander Skutch says:

> One organism invades another, forcing it to yield the requisites of its own existence, to become a living environment for it. Nothing is sacred; no organ, tissue, or fluid, no matter how exquisitely delicate and admirably adapted to an intricate function, no matter how indispensable to the life of the host, is spared the pitiless invasion. Eyes and ears, heart and lungs, the very lifeblood itself — all are at times forced to become the medium of aggressive foreign organisms.[18]

This natural but fragile balance between life and death is a necessity of the planet; but this necessity does not erase the shadow it casts over all creation, contributing in its own ways to the dark night of the planet.

PRACTICE 9.5

Practice in a World of Decay, Violence, and Death

INTENTION   The intention of this practice is to begin thinking about and experiencing decay, violence, and death in the natural world as spiritual practice, formative of Christian identity in the dark night.

---

18. Skutch, *Harmony and Conflict*, 13.

Requiem: Eastern White Pine, Passenger Pigeon, American Beech

> *For three thousand years, till well after the turn of the century, Eastern White Pine was unrivaled as a timber-producing tree. Perhaps no other tree in the world has had so momentous a career. Certainly no other has played so great a role in the life and history of the American people.*
>
> Donald Culross Peattie

Two books about trees were published in the early 1950s: *A Natural History of Eastern and Central Trees of North America* and *A Natural History of Western Trees.*[19] The scope of the books' geographic, botanical, historical, and poetic precision and range is unparalleled in the genre of the natural history of trees. Today a natural history of trees would require a general editor, a managing editor, and dozens of contributors. But in the early 1950s, such a book could be written by one exceptional person: Donald Culross Peattie. Writing before the time of "conservation" or "ecological" consciousness, Peattie was always willing to speak to the better side of human nature in its encounter with North American forest lands. Nonetheless, melancholy seeps into his story here and there: an almost unconscious subplot of human greed and waste follows his primary narrative. Without always being aware of it, Peattie was really writing a natural history of the death of certain magnificent species of tree.

Peattie's writing on the eastern white pine (*Pinus strobus* Linnaeus), for instance, opens his chapter on pines. He writes that it has a "pagoda-like outline and habit of growth" and gives evidence that it was not only majestic in individual size but was also — before European settlement — the most abundant species of tree throughout its range. Pioneers used to claim that squirrels could spend their lifetime in these trees, traveling across states without ever touching the ground. Peattie is hardly an environmentalist; still, he cannot recount the history of these oceanlike forests without a certain lament.

---

19. Donald Culross Peattie, *A Natural History of North American Trees* (Boston and New York: Houghton Mifflin, 2007). This edition brings together for the first time Peattie's original two volumes, which were published in 1950 and 1953. Epigraph is from p. 26. Hereafter, page references to this work appear in parentheses in the text.

Certainly [the white pine] was the first gold that the New England Settlers struck. The exploitation began immediately and was so intensive that it was soon necessary to pass our first forest conservation laws. Not that anyone then could have envisaged the day when the virgin stands would all be gone, so vast and dense was White Pine's empire [nor that anyone would abide by the laws in the slightest], but the wastefulness in the mills began with the first homes, built about 1623 at York, Maine, and was never to cease while virgin timber lasted. (p. 29)

The eastern white pine had a serious flaw: its versatility. Its "uses" were nearly endless. It even had a significant role in the American Revolution: before the first flag that featured stars and stripes, the first flag of our Revolutionary forces bore the eastern white pine as its emblem (pp. 30, 31). After the Revolution, in the days of its greatest exploitation, the white pine only increased in value. It was light and easy to haul. It grew mostly in regions of snow, where it was easy to slide to the mills; it also grew in areas of great systems of rivers, on which the light logs could be guided to the sawmills. It grew in such abundance that a mill only needed to be set up once to ensure its investors a fortune. The eastern white pine, "more than any other tree in the country, built this nation, literally and figuratively" (p. 34). By 1900, all the Paul Bunyans had done their work: the virgin white pine stands were gone, and the lumberjacks "followed the lumber barons and the saws to the 'big sticks' of Oregon" (p. 36).

Today one can spot a single eastern white pine standing, solitary, or maybe in a grove of three to eight, maybe even ten, where once a sea of pines stretched as far as one could see in every direction.

PRACTICE 9.6

The Giving Tree

INTENTION   The intention of this practice is to meditate, using Scripture, *lectio divina,* and nature, on humanity's long history of indifferent stewardship of creation, humanity's apparent denial of creation-pain, and to ask what this long history might mean for us today.

The story of the American beech (*Fagus grandifolia* Ehrhart) is as saddening as that of the eastern pine. The finest, in Peattie's mind, of any tree to be seen, the American beech brings out the poet in him:

> Far down the aisles of the forest the Beech is identifiable by the gleam of its wondrously smooth bark, not furrowed even by extreme old age. . . . And the luxuriant growth of mosses on the north side of such a tree, together with the mottling of its lichens, adds to the look it wears of wisdom and serenity. . . . When the tree stands naked in winter it seems to shine through the forest, almost white in contrast with the dun colors all about it. . . . In very early spring an unearthly pale pure green clothes the tree in a misty nimbus of light (pp. 159-61).

Before Peattie finishes his description of the beech, he has opened his pages to the likes of Virgil, Shakespeare, and Daniel Boone as he lets each one do some justice to this magnificent tree in his own way. The destruction of the American beech was primarily due to its unfortunate preference for the same soil composition that farmers love: rich limestone and deep loams. Thus, as America expanded west, the tree became not much more than a signal of prime cropland to be had only for the cutting. By the early 1950s, a few American beeches still stood; today the tree is very, very rare.

The same cannot be said of the passenger pigeon. They are not very, very rare; they simply are not. Once the most common bird in all of North America (estimates average around five billion birds), it was hunted mercilessly until, on September 1, 1914, the last known passenger pigeon, affectionately named Martha, died in Cincinnati, Ohio. It was the passenger pigeon's fate to enjoy a classic symbiotic relationship with the American beech. These pigeons, by the millions, fed on the mast of beech nuts, in return for which the pigeons spread beech seeds all along their wide North American migration routes.

With the pigeons' fondness for beech nuts, it was not difficult for hunters to determine where to go to kill them — and literally by the millions. They often brought hogs out to the trees to fatten up on birds that were seemingly falling from heaven. Ever humanity's advocate, Peattie nonetheless found it harder and harder, with the passenger pigeon and the American beech, to support the myth of the North American continent as endless resource. We can see a sadness rising in Peattie as he describes the fate of the American beech and the passenger pigeon, expressed in his customary elegant, classical style:

So together they fell, bird and tree, from their supreme place in the history of American Nature. For after the Beech forests were swept away by the man with ax and plow, the fate of the passenger pigeon, the most marvelous bird on the North American continent, perhaps in the world, was sealed.

When Audubon was young, in Kentucky, in love with his young wife, Lucy, he painted his "Passenger Pigeon" — a pair of them — and to some of us it is his greatest picture. The curve of the soft necks, the lift of shining wings, are eloquent, unconsciously, of a tenderness and passion not all theirs. It is on a Beech bough that he has perched his pigeon pair, and two withered beechen leaves tell us that the season is autumn when the mast is ripe. An autumn that will not come again but lingers, immortal, in those leaves that cannot fall. (pp. 164-65)

PRACTICE 9.7

Trees and Birds Never Born

INTENTION   One astute writer has observed that what is saddest about the extinction of species — the word "extinction" itself constricts the throat — is that never again will any individual of that extinct species be born. The intention of this practice is to recognize that the eradication of a species of bird or tree is the eradication of birth and of new life as well.

PRACTICE   For this practice, you will have to do your own exploring. You can carry it out in one (or both) of two ways. First, however, reread the two tender paragraphs above by Peattie. Then —

1. If you have a special connection with a species that has recently become extinct, concentrate the practice on one or a small number of individuals of this species. If you cannot think of one, do some research to find a species of tree or bird or fish or mammal that is either extinct or highly endangered due to human exploitation.
    - Find out all you can about the species in order to know everything that it contributed and everything that has now been lost. Stay with this species for several days or weeks, holding it in prayer and meditation, as if it were a guide to your own sadness. How does it guide you? Where is it now?
    - Notice what, in nature, the absence of this species means to creation. What do you expect this loss means to God?

- As you go about your day, or as you are able to be with nature, try to imagine the rebirth of that species. What would it look like? How would it affect its ecosystem? Notice how you feel about the fact that another member of this species will never again be born. Whatever feelings arise in you — sadness, sorrow, loss, grief, pain, fear, anxiety, anger — let these be prayer.

2. In the second way, walk or sit or work in the natural world until you see an individual of a species of bird or tree that may be numerous and that you have been very attached to over the years.
   - Imagine that the individual to whom you are turning your attention is a member of a species that is becoming extinct. Now imagine that the individual to which you are giving attention is the last member of this species of creation — and that this individual, after a time, also dies. What of the "sacramental" vanishes with this extinction?
   - As above, note how you feel; do not censor yourself. Journal or simply note what emerges and let your feelings come. With the absence of this species that has been so meaningful to you over the years, how do you feel? What does it mean to you that another will never be born? How can you pray this loss? How do you feel about the natural world in general?

CHAPTER TEN

Darkness: Consenting to Creative Love

The wicked thrive before the sun, and their shoots spread over the garden.

Job 8:16

Transformation begins at the point where there is no hope.

James Hillman, *Suicide and the Soul*

At the core of the spiritual journey, religious traditions recognize the inevitability of darkness. Transition from "one degree of glory to another," as the Christian tradition puts it, involves transformation, and transformation means change. Though transformation happens, the journey of letting go is a journey through darkness: it is risk, it is real, and it can be very, very painful as one experiences wandering, trials, a sense of abandonment, becoming lost, often physical and spiritual battles, disorientation, and, as James Hillman puts it so bluntly above, hopelessness. In a previous chapter we saw how Dante Alighieri begins his masterwork at a point where he is lost in his own dark night — lost, significantly, within a forest where the "straight way was lost" and the forest itself was "savage and dark and dense."[1] For Dante, this place of being lost is the beginning of the dark night, but it is also the place and moment where, as he says, "I came to myself." This place is thus the place where transformation begins, but not be-

---

1. Dante Alighieri, *Dante: The Divine Comedy, 1: Inferno*, I.1-6, trans. John D. Sinclair (New York: Oxford University Press, 1961), 23.

fore a long, tortuous journey of darkness. The dark night often has this dual quality: a movement through hopelessness into transformation.

Like Dante, Christian writers, both in Scripture and in the tradition, describe the dark night as an integral part of the spiritual journey and — more importantly — a necessary phase of the Christian formational and transformational process. Saint John of the Cross, in his *Ascent of Mount Carmel, The Dark Night, The Spiritual Canticle, The Living Flame of Love,* and other poems and minor works, describes this dark night journey in vivid detail. The depth of his spiritual and psychological insight is matched only by his memorable images that serve as signposts and counsel for the lost soul. Crucially though, having passed through the dark night himself, he is calling from the "other side" of darkness, offering the compassionate insight of an experienced spiritual director. It is crucial because today this is precisely what we are lacking in the dark night of the planet. To date, we have no idea if or where or how to arrive at this "other side" of the dark night of the planet. Saint John, on the other hand, from this "other side," can point out symptoms or signs by which a dark night of the soul might be distinguished from, say, listlessness, acedia, or depression. For Saint John, the true dark night of the soul is the divine offer of accommodation to a more brilliant, loving light. For the planet — who can say?

Saint John of the Cross was psychologically and spiritually keen and perceptive, even by today's standards. Gerald G. May, a psychiatrist for twenty-five years and later a senior fellow in contemplative theology and psychology at the Shalem Institute for Spiritual Formation, speculates that the reason Saint John was so adept was that he, like other contemplatives, learned his psychology "first hand, through acute, extended and direct attentiveness to his own interior life . . . he reflected on his experience in ways that made sense to others. . . . He was deeply immersed in community . . . [and he had] gifts for communicating his insights through poetry, story, metaphor, and concept."[2]

Obviously, the human soul is not planet earth. Still, Saint John of the Cross's firsthand analysis of the psychological and spiritual processes of the dark night can easily be transposed to illuminate the state of the dark night of the planet today. Whether soul or planet, in the dark night we

---

2. Gerald G. May, *The Dark Night of the Soul: A Psychiatrist Explores the Connection Between Darkness and Spiritual Growth* (San Francisco: HarperSanFrancisco, 2004), 153-54. An equally excellent and clear book on the dark night in both Teresa and John is Thomas H. Green, S.J., *When the Well Runs Dry: Prayer Beyond the Beginnings* (Notre Dame, IN: Ave Maria Press, 1998).

grope our way along, unknowing, trusting our sight not to our own needs alone, but to love. Saint John writes, for instance, that "a soul journeys toward perfect union with God . . . through love."[3] In love we find a common point of contact between the dark night of the soul and the dark night of the planet. We can say with confidence that the "earth's dark journey toward perfect union with God is through love." But the love of which Saint John teaches is a wound:

> O sweet cautery,
>> O delightful wound!
>> O gentle hand! O delicate touch
>> that tastes of eternal life
>> and pays every debt!
>> In killing you changed death to life.[4]

Our hope, our prayer, is that the planet's wound is, finally, a transformative wound of love.

PRACTICE 10.1

Nature Lament

INTENTION The intention of this practice is to enter the dark night of the planet truthfully and honestly by writing a nature lament.

---

3. St. John of the Cross, "Prologue," *The Ascent of Mt. Carmel*, 69. All of what is important for an understanding of St. John's teaching on the dark night are found in two major treatises (actually poems with lengthy commentary on the poems). All citations from these two treatises are from Kieran Kavanaugh, O.C.D., and Otilio Rodriguez, O.C.D., *The Collected Works of John of the Cross* (Washington, DC: Institute of Carmelite Studies, 1979). The two treatises are *The Ascent of Mount Carmel* (*Collected Works*, 65-292) and *The Dark Night* (*Collected Works*, 293-389).

4. St. John of the Cross, "Living Flame of Love," in *Collected Works*, 578-79.

Diagnosis of a Dark Night: Borrowing God's Eyes

> *For, having looked in the direction God is looking, toward the*
> *earth, one seems to know what God is seeing when one looks back*
> *again, as though one were looking into [God's] eyes and seeing*
> *the earth and oneself reflected there.*
>
> John S. Dunne, *The Reasons of the Heart*[5]

The philosopher John S. Dunne writes of our need to "borrow God's eyes" in order to see ourselves and the earth reflected most clearly. Saint John of the Cross sees the human soul as if through God's eyes. By making a shift from Saint John's language of the soul to the language of creation, we can continue to use Saint John of the Cross as a reliable guide in this dark night of the planet.[6] In making this shift, we borrow Saint John's wisdom and teaching and in this sense "borrow God's eyes" as a new way of viewing the planet and its own dark night.

The first thing that we will see if we borrow God's eyes in this way is that (transposing "earth" for "soul") "the dark night is an inflow of God into the [earth]. . . . God teaches the [earth] secretly and instructs it in the perfection of love."[7] Again we see, whether in planet or in soul, that our guide and teacher is Love. The darkness is secret instruction in perfect love that is present to the eyes of the heart, if not the eyes of sight. But we must get used to the fact that in the context of the dark night, Love is perceived initially as a wound of "many miseries" (1.8.3, 312). Don't let anyone try to fool you: the journey to "perfection of love" is not all joy; even the journey to the "messiness of love" is not all joy. Love *is* messy: love can seem to function in reverse just when we think we know it in all its completeness.

> [I]t is at this time that [all earth] is going about its spiritual exercises with delight and satisfaction, when in its opinion the sun of divine favor is

---

5. John S. Dunne, *The Reasons of the Heart: A Journey into Solitude and Back Again into the Human Circle* (Notre Dame, IN: University of Notre Dame Press, 1978), 46.

6. It is helpful, in making a shift from "soul," "spirit," or "senses" to "earth" or "planet," to remember that St. John of the Cross does not actually speak of the dark night of the "soul" *(alma),* but rather of two differentiated but intimately connected elements that together comprise the "soul": the "sense(s)" *(sentido[s])* and the "spirit" *(espiritu).* He thus speaks of the dark night of the senses and the dark night of the spirit.

7. *Dark Night,* 2.5.1, 335. Hereafter, page references to this work appear in parentheses in the text.

shining most brightly on them, that God darkens all this light and closes the door. . . . God now leaves [the earth] in such darkness that [it does] not know which way to turn. . . . This change is a surprise to [all the earth] because everything seems to be functioning in reverse. (2.5.4, 336)

It is in the midst of this seeming backward flow of divine love that the miseries of the dark night come upon us. St. John describes the miseries in three ways: In the first (again transposing "planet" for "soul") the planet's affliction comes about because "the light and wisdom of this contemplation is very bright and pure, and the [planet] in which it shines is dark and impure, [the planet] will be deeply afflicted in receiving it into itself. . . . Because it seems that God has rejected it" (2.5.5, 336). In the second affliction or misery, the experience is that all support, every kindness, is withdrawn, while the memory is of a Creator who held all things in balance: "Under the stress of this oppression and weight, the [planet] feels so much a stranger to being favored that it thinks, and so it is, that even that which previously upheld the [planet] has ended along with everything else" (2.5.7, 337). In a final misery, deprived of these previous consolations and support, "the [planet] at the sight of its miseries feels that it is melting away . . . it feels as if it were swallowed by a beast and being digested in the dark belly, and the [planet] suffers an anguish comparable to Jonah's when in the belly of the whale" (2.6.1, 337).

This is the weight of honestly "borrowing God's eyes." From this divine perspective — and, as illustrated in the preceding chapter, also from the human perspective, if we can turn from denial — our planet today, while yet receiving the inflow of divine love, smolders in the miseries of "the shadow of death and the sorrows of hell, all reflecting the feeling of God's absence" (2.6.2, 338).

<hr>

PRACTICE 10.2

Miseries in This Earth's Dark Night

INTENTION The intention of this practice is to confirm in our minds and hearts the reality of the dark night of the planet and to intentionally acknowledge our part in precipitating or maintaining the planet's miseries. We will acknowledge and affirm about our planet, with our own eyes, what Saint John of the Cross confirms about the human soul.

Desolation and Inability to Pray

The land mourns and wastes away.

Isaiah 33:9

Saint John of the Cross writes not only of the "miseries" of the dark night, but also certain "signs" by which the dark night can be distinguished from other maladies that it resembles, such as grief, pathology, or depression. For Saint John, though the symptoms may be quite similar, careful distinguishing between a dark night (divinely initiated and transformative) and, say, depression (physiologically, psychologically, or socially initiated and destructive) is essential. Saint John of the Cross suggests three signs of a true dark night.

A first and confirming sign of this dark night has to do with consolation: "The [earth] does not get satisfaction or consolation from the things of God, [it does] not get any out of creatures either." Whatever was previously consoling — whether delights from God or connection to creation — no longer gives satisfaction. With regard to the planet, this first sign is not hard to identify: water and ozone depletion, species extinction, ecological imbalance, nature ignorance. But Saint John adds: "The want of satisfaction in earthly or heavenly things could be a product of some indisposition or melancholic humor, which also frequently prevents one from being satisfied with anything" (1.9.2, 313). Thus, a second sign is required in order to identify a true dark night.

Soul depression or ecological imbalance, if the root cause can be determined and an appropriate response made, can be addressed and often cured. This is not true of the second sign: lacking consolation, the earth nonetheless still *longs for contact* with God. There is no cure for longing and desire unfulfilled. Yet in this second sign, despite the lack of consolation, "the [planet] still turns to God solicitously and with painful care" (1.9.3, 313). Like a dog staying with its master long after the master has died, soul or planet keeps turning toward God with "painful care." Paul writes in Romans: "For the creation was subjected to frustration, not by its own choice, but by the will of the one who subjected it, in hope that the creation itself will be liberated from its bondage to decay. . . . We know that the whole creation has been groaning as in the pains of childbirth right up to the present time" (Rom. 8:20-22). Even more than in Paul's time, right up to the present time, the earth longs for contact with God.

In the third sign — again, all three must be present to diagnose a true dark night — the soul or planet is "powerless, in spite of its efforts, to meditate and make use of the imagination, as was the [planet's] previous custom" (1.9.8, 315). Memory of consolation past is as painful as lack of consolation present. Is it the planet's custom to imagine and meditate its Creator? As we have seen, especially in Section 3, Scripture is unequivocal in its answer to this: "Let the earth hear, and all that fills it; the world, and all that comes from it" (Isa. 34:1). "The wilderness and the dry land shall be glad, the desert shall rejoice and blossom" (Isa. 35:1). "Praise the Lord from the earth, you great sea creatures and all ocean depths" (Ps. 148:7). Creation meditates on its maker, and it praises the Lord. But what is creation's praise in the context of degradation and pain. Today, for instance, how do the extinct eastern white pine, the passenger pigeon, or the American beech meditate on or praise God? In what way do forests of pine destroyed by the pine beetle praise God? How do the coho salmon of the Columbia River watershed praise God when these glorious fish are no more? This is powerlessness of meditation and prayer, that "in spite of its efforts to meditate and make use of the imagination, as was the [planet's] previous custom," the planet cannot pray.

PRACTICE 10.3

Signs of the Dark Night of the Planet

INTENTION The intention of this practice is to listen to the earth, hearing in her sighs and groans the three signs of the dark night described above by Saint John of the Cross.

As a young boy I was constantly reminded not to drink from any stream where folks had settled upstream from where I wanted to drink. I believed this, and it was good advice; so I walked up many hills into the mountains where the streams came clean with no intervening sign of humans. I loved that water and remember it, so clear and cold; it had a taste of sweetness and life. It had the sweetness and life and the taste of prayer, which is no longer its custom.

PRACTICE 10.4

The Way of All Earth?

INTENTION One study from the Union of Concerned Scientists lists the "leading consumption-related environmental problems" today as:

- Air pollution
- Global warming
- Habitat alteration
- Water pollution

The same study lists the "most harmful consumer activities" as:

- Cars and light trucks
- Meat and poultry
- Home heating, hot water, and air conditioning
- Household appliances and lighting
- Home construction
- Household water and sewage[8]

The intention of this practice is to consider whether this dark night of the planet is a transformational phase or permanent condition. Explore your own reactions to this phase and/or condition.

PRACTICE Perhaps the most pessimistic (or realistic, depending on perspective and circumstances) portrayal of life, death, and the afterlife in all of Scripture comes from Ecclesiastes 9:1-10. Koheleth, the sage of Ecclesiastes, says that regardless of what we do in this life, we will never understand the meaning of life or death, let alone escape the grasp of death. For Koheleth, human life is a wisp of straw: there is no moral justice in the destiny of men or women; it is vanity to think that there is any sacredness or dignity in human life. The writer concludes that one should enjoy pleasures as they come, because regardless of what we do, "the same fate comes to all" (Eccles. 9:2).

- Read Ecclesiastes 9:1-10.
- What is transformational in this passage?
- Read the passage again. This time apply what is said of humanity to cre-

8. Michael Brower and Warren Leon, *The Consumer's Guide to Effective Environmental Choices: Practical Advice from the Union of Concerned Scientists* (New York: Three Rivers Press, 1999).

ation. That is, bring to mind the reality that all creation meets the same fate as humanity as it is depicted in these verses.

- From this perspective, do you feel the earth is in a transformational phase, or do you feel this dark night of the planet may be a permanent condition, experiencing "the same fate [that] comes to all"?
- How does this perspective affect your own sense of who you are? What does it mean for your relationship with nature? What insight does it shed on your own experience of the dark night?
- Imagine both possibilities. What can or should we do about the dark night of the planet if this is a transformational phase? On the other hand, imagine possible responses if this dark night is a permanent condition.
- Imagine that Saint Francis of Assisi is there beside you. What would he tell you? What would you like to tell him about the dark night?

Moving Forward: Good Friday to . . .

> *A tree gives glory to God simply by being a tree.*
> Thomas Merton, *New Seeds of Contemplation*

In the abyss of the dark night of the soul, one never knows for sure that the transformation will be God's doing or the soul's. The soul sometimes has other options than God's intentions: it can simply walk away from God; it can transfer the darkness onto others; it can even end the despair in suicide. And darkness seldom finds the light it expects to find. In the dark night, if there is to be transformation toward health, it is a Good Friday kind of transformation: death to self, disintegration of familiar patterns of faith and prayer, waiting, mourning. Today this Good Friday crucible intersects the journey of our planet and darkens it. What will be the outcome? Will it make a journey from disintegration to synthesis, from Good Friday to Easter? Or will it — and humanity along with it — choose to walk away from divine intentions?

Humanity is in large part culpable for condemning the planet to this dark night, as culpable as Pilate is of condemning Jesus. Think of it: we are Pilates to the planet's Jesus. We can look to Scripture as, in some sense, calling to us from across the same abyss that Saint John of the Cross called across to the soul. The psalmist says, "Hope in God" (Ps. 42:5). This is helpful, but it is not enough, essential but not complete. If we "hope in God" and leave it at that, the planet weeps while we console ourselves with hope. Paul writes that, through Christ, God is pleased to reconcile all things to God's self (Col. 1:15-17; Eph. 1:3, 8-10). This includes *all* creation. The implication is that this reconciliation is no different for humans than it is for planets: *all things,* Paul says more than once, are reconciled to God "by making peace through the blood of the cross." Good Friday darkness transforms: "all of us . . . are being transformed into the same image [of the Lord] from one degree of glory to another" (2 Cor. 3:18). But this is still not enough. If we honestly borrow the eyes of God, at present the planet's degrees of glory are stained, strained, and dark.

Some are reassured and count their denial trustworthy on the basis of Revelation 22, which assures us of a new heaven and a new earth, with a "river of the water of life" and a "tree of life with crops of fruit and leaves for the healing of nations," where "there will be no more darkness" (Rev. 22:1, 2, 5). Even this is not enough! Using the Good Friday analogy, it is well past three days that the planet has been rotting, the stone is not rolled away, and now even the stone is groaning. Revelation 22 addresses hope (not seen) but circumvents despair (seen in the planet today), a circumvention that is not valid in the dark night.

So where do we look for guidance in this dark night of the planet? Prayer is good. Scripture is good. Creation-care is good. First, however, as I am trying to show in this book, we must ask the earth, learn to listen to the earth, and respond appropriately to her answer: "But ask the animals, and they will teach you, or the birds of the air, and they will tell you; or speak to the earth, and it will teach you, or let the fish of the sea inform you" (Job 12:7-8). Were Saint John of the Cross alive today, he would turn to the earth as his own spiritual director; he would turn to nature as his spiritual guide. He would listen, he would hear, and he would respond.

On Good Friday, Jesus humanized the earth. I believe St. John of the Cross noticed Jesus' sacred presence in creation, while St. Francis noticed Jesus' humanity in creation's love for us. Thomas Merton once wrote:

A tree gives glory to God by being a tree. For in being what God means it to be it is obeying him. It "consents," so to speak, to his creative love. It is expressing an idea which is in God and which is not distinct from the essence of God, and therefore a tree imitates God by being a tree. The more a tree is like itself, the more it is like him.[9]

9. Thomas Merton, *New Seeds of Contemplation* (New York: New Directions, 1961), 29.

The more a tree is like God, the better it prays: a tree united in perfect love to God is a tree in perfect prayer. Creation is very good at being exactly what it is. As we turn to creation, we consent to learn who we are.

PRACTICE 10.5

Consenting to Creative Love

Listen, O heavens, and I will speak;
    hear, O earth, the words of my mouth.
Let my teaching fall like rain
    and my words descend like dew,
like showers on new grass,
    like abundant rain on tender plants.

                                                    Deuteronomy 32:1-2

INTENTION   The intention of this practice is to consent to hear Love speak through nature's consent to be exactly what it is, according to the divine intention.

PRACTICE   In this practice, use the three excerpts cited in the text — Job 12:7-8, the Merton tree quote, and Deuteronomy 32:1-2 — separately or together as you move through the exercise.

- Following Merton, notice how something in nature gives glory to God simply by being itself. In what ways do you notice nature "consenting" to be itself? Consenting to creative love is a vocation as well as a core of prayer. True consent of this kind structures and shapes us for maximum engagement and flourishing for the life given us. True consent in this sense unites us to our Creator. Look again at what you are attending to in nature — a wave or a tree or a red-tailed hawk — and simply notice how readily it consents to be itself, and in this consenting is in fact a deeply sacred form of prayer.
- The Job passage invites you to learn about consenting, vocation, and prayer from nature. Ask the animals, the plants, the mountains what you need to know about consenting to creative love, about your vocation, and about prayer. Give your sacred attention to how nature answers and "declares" to you. The context of the Job passage is that the animals will declare that God is their maker. In your own context, what do nature's an-

swers teach you about God? Ask the animals about how they manage to be themselves in the dark night of the planet.

- From a slightly different perspective, the Deuteronomy passage indicates that nature herself learns from the wisdom of God. How/what do the heavens hear when God speaks? How does the earth listen and learn when creative love opens its mouth? How do the Lord's teachings fall like rain, like dew on the grass and plants? How do these ways of listening and learning form your own senses to listen to and learn from God and nature?

- What are you doing in your life that prevents a tree, a wave, or any part of nature from "consenting" to what God is calling it to be? Expressed another way, what kind of "footprint" do you leave on the earth that contributes to the dark night?

Jesus' Response: Overturn the Tables

> *Creation waits with eager longing*
> *for the revealing of the children of God.*
> **Creation itself will be set free**
> *from its bondage and decay*
> *and share the glorious liberty*
> *of the children of God.*
>
> Response, Ordinary Time,
> St. John's Abbey

This response from Ordinary Time at St. John's Abbey is our hope. This hope, transformed into responses, can help set creation free, release creation from bondage, and give all an opportunity to share in the glorious liberty of the children of God. But today we live in a darkness as yet untraveled by the likes of a Saint John of the Cross or any other. Today the sacred matters in darkness. Christian formation practice does not give way to eschatological visions when those visions become excuses for dreaming, doing nothing, profiting at the expense of creation. Nature as practice shapes attention and wonder; it also shapes activism.

Rather than waiting for a "new heaven, a new earth," wake up! Touch the soil! Be scared! Exercise your "serpent wisdom"! Use your "dove innocence"! (Matt. 10:16) Borrow God's eyes. Ask the animals. Get angry. Jesus did. Jesus fumed at the moneychangers in his Father's temple. He over-turned tables. He didn't wait until he shocked the world by his resurrection from the dead — his own personal "eschatology." Instead, he

> drove out all who were selling and buying in the temple, and he over-turned the tables of the money changers and the seats of those who sold doves. He said to them, "It is written, 'My house shall be called a house of prayer'; but you are making it a den of robbers." (Matt. 21:12-13)

Creation is the Creator's temple; the earth is the Father's house; nature is a house of prayer; the cosmos is the shrine of wisdom. How Jesus Christ's anger would swell at this desecration[10] of his Father's temple, the whole planet as his Father's house of prayer.

The charge against the "money changers" and "dove-sellers" is as much about avarice and greed as it is the decision to break the bonds of trust and belonging that form the sacred temple walls of the dwelling place of God, whom Jesus calls "Father." Avarice and greed deplete creation in an ecological sense. Desecration in the temple of creation violates the earth as a house of prayer in a sacramental sense. In nature's temple, the ecological is sacred; in creation's temple, the sacred is ecological. The moneychangers and dove-sellers desecrate societal bonds of trust; in creation's temple, humanity actually desecrates familial bonds of trust. Adam and Eve's failure to satisfy themselves on their own "earth as it was" is a failure of belonging. By continuing to break the bonds of belonging in the dark night of the planet, humans are once again moneychangers and dove-sellers in the holy temple of the Lord.

PRACTICE 10.6

Belonging and Anger

INTENTION The intention of this practice is threefold: first, to observe feelings and connections associated with belonging within creation; second, to allow transgression of belonging in the natural world to evoke anger as virulent as Jesus' anger in the temple; and third, to question

---

10. Formed from de- ("do the opposite of") + (con)secrate ("make holy"). Dictionary.com: *Online Etymology Dictionary*, Douglas Harper, historian: http://dictionary.reference.com/browse/desecrate (accessed June 24, 2008).

whether both belonging and anger are appropriate ways of participating in ecological and sacred creation.

....

A sacred ecology is a way of belonging that welcomes, invites, and opens as easily into community as into solitude. Reverence in solitude and deference in community are formed by listening: "And the Lord said to me, 'Not only that, but ask the earth and she will tell you, defer to her and she will declare to you" (2 Esdras 7:54). Jesus asked and Jesus listened and Jesus belongs.

Formation in the Dark Night of the Planet

> *Death is one thing, an end to birth is something else.*
> Michael Soule and B. A. Wilcox,
> *Conservation Biology*

Christian spiritual traditions have always recognized "dark nights" as characteristic — even necessary — components of spiritual growth. In their various forms, "dark nights" have generally been interpreted as transforming processes during which the soul is guided into ever deeper chambers of God's heart. The darkness is disorienting, painful, thoroughly unsettling, very real, but finally transformative in that it blinds us to all that is not of God and over time begins to show us ever more innovative ways of connection and belonging.

In the Gospels there is a visual picture of this dark night that appropriately uses images of nature. In one of his parables Jesus compares the kingdom of heaven to a field of wheat interspersed with weeds. The wheat is the kingdom of heaven, the light of God, while the weeds are darkness — all that is not God. Notice in the following parable that Jesus does not suggest that we ignore the weeds, but that we attend to them when the time is ripe. In the context of the parable, to eradicate darkness indiscriminately risks eradicating the light as well:

> "So when the plants came up and bore grain, then the weeds appeared as well. And the slaves of the householder came and said to him, 'Master, did you not sow good seed in your field? Where, then, did these weeds come

from?' He answered, 'An enemy has done this.' The slaves said to him, 'Then do you want us to go and gather them?' But he replied, 'No, for in gathering the weeds you would uproot the wheat along with them. Let both grow together until the harvest; and at harvest time I will tell the reapers, collect the weeds first and bind them in bundles to be burned, but gather the wheat into my barn." (Matt. 13:26-30)

There is a darkness on the face of the planet: weeds are everywhere. Since an episode in a garden long ago, creation has always suffered violence and decay and death. Since then, creation has been groaning until now. But a deeper groaning exists today that is of more recent origin, a groaning traceable to humanity itself. The weeds in the master's fields have become thickly entangled in the wheat. It is well past the time to "collect the weeds first and bind them in bundles to be burned."

PRACTICE 10.7

Creation Confession

INTENTION The philosopher Roger S. Gottlieb has recently written: "People have always had moral failings, but they have never had to confess to devastating creation, or felt the need to pray for the health of the earth as an endangered whole." The intention of this practice is to help us to find our own personal (or communal) languages for confessing our contribution to the dark night of the planet, to ask forgiveness, and to pray for the health of the earth.

Nature as Spiritual Guide

CHAPTER ELEVEN

Nature as Belonging

Paul Tillich, Jonathan Edwards, and My Daughter

> *Humans and nature belong together, in their created glory, in their great tragedy, and in their salvation.*
>
> Paul Tillich's epitaph

A picture I carry shows my beautiful sixteen-year-old daughter, Rachel, during a summer of discovery in Costa Rica. In the picture, a large waterfall forms the backdrop to what is obviously a large, very deep, and inviting pool formed by the falls. Only Rachel's head, her face beaming with pleasure, is visible in the picture; the rest of her body is submerged in the pool. Her head seems to float on the surface of the water. She has her hair in pigtails, both of which shoot off at forty-five-degree angles from the sides of her head into the pool. Did I mention the smile? Indeed, the whole picture smiles.

I know that Rachel felt alive and invigorated and amazed on this trip. But as I look at this picture now, I wonder, as the years progress, what will become of her equally beautiful soul against the dark night of our planet's horizon. Will her beauty of soul and loveliness of body and buoyancy of spirit be enough to keep their shape outlined against this darkening? The theologian Paul Tillich, in what must have been a late-in-life reflection on life and death, arranged for his tombstone to proclaim: "Humans and nature belong together." In death, in the ground, Tillich certainly is together with nature. But he was also referring to his life: human life and nature belong together. I know this lovely daughter of mine also belongs together with nature in this life. In my daughter's smile the horizon of the planet's

163

dark night undergoes something of a restoration: its shadow begins to show signs of a rainbow smile, and I remember a Native American bit of wisdom: "The earth is not an inheritance from our parents, but is given in trust to hand on to our children."

But there are different ways of belonging. Here are two. Richard Seager, a scientist at Columbia University's Lamont Doherty Earth Observatory, works on water-supply models that show current drought conditions in the states of the American Southwest. Recently, when asked whether the drought his models illustrate would be permanent, he replied: "You can't call it a drought anymore, because it's going over to a drier climate. No one says the Sahara is in drought."[1] In this way of belonging, I fear for Rachel's smile, I fear what I will "hand on" to her. Is it a trust or a betrayal? I would like to hand on something more like what Jonathan Edwards describes in his *Personal Narrative:*

> The appearance of everything was altered; there seemed to be, as it were, a calm, sweet cast, or appearance of divine glory, in almost everything. God's excellence, his wisdom, his purity, and love seemed to appear in everything; in the sun, moon, and stars; in the clouds, and blue sky; in the grass, flowers, trees; in the water, and all nature; which used greatly to fix my mind. I used to sit and view the moon for continuance; and in the day, spent much time viewing the clouds and sky, to behold the glory of God in these things.[2]

This would be an honorable trust to hand on: here nature not only heals, but it transfixes, centers, and takes on the appearance of glory and beauty and truth. Most of us have felt something like what Edwards describes, even if we would verbalize it in different ways.

Left to its own healing ways, creation *is* belonging and balance and practice and guidance, a place where beautiful daughters smile and nature-intoxicated theologians glow. Ignored, abused, controlled, and forgotten, nature ignores, abuses, controls, and forgets. Its organic belonging turns ugly, rogue, and rotten. In this chapter we turn back toward a wounded earth, not to batter or be battered, but to remember what she teaches of

---

1. Jon Gertner, "The Future Is Drying Up," *The New York Times Magazine,* October 21, 2007.

2. Jonathan Edwards, *Personal Narrative,* in *Light from Light: An Anthology of Christian Mysticism,* ed. Louis Dupré and James A. Wiseman, 2nd ed. (New York: Paulist, 2001), 391-92.

discernment, healing, intimacy, and belonging before we have entirely forgotten what it is we can hand on to our children in trust. A daughter's smile depends on it.

Nature as Discernment

> *We are many sets of eyes staring out at each other from the same living body.*
>
> Freeman House, *Totem Salmon*

In balance, we belong with nature; belonging with nature, we are in balance. Early lessons in nature's pedagogy of balance and belonging have to do with discernment, whether of self, others, God, or nature. Freeman House presses hard, honestly, and truthfully on the essential senses of intimacy, belonging, balance, and reciprocity in nature. The lessons in this case are between salmon and humans. He frames his experience of nature-intimacy in terms of how salmon guide and heal humans: "There is a way for us humans to be, just as there is a way for salmon to be. . . . We are related by virtue of the places to which we choose to return."[3] Earlier in his book, as he is attending to salmon with what he calls his whole "field of being," Freeman says that on this planet "we are many sets of eyes staring out at each other from the same living body."[4]

This is a perfect image for the kind of belonging through which nature forms and guides human discernment. Discernment generally means sound judgment and tested understanding, keen insight, and sagacity. Discernment is from the Latin *cernere* (to "separate, sift, decide, distinguish, and resolve") and from *discernere* (to "sever, separate, and part"). Discernment thus cuts, separates, and sifts as it distinguishes among values, behaviors, and options. Discernment in nature opens many sets of eyes, all of which are looking at each other from the same living body. Personal discernment affects the body of community; community discernment affects individual lives; together, personal and community discernment affect creation; and the many sets of eyes within creation envision the world in ways that affect humanity. Discernment in this sense is like salmon, which sepa-

---

3. Freeman House, *Totem Salmon: Life Lessons from Another Species* (Boston: Beacon Press, 1999), 217.
4. House, *Totem Salmon*, 14.

rate, sift, decide, and distinguish as they swim faultlessly home. Discernment for salmon is return: it is intimacy and home. Discernment for humanity is also return: it is finding our intimacy and our home in the things of God.

In this sense, the sun setting into the Pacific Ocean, the hypnotic waves, the sounds of colors, the timeless waiting of rock and sand, the day-fish finding sleep in corals and caves and the night-fish stalking the fading light, the miracle of a single cloud, a seagull swimming the sky, the starfish flying the ocean bottom — all are spiritual guides, ritual healers, companions to belonging, solace in solitude, eyes of discernment. All of them are created, redeemed, and sustained in the Word.

Open the Gospels anywhere, and you will find Jesus in intimate discernment with nature — sifting, deciding, resolving. I have just opened randomly to Matthew: "As he walked by the sea of Galilee, he saw two brothers, Simon who is called Peter, and Andrew his brother, casting a net into the sea — for they were fishermen" (Matt. 4:18). Jesus walked beside the sea, beholding all the eyes beholding him, seeing in creation fishes and seas and fishermen and fishers of men. Jesus discerned that the fisherman Peter, this "Rock," would be casting nets that would become homes for men and women gathered in Jesus' name.

PRACTICE 11.1

Balance in Discernment

INTENTION Balance is critical to discernment. The intention of this practice is to recognize balance and imbalance in nature and how you walk with balance or imbalance in nature.

PRACTICE In his book *Drawing Closer to Nature,* the artist Peter London teaches how to pay careful attention to the natural world, in effect how to separate, sift, and decide — how to discern.[5] The book gives practices in both drawing (pictorially) closer to nature and drawing (attentively) closer to nature. Allow yourself at least an hour of uninterrupted time for this practice.

---

5. Peter London, *Drawing Closer to Nature: Making Art in Dialogue with the Natural World* (Boston: Shambala, 2003). For a discussion on balance and most of the balance suggestions, see pp. 210ff.

- Find a place in nature where you are comfortable and where you can spend time exploring the subtle balances and imbalances in creation. Breathe, be still.
- When you are ready, begin going through the list of "balances" below. The idea is to recognize a statement that begins "Balance is . . ." in the natural world around you. Move from one to the next only as you feel the need or as the next catches your attention. Focus on whatever draws your attention: a tree, the ecosystem, colors, a few blades of grass, wind, waves.
- Notice these balances in nature, then do an internal accounting of how you are yourself balanced or imbalanced in a similar way. This internal accounting or "examen of conscious" is a preliminary step in discernment.
- How does nature guide your contemplations and meditations in directions that help you live mindfully, that is, how you walk the earth in balance? Again, you may wish to journal, draw, photograph, or "track," from your field guide, your particular nature interest — birding, for instance. Whatever helps you pay careful attention to nature will help you focus on balance in nature.

"Balances"
  - Balance is to locate the still point at the center of complexity.
  - Balance is to be in a constant state of sensitive fine adjustments.
  - Balance requires exquisite sensitivity to inner and outer forces.
  - Balance requires yielding and resisting, yielding and resisting.
  - Balance appears spontaneous and improvisational, but is utterly responsible and devoted.
  - Balance is thwarted by pretense, also by insistence.
  - Balance knows both this and that, and prefers neither.
  - Balance is opportunistic.
  - Balance finds home anywhere, finds the center everywhere.
  - "Balancing" is more in balance than "balanced."
  - Complete balance is the end of nature.

Slowing Discernment

Careful attention to nature fosters slowing. It calls us into spiritual practice, into formation, and into a path to healing; it calls us as a guide to discernment. How does nature's slowing guide us into discernment?

In the recent best-selling historical novel *Girl with a Pearl Earring,* Tracy
Chevalier writes of the famous seventeenth-century Dutch painter
Johannes Vermeer, and of a peasant girl, Griet, who entered Vermeer's
household at a young age as a maid. Chevalier tells the story through
Griet's eyes. Over the years she manages to gain the trust of Vermeer and,
though still young, is given the important task of cleaning and arranging
Vermeer's studio. Eventually she will become the model for Vermeer's famous painting *Girl with a Pearl Earring.* One of her chores is to lay out the
colors of paint Vermeer requests for the next day. One day Griet lays out
blue paint instead of ultramarine, as Vermeer had asked for. At first an-
noyed, Vermeer soon recovers and walks over to open the studio window.
He invites Griet to look out the window. It is a breezy day, and Griet can
see clouds disappearing behind a church tower. "What color are those
clouds, Griet?" Vermeer asks. Griet looks hard at the clouds and answers,
"Why, white, sir."

"Are they?" he asks. She looks again: "And grey," she says, "perhaps it
will snow."

"Come, Griet, you can do better than that. Think of your vegetables . . .
your turnips and your onions — are they the same white?"

"No. The turnip has green in it, the onion yellow."

"Exactly. Now, what colors do you see in the clouds?"

"There is some blue in them," she says after studying them for some
minutes. "And yellow as well. And there is some green!" In the first-person
narrative of the novel, Griet says, "I became so excited I actually pointed. I
had been looking at clouds all my life, but I felt as if I saw them for the first
time at that moment."[6]

Vermeer teaches Griet contemplative attention, wonder, and slowing,
just as the clouds, over time, had taught Vermeer. Likewise, it is Griet's vegetables — her turnips and her onions, and now the clouds — that slow her
gaze, arouse her curiosity, and will, by the end of the book, teach her a new
way of being on the earth.

---

6. Tracy Chevalier, *The Girl with a Pearl Earring* (New York: Plume, 2001), 99-102.

PRACTICE 11.2

Slowing

INTENTION   In his book *In Praise of Slowness: Challenging the Cult of Speed*, Carl Honoré writes of the ever-increasing speed of contemporary life. He writes: "In this media-drenched, data-rich, channel-surfing, computer-gaming age, we have lost the art of doing nothing . . . of slowing down and simply being alone with our thoughts." He quotes the actress Carrie Fisher, who said that "even instant gratification takes too long."[7] Belonging to nature is a process of slowing, of being willing to attend to a periwinkle or linger with a cloud. The intention of this practice is to begin to restore contemplative connection with creation by slowing down.

In 1857, the painter Frederick Edwin Church completed his spectacular and now famous painting *Niagara*. The foreground of the huge canvas, which is nearly four feet wide and seven feet high, is taken up entirely by the tumultuous water and spray of the falls; land is represented only by two small, nearly imperceptible islands offshore on the far side of the falls, represented by a thin line between water and sky. The sky itself comes forward, thunderous, ominous as the falls, with a small rainbow lending color. One art critic of the period wrote that the painting *was* Niagara Falls — the only thing missing was the sound.

Ten years after its completion the painting was a sensation at the Paris Exposition of 1867. European viewers, normally suspicious of any "art" emerging from the United States, lined up for blocks and blocks outside the Exposition's exhibit hall waiting for a chance to see the painting. Even with the hundreds of people waiting in line behind them, it is reliably reported that men, women, and children spent an average of *one hour* slowing before this spectacular window into nature.

Seeing yellow, green, and blue in clouds and standing before a single painting for an hour — these two examples of attentive slowing are remarkable in part because that kind of intensity of perception is unusual today. Yet attention, slowing, and intensity of perception are components of discernment. Christians are called to disciplineships of discernment: they

---

7. Carl Honoré, *In Praise of Slowness: Challenging the Cult of Speed* (New York: HarperOne, 2004), 11, 12.

are apostles of healing. To see a complete palette of colors in a cloud is an act of discipleship. To be rapt by the spray of water falling from a painting is a way of discernment. All we attend to on this earth is a part of our apostolate. This kind of contemplative perception both sees and acts: it hears the groaning of creation and attends to its healing; creation hears your groaning and attends to your healing.

Intensity of perception leads to curiosity, which may lead to compassion. It is a Christian's baptismal right to be curious. Peter follows Jesus in curiosity. Mary Magdalene is curious as she approaches the tomb. Christ looked at every person he met with the intensity of Vermeer looking at a cloud — curious, rapt, probing. How intensely Jesus must have considered the lilies of the field.

PRACTICE 11.3

Clouds of Discernment

INTENTION   The intention of this practice is to continue to recognize and experience nature as guide in discernment and healing by noticing consolations and desolations in nature.

Participation by Proxy: A Mouse, Trees, a White Beach

> *The Lord created medicines out of the earth, and the sensible will not despise them. And he gave skill to human beings that he might be glorified in his marvelous works. By them [medicines of the earth] the physician heals and takes away the pain; the pharmacist makes a mixture for them.*
>
> Sirach 38:4-8a, 9

For many of us, real intimacy and interconnectedness with creation is a new way of being, a new way of belonging in community. But how do we enter this discipline of relationship and belonging with creation? Not so different, I believe, from relationships entered into with God, relationships we enter into with reverence and awe and trembling, relationships grounded in attention (knowledge of creation being as important as knowledge of God and knowledge of self), and with trust and hope and faith and love. Belonging with creation is likewise not so different, I believe, from belonging with Scripture — expecting nothing, trusting everything.

In the book of Sirach it is written: "The Lord created medicines out of the earth, and the sensible will not despise them." Belonging and relationships are risky, yet relationships born of intimacy are, providentially, also healing and medicinal. This is no less true of creation than of humans. Jay Appleton gives a delightful example of this healing interconnection; notice, though, that he writes, as do many contemporary writers, from the assumption that we have already lost critical connections to the natural world:

> This idea of vicarious involvement, or participation by proxy, presents us with a device which can often help us in our efforts to recapture the experience of our primitive natural environment. . . . The popularity of watching animals in the wild may be at least partially explicable in these terms. A field mouse can find concealment in quite short grass which would afford us no protection whatever, and as we watch him extracting the maximum advantage from his tiny world of prospects and refuges we momentarily live his life for him, participating through him in an environmental experience which we can only enjoy at second hand.[8]

"Participation by proxy" is grace put to practice. We expect nothing from mouse or grass — it is completely free; yet in return we receive a new imagination, a new connection, new discernment, new ways of belonging, healing, and a new spiritual practice.

There are, however, a few cautionary disciplines in the practice of "participation by proxy." Appleton also warns, in a compelling way, against overidentification with nature: "From the vicarious participation in the landscape through identification with the wild animal it is but a short step to the pathetic fallacy: the attribution of feelings to hills, clouds, rivers, trees, or whatever."[9] Though this is often forgotten, the Christian tradition is rich in theological, biblical, and spiritual resources to guard against the pathetic fallacies that are attributed to nature and, by extension, often to Christianity. Creation praises God; but doxology is of a different order from identification.

---

8. Jay Appleton, *The Experience of Landscape*, rev. ed. (New York: John Wiley and Sons, 1996), 168.

9. Appleton, *Experience of Landscape*, 169.

A second cautionary discipline is embedded in the question of how we accept nature's invitation while maintaining the trust necessary to consent to belong. Thomas Merton's reflection on a tree, introduced in a previous chapter, addresses this "discipline of consent" when he reminds us that "[a] tree gives glory to God by being a tree. For me to be a saint means to be myself."[10] This disciplined consent, simply stated, is that we can trust creation's invitation as our "consent" to God to be and become what God intended each to be. Merton implies that we might find more to trust from trees than we do from ourselves, and conversely, less to fear from trees than we do from others. All creation "consents" to be precisely what it is. If a tree imitates God by consenting to be what it is, our own belonging to trees guides us into learning to imitate that and give glory to God simply by being ourselves.

A final cautionary discipline in the practice of participation by proxy is to be aware that nature can guide us into physical, psychological, and spiritual illness rather than health. Loren Eiseley gives us a piece of writing that evokes physical deterioration, violence, death, and spiritual darkness as a kind of demonic presence in creation leading *away* from wellness. In his book *The Night Country* he writes of times and places of wilderness in his own life. In this passage he uses brokenness in nature to highlight a particularly dark night in his own life:

> I walk a half mile to a pathway that descends upon a little beach. Below me is a stretch of white sand. No shell is ever found unbroken, even on quiet days, upon that shore. Everything comes over the rocks to seaward. Wood is riven into splinter; the bones of seamen and of sea lions are pounded equally into white shining sand. Throughout the night the long black rollers, like lines of frothing cavalry, form ranks, drum towering forward, and fall, fall till the mind is dizzy with the spume that fills it. I wait in the shelter of a rock for daybreak. At last the sea eases a trifle. The tide is going out.[11]

In this passage, nature illustrates how relationship carries the risk of loss of personal identity rather than celebrating personal identity through the dignity of difference. How different this is from Appleton's mouse in the grass or Merton's tree! On the white beach, human bone is indistinguish-

10. Thomas Merton, *New Seeds of Contemplation* (New York: New Directions, 1961), 29.
11. Loren Eiseley, *The Night Country* (New York: Charles Scribner's Sons, 1971), 173.

able from wood or shell or stone because pattern is obliterated: all things from the sea are "pounded equally into white shining sand."

If we are to turn to nature for belonging and discernment, if it is to remain a trust we can hand on to our children, we must take a bold, courageous turn. Appleton's mouse is long dead and decomposed. Merton's reflection on trees is true, but too many trees are, in fact, not allowed to be themselves. Many search for grace, identity, and hope, only to find a pounding surf forming dead, white, indiscriminate beaches. And yet the invitation is always open, always present: belonging by proxy in the ecology of a field mouse, learning from an imperfect but complete tree praying consent, gazing into the mirror of a white beach during a dark soul's night.

PRACTICE 11.4

Vocation, Discernment, and Healing

INTENTION Our "vocation" is our listening for, hearing, and response to God's call. The intention of this practice is to discern God's intimate and healing call as it is spoken to us through nature.

CHAPTER TWELVE

Nature as Healing and Solace

Take in their arms the inconsolable sufferings of the world and turn them into song.

Sisters of St. Benedict's Monastery, St. Joseph, Minnesota

I ran across a simple brochure about the Sacred Heart Chapel of the Sisters of the Order of Saint Benedict at St. Benedict's monastery, and the stranglehold of the disconsolate mirror of the dark night of the planet began to brighten. In the brochure's appropriate heading of "Welcome!" I found these words: "The sisters and their friends and neighbors who worship here take in their arms the inconsolable sufferings of the world and turn them into song." With this simple sentence I could breathe. Earth's suffering is "inconsolable," as the sisters say, but perhaps in embracing it we might transform suffering into song. Simple wisdom. "Welcome" indeed!

On the same day that I received the sisters' consolation, I ran across the following story of a twenty-four-year-old veteran at the Veterans' Hospital in Tuscaloosa, Alabama. He had stepped on a land mine in Vietnam and been totally paralyzed by the explosion. Therapists at the hospital were not convinced that his paralysis was permanent, but the patient was in despair and had stopped trying to improve. Paul Mills tells the story:

One sunny day in spring, the horticultural therapist put a small glass jar half filled with peat moss beside the bed, and as the patient watched, planted five bean seeds. A few days later the seeds sprouted. Their roots were visible through the glass as they gradually extended to give life support to the tiny cotyledons working toward the earth's surface.

By the fifth day the growth process was accelerating. The therapist moved the "miraculous" jar to the other side of the patient's bed where he could not see it, and instructed the nurses not to turn the patient as they had been doing. The next morning, the young veteran was lying on his other side, watching his bean seeds. Turning over had been his first voluntary movement since his accident.

From that day on he made steady progress and finally was discharged from the hospital. Though still in a wheel chair, he was able to function in society.[1]

Five small bean seeds embraced a wounded soldier; five small bean seeds join "the sisters and their friends and neighbors who worship here [and] take in their arms the inconsolable sufferings of the world and turn them into song." The sisters — individually and in community — have themselves endured "inconsolable sufferings." Nature, God's creation, is undergoing "inconsolable sufferings." Yet, in the midst of suffering, the wounded heal; the sufferers console the suffering. The sisters, I think, would be humbled to be compared favorably with the healing properties of five small bean seeds.

PRACTICE 12.1

Suffering Into Song

INTENTION   The intention of this practice is, through a process of mutual invitation, to encourage transformational healing through nature by turning suffering into song.

PRACTICE   This is a group process, developed by Eric Law, a consultant on multicultural leadership. I envision it here as a practice that invites turning "suffering into song."[2]

---

1. Paul Mills, "VA's Flower Therapy," *V.F.W. Magazine* 63 (Nov. 1975): 36-37. Cited in Charles A. Lewis, *Green Nature, Human Nature* (Urbana: University of Illinois Press, 1996), 74.

2. The questions have been altered, but this practice otherwise follows a detailed description of Law's "mutual invitation" group processes in Jaco J. Hamman, "Remembering the Dismembered: Teaching for Transformation and Restoration," *The Journal of Pastoral Theology* 16, no. 1 (Spring 2006): 44-59.

- A facilitator provides the group with the following three questions to discuss, introduced one at a time:

  1. What is the deepest suffering or loss you have experienced in nature?
  2. What have you learned since then that speaks to this suffering or loss?
  3. How do you understand God's presence or absence in this suffering or loss?

- The facilitator explains the process of "mutual invitation" as follows: one member of the group is appointed "leader" by the facilitator and empowered to lead off by answering the first question. For each question, sharing is limited to two minutes for each person. When finished, the person sharing invites another person to speak.
- All those invited to share have three options:

  1. They can share for two minutes, answering the question under discussion.
  2. They can say "Pass for now" if they need more time to reflect.
  3. They can say "Pass" if they don't want to say anything at all about the specific question under discussion.

- After the leader has spoken, she or he invites a fellow group member (not necessarily the person sitting next to her or him) to share: "I invite [person's name] to share." The leader functions as the timekeeper for the group.
- The second person either answers the question or responds with "Pass" or "Pass for now" and invites another group member to share.
- The process continues with the first question until every member has had a chance to respond.
- The leader addresses the next question and follows the same procedure.
- After all three questions have been addressed, allow time for open, honest, and nonjudgmental discussion.

The Green Embrace of Suffering

> *[Such people] do not reach out to God. . . . They do not correct the ways of their journey and make them straight, having no greenness* [viriditas] *in their strength.*
>
> Hildegard of Bingen, *Liber vitae meritorum*

Nearly everyone has experienced the earth as a place of healing. Touch the earth, walk along a river, sit beside a tree, watch clouds. Nature seems to understand, seems to fully accept our hurt, and has its own ways of easing pain and offering solace. Hildegard of Bingen, a twelfth-century visionary, reformer, musician, and mystic, referred to this healing power of the earth as *viriditas* (meaning "green" or "green things" or "the greening"). Hildegard also writes as a master herbalist with an intimate knowledge of the healing power of medicinal plants. This healing power of plants is not magic for Hildegard: it is a circle of belonging and faith in which the healing of her Creator encircles the healing goodness in creation. *Viriditas* is simply an imprint of the healing power of the Creator. For Hildegard, the healing power of plants is thus intimately connected to the healing power of their Creator.

For Hildegard, "belonging together" — as Paul Tillich had inscribed on his gravesite memorial — was a given: nature, humanity, God belonging together. Her place in the ancient Christian tradition of *cura animarum* ("care of souls") cannot in fact be separated from her vision of *cura creationis* ("care of creation"). For Hildegard, orientation toward creation is not different from orientation toward God: all things of earth "consent" to the love of God simply, as Thomas Merton says, by being what they are. What they consent to is to reach out, growing ever Godward. This drive, this longing love for a return to God, coordinates the healing powers of all the earth. For Hildegard, the "soul" is to the human as *viriditas* is to creation. In their true selves, both are driven toward wholeness and healing as they consent to their natural longing. As one writer explains it, "[*viriditas* is] the power of youth and of sexuality, the power in seeds, the reproduction of cells, the power of regeneration, freshness, and creativity. . . . Hildegard refers to Mary as *viridissima virga*, the greenest virgin."[3] In Hildegard's cosmology, Mary consents to embrace not only the creative force of the universe, the

---

3. Wighard Strehlow and Gottfried Hertzka, *Hildegard of Bingen's Medicine* (Rochester, VT: Bear and Company, 1988), xxvii.

Word, but also to embrace the absolute center of universal suffering, which in her son becomes, finally, a healing "green" for all creation.[4]

Hildegard of Bingen is anything but naïve in her approach to nature. Humanity suffers; the earth suffers. But in her vision, "greening" is not only the unifying and vital principle of all creation, it is also the vital force that embraces this suffering. It is that power within the earth that helps to console and often dissipate human suffering. In fact, Hildegard is eerily prescient: she recognizes humanity's capacity to create disorder in the order of creation's "greenness." Don't forget that her writing is from the twelfth century, but the following could have been written today: "The winds stink of baseness and do not blow pure air, but blow in a heavy thunderstorm. And the air vomits forth dirt because of the unseemliness of men; it then brings unjust and unworthy moisture that destroys the greenness and fruit that ought to nourish people."[5] The natural cycle of greenness should nourish and guide, but Hildegard of Bingen — five hundred years before the start of the Industrial Revolution — somehow envisions winds that stink, air that vomits dirt, and the destruction of greenness.

Reflecting on Hildegard's stark writing, and still troubled by the dark night of the planet, I go out for a walk. It is late fall. The air is glass, crystal clear — blue and cold and sharp. Most of the leaves are gone from the trees. They form a brittle and crackling trail underfoot. I walk through several smallish wetland areas and out to the larger lake. The loons are gone; Canada geese in ever-larger *V*-patterns still honk and squawk as they head south. This short, crisp season is moving imperceptibly into the dead grays of winter. This is usually my favorite time of year, but I am still unsettled, caught in the dark night of the planet and Hildegard's knowing. Nature is not so prayerful now, not so sermonic, not so easily sacred, hardly consoling. Parker Palmer describes the soul as skittish: like a wild animal, it is resilient, savvy, resourceful, and self-sufficient; yet, despite its toughness, it is also exceedingly shy as it hides in the underbrush as other souls draw near. Today *viriditas* is the same. Palmer suggests sitting patiently by a tree, breathing with the earth. This wild animal of a soul may show itself, if only for a moment.[6] I try this. But today

---

4. *Hildegard of Bingen: The Book of the Rewards of Life (Liber Vitae Meritorum)*, trans. Bruce W. Hozeski (New York: Garland, 1994), xiii.

5. *Hildegard of Bingen: The Book of the Rewards of Life*, 138.

6. Parker Palmer, *A Hidden Wholeness: The Journey Toward an Undivided Life; Welcoming the Soul and Weaving Community in a Wounded World* (San Francisco: Jossey-Bass, 2004), 58.

both soul and greenness are very, very shy: soul and greenness are as dry as the leaves.

I walk out onto a teardrop peninsula that juts out into the lake. As if to protect shy things, the peninsula has only a slender strip linking it to land. I take my place there and lie down with my back on the earth in a bed of oak and maple and beech leaves and stare through the empty branches into the sky. A few wisps of cloud are visible, and I eye them with the eye of Griet, then dare, for just a moment, to try the eye of Vermeer. Then, yes, slowly I do begin to see the colors: first faint, very faint purples, then salmon flesh, and then a faint, waving indigo. Not able to completely slow myself to sunset pace, I don't notice the transitions as they happen, but over time I do notice the shifts into different registers: pale pink, introverted violets, bashful moments of magenta, then a coy turquoise, then what I tremble to call ultramarine. The dark, bare branches form a kind of kaleidoscope for the moving, shape- and color-changing clouds. I close my eyes a while and rest.

Nothing much happens. I do not coax my shy soul from beneath that rock, nor do I manage to cajole the greenness to appear, not even as a mist. After a time, I get up to return — somewhat calmed, but wistful. As I walk back, a single smallish oak leaf descends from a tree above and lands just in front of me, a bit to the left. It is cushioned by the leaves already fallen and seemingly welcomed by them. Then, just for that moment, I am that leaf. *Viriditas* happens with a jolt: my soul kisses a kind of tranquility, a tranquility indistinct from the leaf. As the leaf, I remember how I let go of the oak, my falling away, my floating down, and my sense of dying into *viriditas*. We are — all of us — dying, decaying, composting, waiting for new life as an act of green faith.

A small grace of consensual reconciliation accompanies me home. Returning, I pick up Hildegard one more time and read:

> This image has the form of a woman. At her back, there is a tree standing whose leaves have dried up completely. . . . The tree is without any greenness [*viriditas*] since it does not have the protection of holiness. This image [the woman] is entangled in its branches since this image is as entangled in contrary things as it is in fertile things. For one branch has woven itself over the top of her head. . . . And one branch is around her neck and throat. . . . One branch is around her right arm and another around her left arm. These branches are not spread out but they are very tight around her. . . . In addition, one branch from the right side of the tree and one

from the left side are girded around her stomach and legs and surround them completely. . . . [Such people as this woman] do not reach out to God. . . . They do not correct the ways of their journey and make them straight, having no greenness [*viriditas*] in their strength.[7]

I had gone out walking, having no greenness in my strength. I returned shyer, but greener too, discerning slight but tangible corrections needed in the way of my faith. Hildegard also writes: "Man is nothing without the greenness of faith."[8]

PRACTICE 12.2

The Healing Embrace of Green

INTENTION To experience the healing embrace of green (Hildegard's *viriditas*, the vital source and will to life of nature) and to pray the green.

Jephthah's Daughter and the Consolation of Mountains

They [Joseph and Benjamin] will come back from the land of the enemy. . . . [They] shall come back to their own country.
Jeremiah 31:16, 17

The earth mourns. Out of that mourning, in a green embrace, the earth can be a place of solace and consolation, healing and belonging. In Scripture, the healing boundaries of sorrow and mourning between the earth and humanity are permeable and porous: the earth mourns for itself and mourns for humanity, while humanity mourns for itself and for the earth. Romans 8 declares explicitly that the earth "groans." In 2 Esdras, the earth mourns for the multitudes she has brought forth and which have been lost, as once again we are invited to inquire of the earth, as if more proof were needed: "Now ask the earth, and she will tell you that it is she who ought to mourn over so many who have come into being upon her. . . . Who ought

---

7. *Hildegard of Bingen: The Book of the Rewards of Life*, 5.35, pp. 240-41.
8. *Hildegard of Bingen: The Book of the Rewards of Life*, 3.66, p. 162.

to mourn more, she who lost so great a multitude, or you who are grieving for one alone?" (2 Esdras 10:9, 11)

A prophetic psalmlike section in Isaiah expresses the sorrow of the land, the same land that will later give confidence and deliverance to God's people: "The land mourns and languishes; Lebanon is confounded and withers away; Sharon is like a desert; and Bashan and Carmel shake off their leaves" (Isa. 33:7). No incident is more dramatically shattering for the earth than the moment of Christ's death on the cross. In Matthew's account, the earth grieves Christ's death: "From noon on, darkness came over the whole land until three in the afternoon. . . . At that moment the curtain of the temple was torn in two, from top to bottom. The earth shook, and the rocks were split. The tombs also were opened and many bodies of the saints who had fallen asleep were raised" (Matt. 27:45, 51-52). An example of the porous interchange of mourning and solace between the earth and humanity is also given in Matthew's account, as the grief of the earth brings light to the heart of one of the witnesses: "Now when the centurion and those with him, who were keeping watch over Jesus, saw the earthquake and what took place, they were terrified and said, 'Truly this man was God's Son!'" (Matt. 27:54)

One of the most problematic and provocative stories of how creation provides solace in the midst of its own mourning is the story of Jephthah and his daughter in Judges 11. Jephthah, an illegitimate son of Gilead, is a great warrior and is persuaded to fight on the side of the Israelites against the Ammonites, who have made war against Israel. The "spirit of the Lord [comes] upon Jephthah" (v. 29), and Jephthah makes a vow to the Lord that, should he prevail against the Ammonites, "whatever comes out of the doors of my house to meet me, when I return victorious from the Ammonites, shall be the Lord's, to be offered up as a burnt offering" (vv. 30-31). In the battle, Jephthah prevails and returns home. What first comes out the door to greet him is tragedy itself: as he approaches his house, "there [is] his daughter [his only child] coming out to meet him with timbrels and dancing" (v. 34). Jephthah tears his clothes, wails, and tells his daughter about the vow he has made to the Lord.

Jephthah's daughter (never named) agrees to accept the vow, asking only one thing: "Let this thing be done for me: Grant me two months, so I may go and wander on the mountains and bewail my virginity, my companions and me." Her father agrees. "So she departed, she and her companions, and bewailed her virginity on the mountains" (vv. 37, 38). When she returns home, she is sacrificed. An abominable story: it is patriarchal (though it is unclear what Jephthah would have done had a son come out to greet him); it reminds us of Abraham's willingness to do the same with Isaac; and, ironically, Molech, the god of the Ammonites, whom Jepthah has just beaten, also demands worship through child sacrifice.

The only faintly agreeable aspects of this story are Jephthah's daughter, her companions, and the mountains. For two months, with her closest companions, she gives her grief to the mountains. Jephthah's daughter senses that they do have something to offer: if not life, at least something akin to consolation and a certain tranquility. Ronald Rolheiser has written that one of the most debilitating ills of contemporary society is restlessness. For Rolheiser, very little in contemporary culture invites us to "journey inward, to that quiet center, that central silence, where one's own life and spirit are united with life."[9] That place where one's life and spirit is united by life is indeed a *place*. Jephthah's daughter wanders, but she is not restless. She knows the *place* where she will find the quiet center and the central silence Rolheiser speaks of. She knows where her center is; she knows exactly where she needs to go.

Reciprocal Perception and Wondrous Exchange

> *Naturally, the mountains, the creatures, the entire non-human world is struggling to make contact with us. . . . [O]ur bodies have formed themselves in delicate reciprocity with manifold textures, sounds, and shapes of an animate earth — our eyes have evolved in subtle interaction with other eyes, as our ears are attuned by their very structure to the howling of wolves and the honking of geese. . . . [W]e are human only in contact, and conviviality, with what is not human.*

> David Abram[10]

Jephthah's daughter and her friends are also daughters of *viriditas*, through which, in the words of David Abram, the earth itself is "struggling to make contact with us." In fact, all God's people in the Hebrew Bible are pro-

9. Ronald Rolheiser, *Against an Infinite Horizon: The Finger of God in Our Everyday Lives* (New York: Crossroad, 2001), 24. For an extended critique of restlessness in contemporary culture, see Rolheiser's *The Shattered Lantern*.

10. David Abram, *The Spell of the Sensuous: Perception and Language in a More-Than-Human World* (New York: Pantheon Books, 1996), 22.

foundly aware of the connective parallels between humanity and creation that Abram describes so poetically. In Scripture, land gives identity to individuals and to people, rainbows signal divine covenants, stones are stacked high in sacred places, mountains and vines and water provide sustenance and solace and teachings, and bushes explode in holy flame without being consumed. The philosopher Søren Kierkegaard once asked, "What is a poet?" His answer, paraphrased, would have made complete sense to the Hebrew people: "A poet [let's say, in this case, the earth] is an unhappy person who conceals deep torments in his or her heart, but whose lips are so formed that when a groan or shriek streams over them it sounds like beautiful music."[11] In this sense, the earth is a poet as well as a poem: unhappy, tormented, yet still able to turn these into beautiful music.

Kierkegaard's definition should also make perfect sense to today's Christian communities: the earth's poetry of pain is still beautiful, healing music. And yet many today hear neither the pain nor the poetry. This has not always been the case. In fact, Christians of the past *have* heard the music and poetry of earth, and have heard it as healing and as solace. The Creator breathed spirit (the spiritual) into the clay (the material), and that breath and clay emerge as humanity. The monotheistic traditions — in fact, most religious traditions — affirm creation's healing poetry as that same bond that in effect shapes and molds healing and solace between the human body and human soul. Creation itself mirrors this bond, as we can see in Hildegard of Bingen's inspired depiction of body and soul, in which she uses metaphors of sap and tree:

> The soul in the body is like sap in a tree, the soul's powers are like the form of the tree. How? The intellect in the soul is like the greenery of the tree's branches and leaves, the will like its flowers, the mind like its bursting firstfruits, the reason like the perfected mature fruit, and the senses like its size and shape. And so a person's body is strengthened and sustained by the soul.[12]

The body sustained by the soul, the material tree sustained by the sap, bursts into flower and fruit: between body and soul, between humanity and the earth conjunction is life; separation is death.

---

11. Cited in Rolheiser, *Infinite Horizon*, 57.

12. Hildegard of Bingen, *Scivias*, 1.4.26, trans. Mother Columba Hart and Jane Bishop (New York: Paulist, 1990), 124.

The journey inward to the soul parallels the journey outward into nature. One does not encounter the natural world without encountering the soul. Dissociation from the natural world thus deadens the journey of the soul to God. That dissociation makes the body ill, shrinks the soul, and replaces both with a single, solipsistic, manufactured and commodified self. The results are behaviors that increasingly dull our senses and thus our attentiveness to the natural world. This in turn creates a spiraling loop of pathological and ecological *un*-consciousness that increases destructive and distancing behavior of humans toward nature.

In an earlier chapter we have seen how some contemporary writers use psychological categories to describe our present-day dissociation from nature. Paul Shepard suggests the crippling of the human life cycle, and Ralph Metzner surveys recently suggested pathological characteristics of humanity's dysfunctional relationship with nature that include addiction, narcissism, collective amnesia, and dissociative alienation.

Shierry Weber Nicholsen (also quoted above) recognizes, as does Hildegard of Bingen, that the essential bridge between the material and spiritual realities of creation parallels the essential connective bridge between the material and spiritual lives of individuals or communities. Not only are these two connections mirrored, they are mutually reinforcing in a way that Nicholsen calls "intimate reciprocity." Intimate reciprocity is Nicholsen's way of thinking about and experiencing reconnection between humanity and nature. Much like in Richard Louv's "nature smarts," she is convinced that "the ultimate result of this intimate reciprocity is the growth of consciousness, of human mental structure." Nicholsen uses the relationship between mother and child as the underlying foundation of how "intimate reciprocity" enhances growth of consciousness and intelligence:

> The aesthetic reciprocity in which mother and baby perceive one another as infinitely rich and full of meaning in both body and mind creates a space in which each experience is assimilated and leads on to the next in an ongoing process of growth and development. . . . [Likewise,] relating to the natural world is not a diversion from human concerns . . . it is a journey to the interior at the same time.[13]

---

13. Shierry Weber Nicholsen, *The Love of Nature and the End of the World: The Unspoken Dimensions of Environmental Concern* (Cambridge, MA: MIT Press, 2003), 65.

John Calvin also carried a vision of intimate and reciprocal perception, calling the reciprocity a "wonderful exchange." Initiated by Christ, Calvin's "wonderful exchange" is brought to a point of concentration in the sharing of a meal, in this case the sacrament of the Lord's Supper. Calvin says that through it, by becoming human with us, "[Christ] has made us sons of God with him; that, by his descent to earth, he has prepared an ascent to heaven for us."[14] For Calvin, the "wondrous exchange" is a kind of reciprocal perception between heaven and earth, between the divine and the human, between the material and the spiritual, between the body and the soul, each authenticated and sealed in wine and bread, in grape and wheat, the things of the earth. As David Abram has said, the "earth is rumbling and straining to let us remember that we are of it, that this planet, this macrocosm is our flesh, that the grasses are our hair, the trees our hands, the rivers our blood, that the Earth is our real body and that it is alive." Grape and wheat: the earth is rumbling and straining to let us remember this wondrous exchange.

PRACTICE 12.3

Healing Dialogues and Wondrous Exchange[15]

A Lakota medicine woman may address a stone as *Tunkashila* ("Grandfather"). Similarly, the Omaha may address a rock with the respect and reverence that one pays to an ancient elder. Thus they may address a rock as, for instance:

Unmoved
From time without
End
You rest
There in the midst of the paths
You rest
Covered with the droppings of birds
Grass growing from your feet
Your head decked with down of birds

---

14. John Calvin, *Institutes of the Christian Religion*, IV.XVII.2, ed. John T. McNeill, trans. Ford Lewis Battles (Philadelphia: Westminster, 1960), 1362.

15. This practice is taken mostly from Bill Plotkin, *Soulcraft: Crossing into the Mysteries of Nature and Psyche* (Novato, CA: New World Library, 2003), 167-69.

You rest
In the midst of the winds
You wait
Aged one.[16]

INTENTION The intention of this practice is to help us hear the earth "rumbling and straining" and to sharpen our reciprocal perception by participating in the language of the earth, a language of healing. If you have never traded speech with a lizard, a rattlesnake, an elk, a desert juniper, the wind, or a rock, you have a world-shifting treat in store for you.

Nature's Christic Patterns

The way we return to God across the infinite distance God has crossed to us is through the seed he planted in us that grows into the most beautiful of trees.

Simone Weil[17]

Where I am, where you are, God has crossed an infinite distance, given a wondrous exchange, and planted a seed in us that is growing. It is not just any seed. It is a divine seed, whose growth, as Weil writes, returns us to God. It is the good that is within you and me that will not go away. It is a seed whose identity, when fully grown, is a tree of infinite intimacy, a tree of love. What we had imagined to be an infinite distance is in fact just there outside your window, just there supporting your back, just there reminding you that it is part of you: it is simply the most beautiful of trees. But many of us do, in fact, live an infinite distance from trees, and, though the seed of good is planted in us all, we consequently live an infinite distance from ourselves, an infinite distance from love. It need not be so. Pierre Teilhard de Chardin has written: "By means of all created things, without exception, the divine assails us, penetrates us and molds us." All created things, without exception, are waiting to serve as spiritual guides, to become a part of who we are and what we practice. Teilhard's words are not simply metaphors: in a wondrous exchange, na-

16. Cited in Abram, *Spell of the Sensuous*, 71.
17. Simone Weil, "The Love of God and Affliction," in *The Simone Weil Reader*, ed. George A. Panichas (New York: David McKay, 1977), 451.

ture assails us, penetrates us, molds us. Teilhard adds that "we imagined the Holy as distant and inaccessible, whereas in fact, we live steeped in its burning layers."[18] Just here, on earth as it is, we imagine the holy at an infinite remove, when in fact the seed is already in us, nature is steeped in its burning layers.

Jesus Christ himself lived and grew and took shape in such a milieu of psychic ecology and physical geography and in a particular sacred landscape. At the beginning of Matthew 12 we read: "At that time Jesus went through the grain fields on the sabbath; his disciples were hungry, and they began to pluck heads of grain and to eat" (Matt. 12:1). Already the seeds have grown into beautiful heads of grain. The disciples begin to eat what creation has provided them to eat. They do so on the Sabbath, which is it-self a thing of creation. Even here, relatively early in his ministry, Jesus is growing a beautiful tree; already the disciples are steeped in the holy, though they are not always aware of it; already the layers of creation are burning.

The Pharisees, of course, do not see this and object to the Sabbath plucking. But Jesus says, "I tell you, something greater than the temple is here" (Matt. 12:6). Something greater than the temple! Here? At this time? In this place? Certainly the Son of man, this Jesus, is greater than the tem-ple. But *here*, in this *time*, in this *place*, creation is also something greater than the temple. Creation's burning layers of holy intimacy are happening: layers of grain fields, layers of time, layers of movement, layers of Sabbath, layers of men, of women, and of disciples, layers of hunger and layers of satisfying that hunger, layers of vision, layers of plucking, layers of eating, layers of the Son of man — all are burning in the temple that is already here, in this *place*.

Recognizing and living the unity and holiness of both the "ecological" and "sacramental" realities of nature, all creation becomes a temple. That good seed planted within grows. In reciprocal perception we hear the rum-blings of creation trying once again to remind us that *it* is in fact the tree growing from the seed within.

This section began with a quote from the twentieth-century writer Simone Weil. Listen to Catherine of Siena, a fourteenth-century Christian saint as she anticipates Weil's "infinite distance" (between God and hu-manity) and Weil's inner "seed that grows into the most beautiful tree":

---

18. Pierre Teilhard de Chardin, *The Divine Milieu: An Essay on the Interior Life* (New York: Harper and Row, 1968), 112.

I want you to look at the bridge of my only-begotten Son, and notice its greatness. Look! It stretches from heaven to earth. . . . So the height stooped to the earth, bridging the chasm between us and rebuilding the road. And why should he have made of himself a roadway? So that you might in truth come to the same joy as the angels.[19]

John Calvin called Jesus Christ the "wondrous exchange." Here Catherine of Siena likens Jesus to a bridge accomplishing the same exchange. In the name of the power, wisdom, and beauty of God, Catherine later calls this bridge the "circle of the tree of charity." A circular bridge from heaven to earth, from earth to heaven, from heaven to earth and back again unceasing. Once again we have an image of nature in the form of a tree as guide, in this case as guide to the highest virtue, that of charity. Christ said: "I am the vine and you are the branches. Those who abide in me and I in them bear much fruit" (John 15:5).

PRACTICE 12.4

Christ's Cosmic Exchange: Astronomy Picture of the Day

INTENTION   The intention of this practice is — by using pictures of the universe that were captured by NASA and are available online — to gain perspective on infinite distance and infinite intimacy, and to explore Calvin's "wondrous exchange" initiated by Christ, seen and experienced on a cosmic scale.

---

19. Catherine of Siena, *Catherine of Siena: The Dialogue*, 22, trans. Suzanne Noffke, O.P. (New York: Paulist Press, 1980), 59. For following quote, cf. Catherine, *Dialogue*, 10, pp. 41-42.

Nature's Gift of Healing

> *There's more to flesh than flesh.*
>
> Pattiann Rogers[20]

> *Every creature clearly knows its creator and reaches back to him.*
>
> Hildegard of Bingen[21]

Nature embraces us as teacher and healer through reciprocal perception, across infinite distances, through wondrous exchange, steeped in burning layers, by means of circular trees of compassion. Retrieving the nature-wisdom embedded in the Christian tradition highlights the reciprocity of this embrace. But another component of nature as teacher and healer is more reticent: all of nature's healing components are gifts, but some are simply more shy than others and appear only according to their own timing. One day in a particular place in nature, for instance, may be likened to a "thin place," alive and pulsing with meaning and holiness. The next day this same place, though cherished, may hardly be noticed. It is almost inert. To the careful student, guidance is available on both days. But as gift, nature must both be given and received; and in any given time and place, how and whether the gift is given and received affect the intensity and efficacy of nature as spiritual guide. We are free to be open and to receive the gift; we are equally free to ignore it. If we choose to receive it, we might find that we are on "speaking terms" with nature, or we might not. But nature, over time, transforms even how we perceive its gifts and how we receive them. And over time, as spiritual practices themselves, creation transforms the ability to give and receive to others. The circular tree of compassion and charity grows.

Water, for example, is a gift. It is gift equally as gas and liquid and solid, equally as warm and cold. In any form it is constantly offering itself as a material "door" opening into nature. One snowy day in Michigan, snow offered itself in this way. Each flake came as a precious gift; more than that, each flake was born within a swirl of other white angels, each flake a Gabriel announcing the birth of the Lord within . . . me! The snow joined in, announcing that each flake itself was with child. The pregnant snow was

---

20. From Pattiann Rogers, "The Fallacy of Thinking Flesh Is Flesh," in *Eating Bread and Honey* (Minneapolis: Milkweed, 1997), 9.

21. *Hildegard of Bingen: The Book of the Rewards of Life*, 3.2, p. 125.

participating in a dual mission: announcing the fullness of Gift in all things and accepting themselves as the Gift, each, I thought, with the humility of Mary. As the delicate flakes continued to fall, I noticed the snow piling like elfin caps on thousands of tiny red berries left hanging from the autumn just past. Now covered in the humility of snow, each red berry became itself a new angel-berry announcing to all who would hear: "Greetings, favored one! The Lord is with you" (Luke 1:28). It was a frightening thrill being greeted in this way.

At any given moment and place, the Gift is birthing throughout creation, while announcing, in Pattiann Rogers's phrase, "there's more to flesh than flesh." Echoing Calvin and Weil and Catherine and so many others, Shierry Weber Nicholsen says that the "gift comes across the divide that it helps us penetrate; gifts reveal the underlying community between two sides of a divide; gifts create bonds."[22] Gifts and receiving gifts are a form of belonging. It is from across just such an infinite divide that Jesus Christ is born in each finite flake, each singular berry, forming that infinite bond we know as creation, the very earth upon which we walk. Abram writes that, for ancient cultures and indigenous peoples, this infinite bond is often recognized as finite breath. Breath and air in this case is awareness itself: breath and air "[were] originally felt to be what invisibly *joined* human beings to the other animals and to the plants, the forests and to the mountains."[23] Flakes of snow, berries, air, breath, circular trees, the plants, the forests, the mountains: Jesus is a way of wondrous exchange across infinite divides, a way that joins and wanders paths guided by these finite places in a joining as integral and intricate as breath is to word.

All creation longs for God and reaches back to its Creator. This longing and reaching back is not so different from our own, and reminds us of our own common parentage with the natural world. Perhaps this is why so many people find healing and simple joy in gardening. Julie Moir Messervy says: "I have found, through years of practice, that people garden in order to make something grow, to interact with nature, to share, to find sanctuary, to heal, to honor the earth, to leave a mark. Through gardening, we feel whole as we make our personal work of art upon our land."[24] Art as spiritual practice can never impose a work of art on the land; it shares with

22. Nicholsen, *Love of Nature*, 114.
23. Abram, *Spell of the Sensuous*, 238.
24. Julie Moir Messervy, *The Inward Garden: Creating a Place of Beauty and Meaning* (Boston: Little, Brown and Company, 1995), 19.

the land in co-creating while, as I imagine it, the Author of it all smiles a healing smile. As the earth consoles, men and women relearn earth-language as spiritual practice.

PRACTICE 12.5

Talking Circle: Nature Healing

INTENTION The "talking circle" is a simple yet powerful tradition found in a variety of cultures and religions. Its power is in its simplicity.[25] The talking circle is based on the idea that everyone has something of value to say and something of value to learn. Using the talking circle format, we intend in this practice, within a group, to find healing connections with the natural world.

PRACTICE This is a practice meant for a group of people who have come together with a common expectation: connective, healing relationships with the creation. The purpose of the gathering is to let all express experiences of intimacy, healing, solace, or guidance in nature.

- Participants form a circle, sitting or standing.
- A facilitator, as a model of what might be spoken, begins the conversation. After speaking, the facilitator passes a "speaking stone" or feather or some other object that has special meaning to the group. The facilitator passes the "speaking" object to the person next to him or her, and so on around the circle.
- The ground rules for the talking circle are:
  - Only the person holding the "speaking stone" may speak.
  - Each person may speak for as long as he or she wishes, or not at all.
  - There is no cross-talk; each person gets one opportunity to speak as she or he holds the "speaking stone" and only speaks at that time.
  - The information shared in the circle should be held in confidence unless all participants agree to do otherwise.
- Topics for speaking are up to the person holding the "speaking stone" and might include:
  - Experiences of healing in nature

---

25. This practice is based loosely on "The Talking Circle" in Carl A. Hammerschlag and Howard D. Silverman, *Healing Ceremonies: Creating Personal Rituals for Spiritual, Emotional, Physical and Mental Health* (New York: Perigee, 1996), 145-51.

     – What in nature needs healing
     – Prayer for healing of nature

- The talking circle is a way to have all participants involved in the process, trusting the setting and the Spirit to draw out each individual's truth, thus making it a part of the community's truth as well.
- The group may observe other rituals as a ceremony, or the "speaking stone" may be passed around the circle a number of times with the invitation to speak to different aspects of healing.
- When the circle is completed, the facilitator can pause for a moment of silence, then give a short word or phrase of thanks for something in nature. Then the group passes the stone as before, allowing each person to give the same short prayer of thanks for a particular object or sensation or grace from nature.
- It is appropriate to end with a prayer for healing and guidance by and for creation.

The Moral Senses of Nature

CHAPTER THIRTEEN

Spiritual Practice as Moral Response

Watchfulness is a graceful and radiant virtue when guided by Thee, Christ our God.

Saint Hesychios the Priest,
"On Watchfulness and Holiness"[1]

A brother came to Abba Sisoes and said, "I am aware that the remembrance of God stays with me." Abba Sisoes, the old man of the desert, said to him, "It is no great thing to be with God in your thoughts, but it is a great thing to see yourself inferior to all creatures."[2]

In the third and fourth centuries after Christ, venturing out into the Egyptian desert to seek a "word" from a wise hermit was a pilgrimage of surprises. The brother's encounter with Abba Sisoes is no exception. The unsuspecting brother thought he had "arrived," that he had "obtained" something like a pearl of great price buried in the field: "The remembrance of God stays with me." What a rare and precious pearl! What more could there be? The abba is certain to be impressed. The abba is not impressed. The remembrance of God is all? In itself that is "no great thing," says the abba.

In any case, if God's creative love stays with the brother night and day, in all the brother's thoughts, it is still not the brother's accomplishment —

---

1. St. Hesychios the Priest, "On Watchfulness and Holiness," 50, in *The Philokalia: The Complete Text,* trans. G. E. H. Palmer et al., vol. 1 (London: Faber and Faber, 1979), 171.

2. Abba Sisoes, in *The Desert Christian: The Sayings of the Desert Fathers; The Alphabetical Collection,* trans. Benedicta Ward, S.L.G. (New York: Macmillan, 1975), 214.

it is God's. Ah, but do take that remembrance and do something with it that is indeed great. And what greater thing can there be, coming from the abba, who has his home in the desert, which he shares with the desert creatures? "See yourself as inferior to all creatures." A stone may be present to God, but to remember God and consider yourself least — now *that* is the answer. It is also the answer to Jesus' disciples' puzzled questions, "Lord, when was it that we saw you hungry or thirsty or a stranger or naked or sick or in prison, and did not take care of you?" (Matt. 25:44). To take care of all creatures, to treat yourself as servant to all, that is a "great thing." In that way, Jesus says, you care for me (Matt. 25:45).

Memory of God in all things is a great work of God. A proper balance with creation is the great work of humanity — with God. Seeing oneself as inferior to all creatures is a discipline of balance out of which emerges a disciplined and practical response to creation. Abba Sisoes's answer implies a movement from contemplation to action, or *ascesis*, as the desert monks called it. It was the beginning of this brother's training in living responsibly in a balanced relationship with creation. Later the brother would learn the perpetual circle that flows in and out, back and forth, between contemplation and response. Then he would both remember his Creator *and* respond as a creature inferior to all others of creation.

Practice and formation in Christian spiritual traditions has, from the beginning, recognized this reciprocal, circular relationship between contemplation (attention, wonder, awareness of the presence of God) and action (the practice of moral virtue in imitation of Christ). Both require mindfulness and both, at their core, contain remnants of each other. Thomas Merton once said that everything that is not contemplation is manipulation. If one sees oneself as inferior to all creation, it is difficult to manipulate. In Merton's intended sense, it is a form of nonmanipulative contemplation. In the epigraph to this section, St. Hesychios implies that any true response arising out of attentive contemplation becomes "radiant virtue" to the extent that it is guided by Christ. A thousand years after the young brother encountered the words of Abba Sisoes in the desert, the twelfth-century theologian and mystic Hugh of Saint Victor wrote that the guidance of Christ to restore divine likeness in humanity entails essentially just two things: "contemplation of truth and the practice of virtue."[3] Humanity's restoration to divine likeness in this way is like the perfection of a sphere — the not acci-

---

3. Hugh of St. Victor, *The Didascalicon of Hugh of St. Victor*, I.viii, trans. Jerome Taylor (New York: Columbia University Press, 1961), 54-55.

dental shape of earth — wherein all points, which are equally distant from the core, are intersected simultaneously by the ability to *see* the earth in its truth as a place in which we *respond* to the earth in its virtue. This is a great thing: radiant virtue guided by Christ. Thus Hugh of Saint Victor was keenly aware of the little word "and" and how this small word serves to link contemplation of truth and practice of virtue. The moral or ethical imperative that is the action of the sphere is made whole by the watchful or attentive imperative that is the contemplative practice of the sphere. Both are "great things" to the extent that proportion and balance are maintained between who we are in relationship to God and who we are in relationship to creation. Balanced, green contemplation and balanced, green action *are* truth and virtue.

PRACTICE 13.1

Considering Lilies

INTENTION The intention of this practice is a slight addition to Abba Sisoes's response to the brother: "It is no great thing to be with God in your thoughts, but it is a great thing to see yourself inferior to all creatures" — *and to act accordingly.* Thus we will begin contemplating our moral response to nature by considering the lilies of the field.

Organic Response in the Everyday

> *But how should we turn this need of the everyday around? How do we, in the midst of this everydayness, find our way to the only necessary one who only is God? How can the everyday itself become a song of praise to God, that is, prayer?*
>
> Karl Rahner[4]

As Abba Sisoes was aware, the "hermeneutics of nature" suggests a moral response to creation that shapes Christian life according to everyday patterns that we can read and see clearly. Seeing and reading nature clearly

---

4. Karl Rahner, *The Need and the Blessing of Prayer,* trans. Bruce W. Gillette (Collegeville, MN: Liturgical Press, 1997), 44.

suggests a course in which response is less a matter of will than it is of our organic relationship to the place where we live. Place in nature shapes identity, forms community, and is itself spiritual practice. Nature itself elicits the imperative of our moral actions on the basis of location and place. As mind, body and soul, we "walk" through the natural world in a particular place, called by and attentive to its particular ecological and sacramental realities. And the whole person responds — can only respond — to what it attends to. As we attend to the nature we are "wired" to respond to, that place in turn responds to us. Places in nature respond organically in the sense that they are an interrelational community: open, self-correcting, driven by life and survival.

Our response, in turn, can only be truly organic to a particular place that, in eliciting our attention, reminds us that we, too, are caught up in this particular community of weblike relationships. This is not a limitation. It is liberation of connectivity in which the boundaries of particularity are boundaries only in the sense that they allow contact and connection with other, likewise bounded, elements of an ecological system. Ecologically sustainable living, sacred stewardship, political, economic, cultural, and ethical action on behalf of the natural world are formed on the basis of how we engage a particular patch of earth in the particularity of our true selves as they are organically connected, humanly and humbly, to all creation.

Particular and organic: it sounds paradoxical, but it isn't. There is a black squirrel outside my window. The squirrel itself is an organism, and yet at the same time he is a particular squirrel burying a particular nut in a particular ecology that is itself an organic system. This organic ecological system is a particular place in creation; for example, it is not the planet Venus, where a squirrel would have a difficult time making a living. And yet the boundaries of every particular ecological system are permeable. This particular black squirrel takes in as much from the ecology in which he is embedded as he gives in return: oxygen, food, and much more. If this black squirrel lives balanced in the everyday, he gives as much as he takes: breath for plants, new squirrels, and eventually his own body, perhaps as a meal for a particularly quick red-tailed hawk, or simply back to the earth as nutrient for fertile soil.[5]

---

5. Any ecological system and any closed system within it (such as a black squirrel) is, of course, much more complex than detailed here. Also, adding the dimension of time would require considerations based on the second law of thermodynamics, one aspect of which is that, within any given system, a process occurs that will tend to increase the total entropy of the universe. To a specialist, these considerations would also shape the practice of a moral response to nature.

As a matter of fact, taking into consideration quantum and macro levels of ecological systems, there is a very real sense in which a black squirrel is also connected to Venus and very much else as well. Julian of Norwich had a sense of this when she held a hazelnut in the palm of her hand and saw within it all that was, is, and will be. Given Julian's insight, important considerations emerge from a black squirrel and a hazelnut: (1) the particular and the organic together define the simple complexities of that place in creation in which we find ourselves; (2) where we are placed on the earth determines what we pay attention to; and (3) what we pay attention to shapes our moral response to creation. All these considerations involve spiritual practice, the doing of which awakens our true relationship to creation, which forms moral response; that response, in turn, transforms practice. As Hugh of Saint Victor again reminds us, Christ's radiant virtue is found in "contemplation of truth [spiritual awakening] and practice of virtue [moral response]."

Spiritual awakening and moral response also include the capacity for astonishment, wonder, awe — all of which in nature are nearly equivalent to the life force itself and give hints of the presence of God. Wonder is akin to the energy that pulses throughout the universe, which as spiritual practice forms a moral response. Imagine the wonder evoked by Abba Sisoes's brother as the brother learns to transform being "inferior to all creatures" into a moral response. In his book *The Embers and the Stars*, Erazim Kohák says that "an evening, unlike an argument, does not lead to a conclusion. . . . Clues, though, do arise within it. Perhaps the most basic among them is that *God is.*"[6] Keeping this difference between an evening and an argument in mind, we might say that the correspondence between attention, wonder, and the sacred in creation is a correspondence of an evening: like an evening, they lead, not to conclusions, only to clues, gentle hints (if we are fortunate) that God is. Finally, a moral response to nature formed and shaped by attention and wonder is a sacramental response. Like the evening, a sacramental response of receiving the bread and the wine is our fundamental clue that God is.

6. Erazim Kohák, *The Embers and the Stars: A Philosophical Inquiry into the Moral Sense of Nature* (Chicago: The University of Chicago Press, 1987), 195.

Bread and Wine

INTENTION   To evoke a moral response to nature equivalent to the response of receiving the bread and the wine.

PRACTICE   We receive the bread and the wine out of our own freedom, and yet they are gifts that actually create and reciprocate freedom.

- During the next few times during Mass or Eucharist or Lord's Supper, notice how you receive the bread and the wine. What does your reception and partaking of them mean to you? What do you experience?
- Noticing your experience of the elements, also consider and wonder at the fact that both bread and wine are themselves pure elements of creation. Jesus could have made any number of things into sacraments representing his body and blood. Why did he choose bread and wine?
- What does it mean to you that the body of Jesus Christ is a part of nature, a part of creation?
- A few attributes of a moral response to nature at any time include humility, compassion, kindness, perseverance, hospitality, mindfulness, and love. Find a personal response to nature that is similar to or even re-creates your response of receiving the bread and the wine. Act on that response.

The Complications of One Moral Walk

> *Treat the earth well; it was not given to you by your parents; it was loaned to you by your children.*
>
> African Proverb

An appropriate moral response to nature is not easy. Though we often receive the bread and wine without giving them much thought, if we took them as the contemplation of truth and the practice of virtue, the reception of the elements, too, might give us pause. What is the "practice of virtue," having shared the elements? Without grace we would not even be in a position to receive the bread or the wine. Having received the elements with grace again, what is to be our "practice of virtue"? Similarly, having had our eyes opened by grace to the dark night of the planet, what is to be our "practice of virtue"?

To show some of the complications of moral response, what follows is one possible encounter with nature, as we contemplate truth and wonder about the practice of virtue. Let's take a walk through a forest. As all walks must be, this walk is local: through a particular forest, along a particular path, particular step by particular step, breath by breath, tree by tree, perception by perception.

We are walking through one of the few remaining old-growth forests of the coastal redwood *(sequoia sempervirens)* in that narrow strip of land — not more than twenty miles wide — between the Pacific Ocean and the Pacific Coastal Range, just a few miles south of Eureka, California. Of course, we don't see all there is to see, but suppose we notice a few things in addition to the redwoods themselves: tan oak, Douglas fir, red and black huckleberry, salmonberry, blackberry, thimbleberry, bracken fern, sword fern, rhododendron, various forms of mosses and ivies, blue jays, crows, deer, chipmunks, streams, flies, and yellow jackets — just to name a few. The forest is soaking up the moist fog that rolls in from the Pacific in this part of the early morning, just after the dawn. There is a slight breeze, not enough yet to dissipate the fog. The redwoods, of course, are huge, bursting with physicality and sacred stillness: the words "cathedrals," "groves," "grottoes," "holy places" are often used to describe them.

While walking, the subject of the spotted owl *(Strix occidentalis)* comes up, and we talk a bit about that now notorious endangered raptor whose name has become a rallying cry for both environmentalists and lumber producers. The spotted owl is not native to coastal redwood forests, but we talk of it as a kind of symbol of the misunderstanding and mistrust that can arise between communities who have competing interests within the same forest. We walk a while in silence. You mention Abraham, the person we both know and like: he owns the company that "owns" these few local remaining acres of harvestable coastal redwoods. We have learned that Abraham has decided, finally, to "harvest" these first-growth trees, then replant. Abraham is not a bad person: he thinks in terms of what he considers to be a legitimate and necessary profit for his company and in terms of jobs for the community we are all connected to. But as we walk, both of us realize how differently we see things from the way Abraham does: we are both opposed to coastal redwood logging of any kind, especially here.

The redwood smells like the queen of cedars. As we sniff the air, you pick a few huckleberries that leave purple stains on your fingers. The sun-

light pierces the forest canopy, highlighting dust particles, white butterflies, and some gray-and-black moths. I bend down to pick a sword fern
because I admire the pattern of the dustlike spores of seed running along
the back of the leaves: simple and unique.

Then, at the same instant, we both sense slow movement down the trail.
Of all people, it is Abraham. We both instinctively want to give him wide
berth, and so we quickly move behind two trees, certain we are out of sight.
Abraham is preoccupied anyway. We see him coming, walking this trail in
the forestland he owns. He seems to be making an early survey of which trees
to cut based on a quick estimate of the maximum board-feet of lumber he
can get from each tree. In order to make these calculations he measures the
girth and estimates the height of each tree. To move around and make his
measurements, he is carrying a small chain saw that he uses to clear away
brush in order to get close enough to the trunk to measure each tree. For the
first time, we hear the little chain saw as he cuts indiscriminately (he knows
his forest and that any scar he makes during the measuring recovers quickly).
I think that this is one moral response Abraham has chosen to make toward
nature. And so he goes crashing through rhododendron, cutting fallen
limbs, slicing small fir and alder that bar his way. As he gets closer to us, the
fog remains and is good cover, and he is entirely focused on his work.

After he has cleared an area around a tree, he measures it, walks around
it three or four times, jots down a few notes, then nails a blue plastic ribbon that will be a signal to his loggers that this tree is to come down. With
the noise of the chain saw and the fog protecting us, we follow Abraham
for a while as he focuses on one tree after another. He *is* attentive in his
own way, but to board-feet and other numbers. He never notices us.

After a short time we signal each other silently, knowing we have had
enough of hiding, and we move off in the opposite direction from Abraham and his incessant work. After we have regrouped our senses and ourselves, you mention that each blue plastic ribbon marks the end of a near
two-thousand-year-old redwood. There are hundreds of blue ribbons as
we circle around behind Abraham and retrace his path through the forest.
As we go along, we each tear off a few blue plastic ribbons, feeling a kind of
adrenaline rush of righteousness with each blue ribbon we pluck. I have
done this same act in the past; unfortunately, it has always seemed to result
in even more trees being hacked down and removed — almost a spiteful
reaction. Yet I cannot help myself. Neither can you, it seems, as we return
along the path back to our car and head for our favorite coffee shop/bak-
ery, The Ram's Horns.

Nature as practice is often a "path" of conflict. The forest knows this conflict and the suffering it entails. Saint Paul says in Romans 8:

> I consider that the sufferings of this present time are not worth comparing with the glory about to be revealed to us. For the creation waits with eager longing for the revealing of the children of God; for the creation was subjected to futility, not of its own will but by the will of the one who subjected it, in hope that the creation itself will be set free from its bondage to decay and will obtain the freedom of the glory of the children of God. We know that the whole creation has been groaning in labor pains until now; and not only the creation, but we ourselves, who have the first fruits of the Spirit, groan inwardly while we wait for adoption, the redemption of our bodies. (8:18-23)

Creation itself is conflicted. Though differently attentive, both the "owner" of the forest land and we are conflicted as well. Paul, before he wrote about creation's eager longing to be set free from the conflictive bondage of decay (sin and death), wrote about a parallel conflict in another of God's creations: humanity.

> I do not understand my own actions. For I do not do what I want, but I do the very thing I hate. . . . I can will what is right, but I cannot do it. For I do not do the good I want, but the evil I do not want is what I do. Now if I do what I do not want, it is no longer I that do it, but sin that dwells in me. So I find it to be a law that when I want to do what is good, evil lies close at hand. . . . Wretched man that I am! Who will rescue me from this body of death? Thanks be to God through Jesus Christ our Lord! . . . There is therefore now no condemnation for those who are in Christ Jesus. (Rom. 7:15, 18-21, 24-25; 8:1)

The conflict and the split for Paul is doing the thing he hates while he wills to do the good. This conflict is played out once again in this coastal redwood forest. The conflict is compounded a hundredfold by the aspirations of will and action within me, within the lumber owner, within you, and within creation's bondage to decay. The coastal redwoods live to be 3,000 years old, but this is only a pretense of escaping all creation's bondage to decay.

It is striking how similarly Saint Paul chooses to phrase the conflictive dilemma that exists within the creation with the conflictive dilemma within humanity. Creation "subjected to futility" is equivalent to humanity "sold into slavery under sin." Creation, under the condition of existing "not of its own will but by the will of the one who subjected it," is equivalent to humanity, which is "at war with the law of the mind, making me captive to the law of sin." Paul then continues the equivalency, but this time through the equivalency of contrast. "Creation itself will be set free from its bondage to decay and will obtain freedom," but even Paul's own bondage and moans, like creation's, are subject to an answer lingering within his question: "Wretched man that I am! Who will rescue me from this body of death?"

Sitting in The Ram's Horns having coffee and a doughnut, we have set the blue plastic ribbons we have torn off the trees on the table: of the hundreds we saw, there are only twelve of them on the table. We talk a while about what, if anything, to do. For some reason, you mention the apostle Paul and the evil we do defeating the good we want to do but do not do. I think I understand what you mean, but say nothing.

Whatever you meant, we talk about the redwood forest and what *it* would like us to do. We come up with some ideas, and I write them down on a napkin: (1) tear away all the ribbons, knowing that eventually the destruction will be even worse; (2) try to talk with Abraham about our stories and the stories we hear from the redwoods, the strata of narratives that make up the forest; (3) camp out in the tree until the company backs away or decides to cut and kill the tree and us along with it; (4) round up friends we know who are sympathetic to our cause and together try to decide what action to take; (5) start a political action group that focuses on informing the public what is going on and what will be lost when the trees are logged; (6) develop strategies with local employment agencies about finding alternative jobs for the logging personnel so that not only their environmental awareness, but their livelihoods, are assured; (7) pound spikes into all the marked trees so as to ruin any chainsaws that dare to bite into the tree and pour sugar in the gas tanks of all trucks and logging equipment brought to the site; (8) gather a group of like-minded people and conduct worship/liturgy/prayer services in the forest, ritually praying in turn for each marked tree and for a change in the consciousness of the loggers; (9) together decide that we can become architect and/or builder in a firm specializing in houses that are environmentally organic, use a minimum of new wood, are designed and built primarily with found or reused products; (10) get to know the forest so well that we find a species that legitimately belongs on the federal endangered species list and would face extinction should Abraham's company log off the first-growth redwoods; (11) raise money to buy the land over time from Abraham and retrain his loggers; (12) walk away, a little sad.

In this one patch of forest alone, here in the everyday, there are many forms of moral response. The German theologian Karl Rahner once wrote, in a sermon just after World War II, that we cannot flee from the everyday because we are, ourselves, a part of it. By the "everyday" Rahner meant the place where we find ourselves as God communicates with us, *even prior to any human response.*[7] In Rahner's case, this meant the gutted Saint Michael's church in the middle of a completely bombed-out city, Munich, during the first Lenten service after the war. In our case, it means one of the last uncut cathedrals of first-growth coastal redwoods in the world. Seven of Rahner's sermons during that postwar time have been gathered into a little book entitled *Prayer.* We cannot walk away from the "everyday," whether it be a burned-out city or an endangered forest, because we are a part of it. Perhaps, then, prayer is the link between contemplation of truth and practice of virtue. It is not the kind of prayer that closes its eyes, asks for a miracle, and walks away. Rather, it is a prayer of everyday life that challenges each of us to look more closely at what is actually going on in the depths of our daily life, in the depths of creation, a prayer that gives us a clue that *God is* and that God's way in the everyday is the "more excellent way" of love (described in 1 Cor. 13).[8]

PRACTICE 13.3

Nature and Moral Discernment

INTENTION   Given the complications of determining an appropriate moral response to nature, the intention of this practice is to apply a model of discernment to the natural world that grounds moral response in contemplation, prayer, and love.

---

7. Karl Rahner, "Prayer in the Everyday," in *The Need and the Blessing of Prayer,* 37.
8. See Harvey D. Egan, "Introduction," in Rahner, *Need and Blessing,* xvii.

CHAPTER FOURTEEN

Transforming Perspectives and Earth Insights

There are obviously enormous differences across the spectrum of belief [i.e., between conservative, moderate, liberal, and radical representatives of the Judeo-Christian tradition], but caring for creation is a central metaphor that might serve to unite all traditions of faith in setting an environmental agenda.

Max Oelschlaeger[1]

Modern environmental ethics, whether secular or grounded in a sacred tradition, are slowly transforming how we perceive and interact with the earth. Most are committed to responding in a reciprocal relationship to the earth as a subject with needs and desires and as a subject that communicates these needs as insights concerning health, healing, and care of earth, self, and others. To those grounded in sacred traditions, the earth communicates new ways of being in relationship with God. Contemplation, attention, prayer, a capacity to sense and to navigate the intricacies of a reciprocal and loving relationship with nature are essential to "hearing" the earth as she speaks both her needs and her insights. These needs and insights call us to what Oelschlaeger calls *the* central metaphor behind all traditions of faith today: caring for creation.

Psychologist Howard Clinebell hears the voice of the earth and is skilled at applying what he hears to earth-care. Clinebell lists at least six transforming perspectives in service of what he calls ecotherapy and ecoeduca-

---

1. Max Oelschlaeger, *Caring for Creation: An Ecumenical Approach to the Environmental Crisis* (New Haven: Yale University Press, 1994), 120.

tion.[2] His perspectives are also, in essence, contemplative practices that circle back and inform a way of life that honors the integrity of the earth and responds with care of the earth as the living organism that it is. Clinebell's perspectives include:

1. The *view-from-the-moon* perspective. This is seen in the now iconic photographs of earth taken both from the moon's surface and from space. The beauty and fragility of our earth seen from space is an earth without borders, boundaries, and barriers.

2. The *transgenerational well-being* perspective. This perspective involves the growing realization that we are squandering resources for our children, our children's children, and beyond. This perspective is captured well by Carl Sagan and Ann Drunyan: "It is no longer enough to love, feed, shelter, clothe and educate a child — not when the future itself is in danger. . . . We have been treating the environment as if there were no tomorrow — as if there were no new generations to be sustained by the bounties of earth. But they, and we, must drink the water and breathe the air."[3]

3. The *whole-biosphere well-being* perspective. This perspective represents the growing awareness that one species can have optimal health only to the degree that the whole biosphere is made healthier. Thomas Berry has written: "Our best procedure might be to consider that we need not find a human answer to an earth problem, but an earth answer to the earth problem."[4]

4. The *whole-human-family well-being* perspective. A logical extension of the earlier perspectives, this perspective recognizes that single exclusivist worldviews — whether of individuals, ethnic groups, regions, nations, or any other self-focused group — are no longer beneficial to our interdependent world.

5. The *wise woman/wise man* perspective. The psychologist Lesley Irene Shore writes: "The wise woman tradition is an old tradition. . . . Healing was linked with the tasks and spirit of motherhood." We have already seen traces of this vibrant tradition both within Christian and Hebrew Scriptures and within the Christian spiritual traditions. Howard

---

2. The following six "transformational perspectives" are from Howard Clinebell, *Ecotherapy: Healing Ourselves, Healing the Earth* (Minneapolis: Fortress, 1996), 76-83.

3. From "Give Us Hope," Boston Council for a Livable World Education Fund pamphlet (1988, 1, 3), cited in Clinebell, *Ecotherapy*, 78-79.

4. Thomas Berry, *The Dream of the Earth* (San Francisco: Sierra Club Books, 1988), 35.

Clinebell adds that "playing the blame game between the genders is counterproductive."[5]

6. The *interfaith, inclusive ecological spirituality* perspective. Since the environmental crisis is a global crisis, it must be addressed globally, meaning that no one religion has a uniquely valid way of understanding the earth. Cooperation and peacemaking are required values in moving toward balanced, healing lifestyles and beliefs.

As a counterpoint to these new, more contemporary perspectives, premodern indigenous cultures can also facilitate a shift in perspective to reverence for the earth and, as such, view the earth as a subject to whom respect and care are due. The ethicist J. Baird Callicott writes:

> A reexamination of human history and prehistory also reveals the existence of culturally evolved and integrated environmental ethics that served to limit environmental impact of pre-industrial human technologies. . . . [I]n many indigenous cultures nature was represented as inspirited or divine, and was therefore the direct object of respect or of reverence; that in some traditional cultures nature was the creation of God, and thus was to be used with care and passed on with respect.[6]

As I have pointed out in earlier chapters, this perspective of reverence and respect is precisely what we encounter in both Christian testaments and in Christian spiritual teaching. Callicott, for instance, finds three readings of creation narratives in Judeo-Christian scriptures consonant with three interpretations of the human/creation relationship:

> (1) an indirect human interest/human rights environmental ethic associated with the *"despotic"* [or *"dominion"*] reading; (2) a more direct, ecocentric environmental ethic associated with *"stewardship";* and (3) an uncompromising ecocentric environmental ethic associated with *"citizenship"* — a radical biblical biotic communitarianism.

Based on his choice of words ("despotic," "uncompromising," "radical"), it is not surprising that Callicott interprets "stewardship" as the perspec-

---

5. Lesley Irene Shore, *The Healing Art of Feminist Psychology* (New York: Harrington Park Press, 1995), 35, cited in Clinebell, *Ecotherapy*, 81-82; Clinebell quote from *Ecotherapy*, 82-83.

6. J. Baird Callicott, *Earth's Insights: A Survey of Ecological Ethics from the Mediterranean Basin to the Australian Outback* (Berkeley: University of California Press, 1994), 8.

tive most consonant with Judeo-Christian writing. Unfortunately, Callicott's interpretation of biblical creation narratives as *either* anthropocentric (his first interpretation) *or* ecocentric (his second and third interpretation) is itself "radically" narrow. Christian nature practice is in fact not "centric" at all; rather, it is "morphic," that is, fluid and changing as relationships between humanity and creation inform Christian practice and moral response.

H. Paul Santmire has been in the forefront of reclaiming and re-envisioning a specifically Christian theology in the context of contemporary ecological dialogue, spirituality, and ethical practice. Wisely, Santmire proposes that we "retire" outmoded and unhelpful words from our vocabulary of creation practice: "I now believe that it is best to retire them [words like *dominion* and *stewardship*] for the foreseeable future, so that we do not have to explain constantly to others and to ourselves what they really mean."[7] Instead, Santmire suggests "righteous cooperation with nature" and "sensitive care of nature" as alternatives. Both are consonant with images of the human/creation relationship that I have laid out and advocated in *Nature as Spiritual Practice*, though I would advocate more than "cooperation" with nature. This points out, for instance, that nature is herself guide, teacher, and healer, responding not just to "sensitive care," but equally to listening, mutual perception, and reciprocal prayer.

Max Oelschlaeger is a writer especially helpful in charting the ecumenical range of ethical perspectives of earth-care as they are interpreted by what he calls conservative, moderate, liberal, and radical constituencies within the Judeo-Christian tradition and within the church today. After meticulously defining what he means by each of these four groups, how they fit and contribute to the Judeo-Christian traditions of environmental ethics, and how they tell their stories of creation and humanity's role in relationship with nature, Oelschlaeger adds to what I have quoted as the epigraph to this chapter: "Few if any contemporary traditions of faith [from conservative to radical] could not develop a rationale, consistent with their core doctrines, to care for creation."[8] Oelschlaeger's particular gift is the ability to honor the distinctions within the different traditions while providing each with a language that has potential for opening constructive,

---

7. H. Paul Santmire, *Nature Reborn: The Ecological and Cosmic Promise of Christian Theology* (Minneapolis: Fortress, 2000), 120. See pp. 120-26 for Santmire's particular slant on "righteous cooperation" and "sensitive care."

8. Oelschlaeger, *Caring for Creation*, 120, 123. Hereafter, page references to this work appear in parentheses in the text.

informed dialogue. In giving honest accounts of the similarities and differences in the Roman Catholic, Protestant, and Jewish traditions (pp. 128-83), Oelschlaeger notes, for instance, that in each tradition creation stories do in fact have the following shared characteristics:

- Account for a Creator or creative principle
- Offer a spatial-temporal narrative
- Account for the origin of life and human beings
- Define the relationship of human beings to the Creator or creative principle and other life-forms
- Prescribe appropriate and proscribe inappropriate behavior
- Explain the great mysteries or core concerns of life, such as death (p. 125)

With these characteristics in mind, he then offers an "ecotheological spectrum" for interpreting creation stories within the Judeo-Christian traditions:

- Conservative: exclusively Bible-based creation stories
- Moderate: biblically supported creation stories
- Liberal: scientifically informed creation stories in a biblical context
- Radical: Judeo-Christianity in the context of the new cosmology (p. 124)

Oelschlaeger's reasoned approach indicates that not all scientific and religious accounts of creation are intrinsically antithetical. Generously (in comparison to many critics of the impact of religion on the environment), he notes that even conservative Christians operate with a basic "care for creation" model and that conservatives argue that the Bible explicitly mandates that humankind is to *care for creation* (p. 128).[9]

Ultimately, whether one prefers the metaphor of "care for creation," "mutual participation," "citizenship," "transformational perspective," or "reciprocal perception" is not crucial. What is crucial is that we 1) recognize that the earth is at risk; 2) hear/see and reverence the earth's own abil-

9. By focusing on the most conservative Christians, Oelschlaeger is here confronting the Charles White thesis that Christianity itself is the primary contributor to global environmental degradation with a "worst-case scenario" that in fact represents a tradition very much at odds with White's thesis.

ity to "speak" its own insights as to how best to respond to earth-pain; and 3) respond to those insights out of contemplative practice, prayer, and that "better way of love" described in 1 Corinthians 13. Again, however, the enormity of the problem can itself be debilitating. Richard Fern, for instance, leaves this as the final chapter title of his excellent book on environmental ethics: "What do we do?" In creation as in any other context, Christian spiritual practice informs how we act, and how we act gives shape and pattern to our formation. Remembering Rahner, we are placed in the everyday; in the context of our "place," what we do depends on our prayer becoming action and our action becoming prayer. Richard Fern puts it well when he says that justice, love, and prayer must intertwine with genuine creativity:

> While theistic naturalism [his term for a Christian ethics of nature] puts these many tensions in perspective, holding out hope of their harmonious resolution, it does not tell us what we are to do here and now. Nor should it. Just as there are no obvious or easy answers to the social and ecological crises of our time, so there are no pre-ordained answers. The task with which we are confronted calls for not only a channeling of divine love and justice but, no less, genuine creativity.[10]

No Christian assumption, dogma, creed, ethic, Scripture, sacrament, or process of spiritual practice and formational identity "tell[s] us what we are to do here and now. Nor should it." All these can inform what we do here and now. But human-centered information alone will not tell us precisely what to do or how. Only the place (the here) and the moment (the now) can teach us the wisdom of growth and change that we find in Thomas Merton's tree that gives glory to God simply by being a tree. And the here and now is everywhere and always an opening to consent to the presence of God, even to consent, in Abba Sisoes's words, to "seeing yourself inferior to all creatures."

A ruby-throated hummingbird flits through the gray borders of my peripheral vision. My senses twitch as I catch the silver-green reflection of sun. The power of the slowing, tireless tremor of the laser-straight hummingbird in flight hangs on the meaning of an evening, an evening dispelling arguments like shadows. The real question is not "What do you do?" It

---

10. Richard L. Fern, *Nature, God and Humanity: Envisioning an Ethics of Nature* (Cambridge: Cambridge University Press, 2002), 215.

is "What do you love?" As creation is a companion to us in finding what we love, whatever we do is the moral equivalent of creative love.

PRACTICE 14.1

Divine Provision and Human Degradation

INTENTION   The intention of this practice is to attend to, pray over, and respond as needed to seven divine provisions laid out in Scripture that make the earth a livable, self-sustaining, health-giving environment, and seven corresponding degradations that humans have imposed on these divine provisions. The practice is effective whether done in solitude or with a group, though a group will lend a variety of perspectives.

PRACTICE   Calvin B. DeWitt lists seven *God-given* "provisions of creation" and seven *human-created* "degradations of creation," each biblically based.[11] Holding the degradations and the provisions together functions in itself as a contemplative exercise that can lead in turn to organic moral responses to earth-needs.

- Notice and attend to each of the divine provisions and human degradations listed below. Attend first to one provision, then concentrate on its corresponding degradation. Visit locations of as many of both as you are able and find out as much as you can about the genesis of each (especially the degradations).
- DeWitt gives biblical support for each of the divine provisions. Where do you find in Scripture that God has provided these gifts? Spend time in creation with these gifts, imagining what God intends in providing each of them.
- In prayer, first pray about the goodness, beauty, plentitude, and giftedness of the world as God has provided it. After this, pray about how we have degraded so many of these gifts and contemplate active ways to heal them. In the midst of this prayer, leave some quiet time to listen for and/or imagine how God is speaking to you about these same issues. Do not be hesitant to tell the earth how you feel and how you are talking with God about it. This, too, is prayer.

---

11. Calvin B. DeWitt, "Creation's Environmental Challenge to Evangelical Christianity," in *The Care of Creation: Focusing Concern and Action,* ed. R. J. Berry (Leicester, UK: InterVarsity, 2000), 60-73.

- It has been said that vocation is where the needs of the world intersect your own gifts or deepest longings. How are the needs of the earth, your own gifts, and God's guidance calling you to respond to earth-pain?

Provisions of Creation: Upon which all creation, all creatures, and all human life depend. Many are celebrated in Psalm 104.[12]

1. Regulation of earth's energy exchange with the sun, which keeps earth's temperatures at a level supportive of life through the long-standing greenhouse effect, and which protects life from the sun's lethal ultraviolet radiation by filtering sunlight through the stratospheric ozone layer.
2. Biogeochemical cycles and soil-building processes, which cycle oxygen, carbon, water, and other vital materials through living things and their habitats and build life-supporting soils and soil structure.
3. Ecosystem energy transfer and materials recycling, which continually energizes life on earth and incessantly allocates life-sustaining materials.
4. Water purification systems of the biosphere, which distill, filter, and purify surface waters and ground water — on which all life depends.
5. Biological and ecological fruitfulness, which supports and maintains the rich biodiversity of life on earth by means of responsive and adaptive physiologies and behaviors.
6. Global circulations of water and air, which distribute water, oxygen, carbon dioxide, and other vital materials between living systems across the planet.
7. The human ability to learn from creation and live in accordance with its laws, which makes it possible for people to live sustainably on earth and safeguard creation.

Degradations of Creation:[13]

1. Alteration of earth's energy exchange with the sun, which results in accelerated global warming and destruction of the Earth's protective ozone shield.
2. Land degradation, which destroys land by erosion, salinization, and desertification, and reduces available land for creatures and crops.

---

12. DeWitt, "Creation's Environmental Challenge," 62.
13. DeWitt, "Creation's Environmental Challenge," 61-62.

3. Deforestation, which annually removes some 100,000 square kilometers of primary forest — an area the size of Iceland — and degrades an equal amount by overuse.
4. Species extinction, which witnesses the elimination of more than three species of plants and animals from the earth each day.
5. Water quality degradation, which defiles ground water, lakes, rivers, and oceans.
6. Waste generation and global toxification, which result from atmospheric and oceanic circulation of the materials that people inject into the air and water.
7. Human and cultural degradation, which threatens and eliminates long-standing human communities that have lived sustainably and co-operatively with creation, and also eliminates a multitude of long-standing varieties of food and garden plants.

Organic, Ethical Practice

> *There is a resonance of humility that has evolved with the earth.*
> Terry Tempest Williams,
> *Red: Passion and Patience in the Desert*[14]

The cosmos is not a proving ground for some misguided eschatology in which all that humanity does to degrade God's provisions will someday, in the future, be put right with a "new" heaven and a "new" earth. As Terry Tempest Williams writes, a resonance of humility has evolved along with the earth, not a resonance of pride or folly. What we have here and now is the earth as it is. Nature practice helps us hear and live out that resonance of Williams's humility. Albert Einstein once said, "God is subtle but he is not malicious." The earth, too, is subtle: it resonates with humility, not maliciousness. Nature as spiritual practice is an organic process that happens in a particular place and time; that same practice becomes misguided, degraded, and malicious if it is undertaken from the standpoint of some future earthly perfection. Another way of saying this is that, from either a small-quantum or a large-cosmic perspective, the

14. Terry Tempest Williams, *Red: Passion and Patience in the Desert* (New York: Vintage Books, 2001), 17.

earth is a burning bush now — just as it is and right where you are. The earth is a place of radiant virtue, sacred participation, and constant doxology — here and now.

This chapter moves toward an ecological ethic, but for several reasons that I have laid out in the preceding section, it stops short of proposing exactly what to *do* about any particular degradation of divine provisions. What to do is the decision and task of particular persons and particular communities where they find themselves, in a particular place. Leaving open the question "What do we do?" honors the fact that practice in nature is practice as organic process. In nature, every element and particle, every being and molecule live, grow, die, and are reborn as integral members of community. There are what we could call "singularities" — if there were not, the concept of incarnation would be meaningless — a field mouse, for instance, a blade of grass, that rock, that person walking through the door. But each "singularity" is sustainable only in community, in the "complexity" of organic systems.

That Christian nature-practice is organic means that practice is analogous to the growth and characteristics of living organisms in the complexity of community. Likewise, the structure or "architecture" of organic practice is analogous to the structure and "architecture" of both living and nonliving beings in that it fulfills perfectly the functional requirements of practice. In nature, for instance, the shape, structure, and organism of a fish perfectly performs the requirements of swimming through water, drawing oxygen from that water, finding and eating food, and reproducing new fish. In a similar way, in the organic practices of persons and communities, structure can be envisioned as the actions and spiritual states of the practice such as attention, mindfulness, and contemplation.

The function of that practice is transformational, identity-forming, and responsive. Together, the structure and function of Christian practice sees this same fish as an intimate member of an organic community (of which the persons attending to the fish are likewise members). Christian practice sees the fish as it sustains persons and communities and thus approaches fish humbly as food; it recognizes and participates in the beauty of fish and thus approaches the fish with reverence; it encounters the fish as representative of their Creator and thus acknowledges the fish as sacred; it attends to fish and becomes acquainted with the habits of fish because the fish is a member of our family of creation; it notices when a species of fish is at risk due to overfishing or polluted water and thus works to find and implement ways to reduce and eliminate that risk; and it knows and shares the reality that fish swim and exist as prayer and praise, giving glory to their Creator, and thus gives itself to doing the same.

"What do we do?" is thus a question dependent on organic spiritual practice in a particular place and time. If our habitat is a desert region, it is unlikely that we would need to be equipped to "see" a fish, while people and communities along the coast of Maine or living on a small island in the Philippines will likely be formed by, participate in the structure of, and function in accordance with the organic communities of fish.

Another way to recognize the organic quality of Christian practice in nature is to notice how we are systemically connected to creation in body, mind, and spirit. For instance, the astoundingly beautiful male Cramer's blue morpho butterfly *(Morpho rhetenor)*, which has a six-inch wingspan, is — in the full organic sense — really no different in structure and function and holiness than the practice of mindfulness or compassion or rainforest preservation. Systematic, organic spiritual practice is prayer in rhythm with the breath and capacity of the almost unimaginably small lungs of the ruby-throated hummingbird *(Archilochus colubris)*, as it inhales the love of Christ with each breath. The structure and function of systematic, organic spiritual practice is really no different from a walk through sparse forests of prickly pear cactus *(Opuntia humifusa)*, which bear round yellowing flowers with reddish centers and flat, fleshy green pads covered with clusters of minute reddish-brown barbed bristles. It is a walk in the midst of which we must stop to take off our shoes as we see that this cactus, in all its particularity and community, imitates the organic texture of the Trinity itself.

Organic practice through nature invites Christians to participate in the holiness of the natural world at all levels. We see the world as rational, explainable, decipherable, perceptible, and quantifiable structures, while at the same time we experience it as transrational, noetic, unreadable, poetic, invisible, and beyond quantifiable functions. In short, we see the world as both ecological and sacramental, and formational practice through nature reflects these two different but complementary perspectives. Organic formation in nature is ecological: it is perceptually recognizable, tactile, and as physical as you and I are. And organic formation in nature is sacramental: it points to what is not immediately recognizable, not immediately tactile in the physical sense. It is invisible, spiritual, Jesus in the womb of Mary, a burning bush not consumed in the new understanding of Moses.

In practice, ecological and sacramental realities each rely on the other: if one dies, so dies the other. While creation waits with eager longing, groaning for adoption into the life of Christ (Rom. 8:19-23), we are today, as H. Paul Santmire writes, "free to allow the love of God in Christ Jesus so to pour into our hearts by the indwelling of the Holy Spirit that it overflows abundantly, not only to persons, especially to those in great need, but also to all the creatures of nature."[15] Or as Terry Tempest Williams puts it so plainly, in organic practice we are free to explore creation as that in which "the external space I see is the internal space I feel."[16] As the love of God pours into all creation, in structure and in form, in attention and in wonder, external space is really no different from the internal space of our experience of the creative love of God.

Creation teaches ecological virtues such as sustainability, adaptability, relationality, frugality, equity, biodiversity, sufficiency, humility.[17] Nature invites us to trust justice, sufficiency, participation, solidarity.[18] In the *Earth Charter* of 2000, which emerged from the Earth Day program, the organic quality of Scripture merges with the organic qualities of creation, emphasizing human well-being, the well-being of species and ecosystems, principles of respect and care, ecological integrity, social and economic justice, nonviolence, and peace for humans and creation.[19]

There are numerous and varied communities today dedicated to practicing these values in creation, each in its own way addressing particular longings, consents, and needs. An example of one such community is Heartland Farm's commitment to small-scale sustainable organic agriculture near Pawnee Rock in central Kansas. Another is the Franciscan Sisters of Perpetual Adoration's (FSPA) ecumenical community named Prairiewood, near La Crosse, Wisconsin, which is dedicated to integrating relationships with earth, self, God, and others. Yet another is the community-supported agriculture of Michaela Farm near Oldenburg, Indiana. The Benedictine monastery of St. John the Baptist in Collegeville, Minnesota,

15. Santmire, *Nature Reborn*, 119.

16. Williams, *Red*, 158.

17. Suggested in James A. Nash, *Loving Nature: Ecological Integrity and Christian Responsibility* (Nashville: Abingdon, 1991), 63-67.

18. Suggested in James B. Martin-Schramm and Robert L. Stivers, *Christian Environmental Ethics: A Case Method Approach* (New York: Orbis, 2003), 37-45, 101-9. This is an excellent book for practical case studies and for obtaining other resources on Christian environmental ethics.

19. Earth Charter Commission, *The Earth Charter: Values and Principles for a Sustainable Future*, 2000. The website of the Earth Council: http://www.earthcharter.org (accessed December 2008).

is in the process of restoring three major native habitats that were formerly all but lost to the area. John E. Carroll surveys many more such communities in detail in his book *Sustainability and Spirituality*.[20] Many of these communities are inspired by the work of "ecologian" Thomas Berry, who suggests three basic principles of creation:

1. *Differentiation:* the universe is not homogeneous but is rather composed of clearly articulated entities, each of which is unique and irreplaceable.
2. *Subjectivity:* each of the component members of the universe has its own interiority, its spontaneity, its subjectivity.
3. *Communion:* each member of the universe community is bonded inseparably with every other member of the community; each member is immediately present to and influencing every other being in the universe, without, we are told by modern physics, crossing the intervening space.[21]

Prairiewood, for example, reflects Berry's contemplatively practical insights in their own "rule of creation life":

- To be open to the divine presence within all members of the earth community
- To integrate the principles of the universe: interiority, diversity, and communion
- To reverence all of creation as sacred and revelatory of the holy
- To embody a lifestyle that cares for the earth and celebrates the human
- To extend hospitality to all
- To impact ecological consciousness[22]

The possibilities of doing are as infinite as the needs distilled into a single moment in a single place: a forest clearing on a snowy evening, the opening sky, every flake of snow, the straight, true trunks of Sitka spruce — each needle, each cone — the dry air, the smell and touch and taste, the memory, the gentleness of white snow piling on green and the memory

---

20. John E. Carroll, *Sustainability and Spirituality* (Albany: State University of New York Press, 2004). Carroll surveys model communities of sustainability, esp. pp. 21-43 and 74-93.

21. Carroll, *Sustainability and Spirituality,* 45.

22. Carroll, *Sustainability and Spirituality,* 36.

that the tender, piercing softness of snow can kill. Each of these is singular; each is complex. Each is an Easter of ordinary things. As the snowflake and the snow become "an atmosphere ever more luminous and ever more charged with God," we will begin to know what we have to do.[23]

PRACTICE 14.2

A Creation Rule of Life

INTENTION Monastic communities and lay communities and individuals practice a "rule of life" to orient their work, prayer, and community toward God. The intention of this practice is to create and commit to practicing a "creation rule of life" that orients us toward God without neglecting the basis of the rule: creation itself.

Organic Contemplation/Organic Ethics: Water and a White Moth

Teresa of Avila, in her *Interior Castle,* guides her readers into a journey of contemplation and transformation that leads into the center, the most sacred heart of the soul, where Teresa has found — and tells us we will find — God in all God's goodness and clarity and wisdom. God is that close, closer to soul than the soul. Teresa often uses illustrations from nature that serve as signposts for the various points along the spiritual journey. Early on, for instance, she introduces a caterpillar, which, later in the journey, is weaving a silk cocoon, from which will emerge, much later still in the journey, a beautiful white moth. When the white moth emerges from the cocoon in her castle, the journey is already well along. Representing the soul, at first the moth is ecstatic: everything it touches is sweet; everything on which it alights is sacred beauty. But after a while,

---

23. Pierre Teilhard de Chardin, *The Divine Milieu: An Essay on the Interior Life* (New York: Harper, 1960), 112. In keeping with the theme of this section, that the organic is both a natural and formational quality, it is helpful to note that Teilhard's book is "about" creation, the "divine milieu," yet it is subtitled "An Essay on the Interior Life." Teilhard, too, understands that the exterior world mirrors and is mirrored by the inner life. The dedication of his book reads: *Sic Deus Dilexit Mundum* ("for those who love the world").

initial ecstasy gives way to the everyday, and eventually any place the moth lands begins to seem empty, made worse by the memory of its former ecstatic and sacred brilliance.

More time on the journey, more prayer, further transformation, and the moth appears again. At this time the journey has drawn the soul into its most interior "castle," the core of its being, where it is betrothed to Christ and wedded to Love in the Holy Trinity. This is the untouchable, unchangeable nature of the soul, the indestructible imprint of Love as good, the divine spark of the good at the core of all creation. And the moth now has changed. Each place where it settles is not a place of ecstasy but a place of settling, centering, stillness, peace, and shalom. Teresa compares this finally calmed, settled moth to an image of union between the human soul and God. This image is not of two flames from two candles uniting as one (which she had used earlier), a flame that could separate, returning to two flames as the candles are drawn apart. Rather, this prayerful journey through the castle of the soul finds its only Love as a drop of rain falling into the ocean, completely merged in God. Thus, wherever it alights, the white moth rests in Love; unlike its previous ecstasy, it really does not matter where it alights, because the result is the same.

Teresa loves images of water; she uses them many times and in many different ways to teach of work, grace, prayer, the spiritual journey, and more. In *Interior Castle,* the trials of life, wandering, contemplation, and longing for God have brought her to this ocean place. Yet this is not the end of the journey, at least not in this life. Out of this centering, this peace and shalom, this stilling — and in large part because of them — even as the soul disperses throughout the whole ocean, the moth hears whispers of need, the cries of the lost, the bellows of the degraded. Therefore, as naturally as removing one's shoes when one is on holy ground, "what to do" is the same as where the moth has landed. Service, justice, moral response now become the holy ground: the moth/soul gathers herself once again, even from the ends of the oceans, in response to those cries and whispers and bellows. Wherever she lands, that peace — so essential to healing — remains. She is, after all, wedded to Christ, to the Trinity, wedded even to the oceans. With her beloved, centered, responsive, active, and alive ministering, the moth/soul alights where the trees are groaning, where the melting ices are crying, even where the passenger pigeon and the beech trees are silent.

Teresa of Avila would have cherished the water image of this vesper antiphon and its affirmation of the salvation of all creation: "Like rain upon the grass, you descended to save humankind and all creation. Oh God, we praise you."[24] You have a white moth within. God waters the garden of your soul: where your white moth lands determines what you do, your organic ethic. How you function as the great Gardener's helper in tending the garden of your soul is the quality of your attention, of your contemplation. Let your white moth look, listen, hear, and respond. What you do depends on where your white moth lands.

24. "Solemnity of Mary, Mother of God," in *Benedictine Daily Prayer: A Short Breviary*, comp. and ed. Maxwell E. Johnson and the Monks of St. John's Abbey (Collegeville, MN: Liturgical Press, 2005), 1404.

The Green Beatitudes

Wisdom and the Green Beatitudes

I, wisdom, live with prudence, and I attain knowledge and discretion. I walk in the way of righteousness, along the paths of justice. My fruit is better than gold, even fine gold, and my yield than choice silver.

Proverbs 8:12, 20, 19

"What do we do?" This is the question I ended up asking in the last chapter. Another way to phrase the question is: How does wisdom "walk in the way of righteousness, along the paths of justice"? How do we give contemplative attention to nature, share in the wonder of creation, experience nature as spiritual practice, and choose moral responses to the earth's needs?

Two stories of creation in Genesis are complemented by a third in Proverbs 8:22-31. In this third story, Wisdom is the first of God's creation: "The Lord created me at the beginning of his work" (Prov. 8:22; cf. Sir. 1:4; 24:9). This short creation story in Proverbs is clear, straightforward, and unambiguous: Wisdom is God's first creation, serves beside God as a "master worker" (8:30; cf. Sir 1:9-10; Wis. 8:22), and in fact assists in all works of creation. More than merely an assistant or master worker, Wisdom sees God as "daily her delight"; she rejoices before God always, and along with God she "rejoices" in the "inhabited world," "delighting in the human race" (vv. 30-31). This is how Wisdom herself describes it (vv. 24-30):

When there were no depths I was brought forth,
    when there were no springs abounding with water.
Before the mountains had been shaped,

before the hills, I was brought forth —
when God had not yet made earth and fields,
     or the world's first bits of soil.
When God established the heavens, I was there,
     when God drew a circle on the face of the deep,
when God made firm the skies above,
     when God established the fountains of the deep . . .
     I was beside God, like a master worker.

What is Wisdom? Words don't really do her justice; there is something of the paradox, something of the riddle in her. We can say that Wisdom was *there,* at the beginning. Wisdom was created before any words by which she might be described, and in that sense she is not really describable. Appropriately, then, the book of Proverbs does not try to "capture" Wisdom in words, but rather to "understand [her in] a proverb and a figure, [in] the words of the wise and their riddles" (Prov. 1:6). The writer of Proverbs simply admits that only Wisdom brings knowledge of Wisdom. As I have pointed out throughout this book, this is very much the quality of creation itself: only creation brings knowledge of creation.

The Wisdom we find in Proverbs is very much like the kind of understanding Erazim Kohák pursues when he makes the point that an evening, unlike an argument, does not end in a conclusion. Wisdom does not end with an answer, but rather with a way of life, as a "walk in the way of righteousness, along the paths of justice."

Scripture is our best aid to finding how both Wisdom and nature can be understood as a way of life. I believe that one of the best places to go in Scripture to find how nature can become a way of life that is shaped in terms of a "walk in the way of righteousness, along the paths of justice" would be the Beatitudes found in Jesus' Sermon on the Mount. In the first five verses of Proverbs (1:1-5), Wisdom gives hints of her way of life, hints that are further illuminated in the Beatitudes. In those first five verses of Proverbs, Wisdom produces an abundance of children, including learning, instruction, understanding, insight, wise dealing and acting, righteousness, justice, equity, shrewdness, simplicity, knowledge, prudence, listening, learning, discernment, and guidance. The Beatitudes produce their own — yet similar — abundance of children.

These "children" of the Beatitudes, as they are put into practice, serve as models and guides for compassionate creation-care. Creation contemplation centers on the Beatitudes: nature as spiritual practice emerges from the Beatitudes, and the moral responses based on the Beatitudes all converge to form a way of life in which the ways and paths of righteousness and justice lead directly through "the Green Beatitudes." Like nature itself, the Beatitudes function as a still point or place of balance that integrates contemplation and care, prayer and justice, spiritual practice and the paths of righteousness.

Wisdom herself is green, and when her creation, daily the delight of God, begins to go brown, "Does not wisdom call, and does not understanding raise her voice?" (Prov. 8:1). Today Wisdom is calling and creation is raising her voice. The Beatitudes — greened like Hildegard's *viriditas* — give us ears to hear Wisdom's call and pathways to respond to creation's voice. Matthew's much longer version of the Beatitudes begins by orienting us in a *place:* seeing the crowds, Jesus "went up the mountain, and sat down" (Matt. 5:1). In many ways, Jesus is the form and practice of Wisdom, and even before he calls or raises his voice, he is situated in nature. He is sitting in places — on the mountain, upon the earth. In the shorter version in Luke, Jesus is also situated: in Luke's rendering he is coming down from a mountain, where he "stood on a level place" (Matt. 6:17). In both places — on the mountain and on the plain — Jesus is surrounded by great crowds of people who have come to "listen" and to "understand," as Jesus "raises his voice" ever so gently.

Matthew gives us what I consider to be nine Beatitudes, each of which raise Wisdom's voice and suggest ways that we might, with creation, "walk in the way of righteousness, along the paths of justice." All but one of the Beatitudes (Matt. 5:11) are stated in a conditional form: "Blessed are you if . . ." Some of these conditional forms are stated in the simple present: "is" (5:3, 10); some are stated in the simple future: "will" (5:5, 7, 8); others are stated in the future passive: "will be" (5:4, 6, 9, 10). What is important to note is that in all of the Beatitudes there is a sense in which the condition of blessing is already present, while the fullness of the blessing is a promise yet to be filled. That, I believe, is how we "walk in the way of righteousness, along the paths of justice." The ways of righteousness and the paths of justice honor, cherish, revere, and care for every blessing present, while waiting with eager longing for fuller blessings yet to come. Regardless of the time of fulfillment, Jesus, at the end of the nine Beatitudes, raises his voice to its highest pitch of Wisdom when he says, probably in a very gentle voice, "Rejoice, be glad" as a blessing (v. 12). Filled with the health of Wisdom, this is nature's voice as well: throughout Scripture nature rejoices and is glad simply because it is a blessing to consent to be what it is.

The nine Green Beatitudes are themselves lifelong conditions of spiritual practice and creation care. Each can be interpreted in terms of "nature's wisdom" and "listening to nature: human wisdom as creation care." Read in this way, they are gems of spiritual practice, each in turn greening the voice of Wisdom.

The Green Beatitudes

> *Our first wisdom as a species, that unique metaphorical knowledge that distinguishes us, grew out of such an intimacy with the earth. . . . Whatever wisdom I would find, I knew, would grow out of the land.*
>
> Barry Lopez, *Arctic Dreams*[1]

The First Beatitude

"Blessed [happy] are the poor in spirit (πνεύματι), for theirs is (ἐστιν) the kingdom of heaven" (Matt. 5:3).

Nature's Wisdom

Blessed, happy is creation: she is poor in spirit, she receives the kingdom of heaven. We have seen how nature is doxological, blessed, praising; this is an attribute of nature expressed throughout Scripture. As divine creation, nature is, in both her material and spiritual aspects, imprinted and infused with the Spirit *(pneuma)*. The Spirit has special activity in the Trinitarian acts of creation in Genesis: "Let *us* make" of Genesis 1:26. Nature is "poor" in spirit not in the sense of lacking, but in the sense of "purity of heart," as she seeks and consents to be only, yet fully, what she is created to be. In this sense also, nature is humble, emptying herself such that only the Spirit may fill her. Consenting to become what she is blessed to be in the present, creation remains poor in spirit as she nonetheless longs to return to the Creator and the fullness of blessing, or "kingdom of heaven." In these senses, nature's poverty of spirit is one of her most profound teachings: in her poverty of spirit, her highest aspiration is to "walk in the way of righteousness, along the paths of justice." As the exemplar of poverty of spirit (after Jesus

---

1. Barry Lopez, *Arctic Dreams* (New York: Vintage Books, 1986), 40.

and Wisdom), nature guides humanity in the pathways of consent to divine intention. That this book is focused "on earth as it is" in no way contradicts this Green Beatitude's wisdom that poverty of spirit is a blessing that *will* result in the kingdom of heaven. The "is" (ἐστίν) of this verse indicates that the kingdom is present in a certain sense already — here, today.

Listening to Nature: Human Wisdom as Creation-Care

Wisdom speaks to human understanding in this Beatitude, counseling blessing, happiness, and poverty of spirit as exemplified by the natural world. Nature's poverty of spirit is a model of humility for humanity (the two words are related in etymology: *humus* means "earth"). As nature shows poverty of spirit, so too might humanity consent to empty itself of the false self, walking in righteousness and justice in its true self, its true *humus*. The "dark side" of nature's poverty of spirit is that she can be taken advantage of. Emptied of all but what she is created to be, she is often defenseless against sustained assaults by human avarice, gluttony, pride, and foolish ignorance. There is a certain kind of naïve trust implicit in poverty of spirit, a trust that can be violated. And humanity *has* violated that trust. Still, creation's poverty of spirit is so wrapped up in what creation is that she will continue in poverty of spirit even if humanity succeeds in destroying much of her. If humanity does succeed in such earth-destruction so severe as to annihilate itself in the process, nature and earth will survive in some form beyond human extinction. But she will not rejoice in that: her blessing will be much compromised. The wisdom for humanity in this is to pay extremely close attention to nature's poverty of spirit and to do all it can do to imitate that poverty. Watch nature; notice her empty herself of all that she is not.

THE SECOND BEATITUDE

"Blessed [happy] are those who mourn (πενθοῦντες), for they will be comforted" (Matt. 5:4).

Nature's Wisdom

Mourning, creation will be comforted. In the chapters on the dark night of the planet, I explored the depth and degree of nature's mourning. Nature is in deep mourning. From our perspective, it is difficult to see this as a blessing, but in her mourning, nature will be comforted. Nature mourns the natural loss of individuals and species; but today nature mourns — even more deeply — the "unnatural" stress, degradation, crisis, pain, and loss inflicted on it by human *dis*-comfort. Nature has been groaning, and the Greek participle indicates current and continuing mourning: "those who are mourning." "Comfort" may be translated also as "invite" or "console." Those in mourning find the open hand of invitation they need, and as they reorient themselves toward consolation, they find simple forms of comfort. As a Green Beatitude, nature's wisdom speaks of righteousness and justice in that even in the midst of her mourning, nature finds ways to comfort herself even as she reaches out to comfort, invite, and console even those who inflict pain. In this she is impartial and forgiving. Creation is a lesson in turning the other cheek. Nature, in her ability to mourn and yet to console those who abuse her, is a voice of comfort.

Listening to Nature: Human Wisdom as Creation-Care

In those same chapters on the dark night of the planet, we noted how many psychologists and psychoanalysts have observed personal and societal denial of the current ecological crisis. The mechanisms of this denial are similar to those of our culture's own denial of death. One of the components or mechanisms is the inability or unwillingness to mourn, which blocks healing or undermines forgiveness. Certainly there are a few voices today calling us to confession, to contrition, to tears, to recognition of loss, to the genuine mourning, grief, and sadness of the creation. Yet the continued degradation of the planet indicates that, for the vast majority of humanity, the primary response to creation crisis is denial. This is, as Wisdom would say, the response of the "fool." Those who acknowledge pain and loss, and those who mourn, *will* be comforted. A primary source of comfort for the human species is the consolation and forgiveness offered by the natural world herself.

THE THIRD BEATITUDE
"Blessed [happy] are the meek (πραεῖς), for they will inherit the earth (τὴν γῆν)" (Matt. 5:5).

Nature's Wisdom

Those who have spent time in nature know immediately that "meek" in this verse does not mean "submissive" or "inconsequential." "Meek" can mean "gentle," and that is perhaps closer to the blessings of creation "meekness." But "gentle" is not quite right either: we know that the natural world is at times anything but gentle. "Meek," as the wisdom of the natural world itself teaches us, is more akin to divine order — that is, finding one's place and living within it. Creation's divine order is not hierarchical order, but rather organic order. Thus a mouse is "meek" by living as a mouse; a whale is "meek" by living as a whale. The same is true for humanity, though humanity generally has a difficult time with "meekness" in this sense. If we set humanity aside, however, nature lives in perfect meekness. A sun rising on a cold December morning into a crystal-blue sky, with perhaps a few clouds on the horizon, burning in pinks and violets and reds, is not "submissive"; it is not "inconsequential." It is "meek" with the blessing of emerging into its organic order within creation. As a Beatitude, as a blessing, in its meekness the earth will inherit the earth; the organic order of creation speaks of the blessing of earth as home.

Listening to Nature: Human Wisdom as Creation-Care

In understanding nature as "meek" and the earth as "inheritance," Wisdom raises her voice. Hearing that voice, we know that for humanity as well as all of nature, "meek" does not mean "submissive." There is an imperative contained in a meek and moral response to nature that insists on robust creation-care. Hearing Wisdom's voice, we also know that "meek" is not equivalent to our response to nature as "inconsequential" and thus absolved from making hard decisions and necessary changes regarding how we live within the natural world. As we listen to the wisdom of creation, hearing "meekness" is hearing balance, learning needs, addressing needs, and working to heal damage — even aggressively, if we must. Nature is an expert at caring for itself in ordered, organic ways. "Inconsequential" means, literally, to be out of sequence, to be out of order. The ordered, organic sequences of nature (her meekness) bespeak an earth we would want to hand on to our children as an inheritance, as a blessing.

THE FOURTH BEATITUDE

"Blessed [happy] are those who hunger and thirst for righteousness (δικαιοσύνην), for they will be filled" (5:6).

Nature's Wisdom

Animals and plants, fish and birds, insects and lizards — all are driven by hunger and thirst. These and all of creation, animate or inanimate, are driven by a larger hunger and thirst: the blessings of righteousness. Righteousness is not a prim and proper, pinched moral code. It is, we can say, the place where justice and peace kiss. Creation longs to return to its maker, to that place where justice and peace kiss, where the lion and the lamb lie down together. This Beatitude does not say, "Blessed are those who are righteous"; rather, it says, "Blessed are those who *hunger and thirst* for righteousness." The lion and the lamb hunger and thirst to lie down together; they do not as yet, on this earth as it is, but they are blessed still. Even mountains and galaxies and stars and oceans and stones — in their gravitational forces and their strong forces and their weak forces and their electromagnetic forces and their nuclear forces — hunger and thirst for righteousness. The kiss of justice and peace is the glue that holds, the food that satisfies. Spend time watching a mountain hunger and thirst for righteousness. Creation "waits with eager longing" (Rom. 8:19) for righteousness, for liberation from "its bondage to decay and [to be] brought into the glorious freedom of the children of God" (Rom. 8:21). In hunger and thirst of righteousness, "the whole creation has been groaning in labor pains until now" (Rom. 8:22). Creation can be savage; still, it hungers and thirsts for righteousness.

> May he judge your people with righteousness,
>   and your poor with justice.
> May the mountains yield prosperity for the people,
>   and the hills, righteousness.
>
>   Psalm 72:2-3

Listening to Nature: Human Wisdom as Creation-Care

For men and women, righteousness is a difficult term to understand fully, let alone live. "Hunger and thirst" are of a different order: fully understandable, daily lived. On earth as it is, we see creation in an organic, rhythmic, dynamic revolution of hunger and thirst. Everywhere we look, creation is moving, seeking to fill these needs. The hunger and thirst for righteousness is no less a need. Unfortunately, humanity has the power and will to *create* conditions of hunger and thirst, not just address them. Humanity can create conditions of dire need for food and water; and it can create conditions in dire need of righteousness. In fact, we even create unnatural appetites that over time become first unhealthy and, in time, lethal. As Wisdom raises her voice, our call to righteousness, justice, and peace is a call to maintain relationships with the natural world in which we fill what asks for filling and empty only what offers itself to be emptied.

THE FIFTH BEATITUDE

"Blessed [happy] are the merciful (ἐλεήμονες), for they will receive mercy (αὐτοὶ ἐλεηθήσονται)" (Matt. 5:7).

Nature's Wisdom

With certain virtues, you receive what you are: because she is merciful, creation receives mercy. Mercy is compassion, forgiving, and loving-kindness: compassion seems to be a rare commodity, even in nature. But mercy can refer both to compassionate behavior on the part of those in power (mercy shown by a judge toward a convict) or compassionate behavior on the part of a third party oppressed by another (a mission of mercy intended to treat war victims). But what about nature? Does she hear Wisdom's voice only as a set of "laws" that regulate against mercy? No, but at times it may seem so. A male lion who is the head of a pride seems to show no mercy — in either of the two senses — toward another male who transgresses his territory. A peregrine falcon seems to show little mercy toward the duck she has separated from the flock and is about to slash from the sky. A snowstorm seems to show no mercy to the lost hiker. We say an earthquake or a tsunami "is merciless." But here is Portia asking Shylock for mercy in Shakespeare's *Merchant of Venice:*

> Shylock: "On what compulsion must I?"
> Portia: "The quality of mercy is not strained."

As Portia knows, mercy is a virtue that cannot be compelled, it is not a behavior that "strains" against a natural inclination. The illustrations of creation given above do not "strain" against natural inclination or natural law. Rather than straining against mercy, they take their place within this Green Beatitude's concept of mercy, a third form of mercy to which creation gives clear voice: the mercy that the merciful receive in return. The duck gives its life for the peregrine and the peregrine's young. This is the mercy of the duck to the peregrine, on earth as it is — today. Though hardest to understand, this Beatitude of the merciful receiving mercy may be the voice Wisdom wishes us most to hear today.

Listening to Nature: Human Wisdom as Creation-Care

Mercy in nature is not what we would expect, or perhaps even want it to be. And often mercy means some hard choices, but it cannot be constrained or compelled. We can, out of mercy, seek to save a flock of ducks by capturing the adult peregrine and removing it far from the area. Or we could, out of mercy, kill a duck ourselves as the only way to sustain a starving and recently abandoned nest of falcon chicks. Meditating on mercy in nature, we must accept nature's groaning. Within this groaning, we might still catch a glimpse of mercy as a part of the larger, organic system of righteous conflict and harmony. Where we choose to enter into that system of mercy can often be difficult. What we can say is that, of both the definitions of mercy given above, in nature there is no "higher" authority that needs to grant leniency to a "lower" subject, and there are no wars requiring missions of mercy. Still, humans can exert a position of power in the natural world: the power of compassion, forgiveness, and mercy that sometimes *must* be strained as a caring response to the natural world. This is a difficult blessing.

THE SIXTH BEATITUDE
"Blessed [happy] are the pure in heart (καθαροὶ τῇ καρδίᾳ), for they will see God" (Matt. 5:8).

Nature's Wisdom

What an extraordinary claim! What a bountiful hope! The Greek word for heart, καρδία, is a dative form of "respect," and at the time the Gospels where written, "heart" was equivalent to the seat of the will, intellect, passions, and love. The heart of creation burns for her Creator. A tree gives glory to God simply by being a tree: creation groans, yet creation in another sense is "pure in heart": it sees God. The spirituality of the Christian desert fathers and mothers included the practice of dispassion (ἀπάθεια — *apatheia*), and they also linked dispassion as a path to the vision of God. When translating "dispassion" into Latin at the beginning of the fifth century, Cassian rendered it "purity of heart." Dispassion is not the opposite of passion. For example, the desert fathers and mothers regarded the passions as fundamentally good. For these monks, dispassion (or purity of heart) is a state in which passions are exercised in their original purity.

> [D]ispassion [or purity of heart] is a state of reintegration and spiritual freedom; . . . such a state may imply impartiality and detachment, but not indifference, for a dispassionate man does not suffer on his own account, he suffers for his fellow creatures.[2]

Such a state of reintegration and spiritual freedom, in which a person may suffer with fellow creatures — the true meaning of *com*passion — is suggested by Saint Diadochos of Photiki: "The qualities of a pure heart are intelligence devoid of envy, ambition free from malice, and unceasing love for the Lord of glory."[3] Such a pure heart will see God, and such I believe are the qualities of creation: creation is "devoid of envy"; creation does have ambition in the sense of a drive to live, thrive, and reproduce, but it is an "ambition free from malice." In the "mountains and all the hills, fruit trees and all cedars! [w]ild animals, and all cattle, creeping things and flying birds!" (Ps. 148:9-10) we find the declaration of unceasing love for the Lord of glory. Creation is a perfect model for purity of heart. Creation does not renounce the world; she *is* the world. Creation's dispassion is an attainment of love. In purity of heart, creation does see and will see God. This Green Beatitude is a yes: in seeing creation seeing God, we will see God.

2. G. E. H. Palmer et al., trans. and eds., *The Philokalia: The Complete Text,* 5 vols. (London: Faber and Faber, 1979-1995), Glossary: "Dispassion."

3. St. Diadochos of Photiki, "On Spiritual Knowledge," 19, in *The Philokalia: The Complete Text,* trans. and ed. G. E. H. Palmer et al., vol. 1 (London: Faber and Faber, 1979), 258.

Listening to Nature: Human Wisdom as Creation-Care

The Christian desert tradition also helps us see the natural world as "purity of heart" and helps us to allow nature's "purity of heart" to shape and form our own hearts. Dispassion and purity of heart in this tradition are always described in the context of the mutually supportive practices of contemplation and virtue and in the context of illumination by the Holy Spirit. Abba Nikitas Stithatos writes:

> The first [factor] is the freedom — that is to say, the dispassion of soul [purity of heart], which as a result of ascetic practice raises the aspirant to the contemplation of the spiritual essences of the created world. . . . When you attain a right view of God and the nature of things, . . . you will be illuminated by the Holy Spirit.[4]

For Abba Nikitas, the pure in heart ascend to a vision of the Creator through the beauty of his creatures. Purity of heart is thus both a practice of ascent leading through the beauty of the created world to a vision of God (contemplation) and a practice of moral response as a way of being in the world (virtue). "Blessed are the pure in heart, for they will see God." The Beatitudes are green in part because the natural world *is* purity of heart.

The Seventh Beatitude
"Blessed [happy] are the peacemakers (εἰρηνοποιοί), for they will be called (κληθήσονται) children of God" (Matt. 5:9).

Nature's Wisdom

Aggressive in the positive sense in her hunger and thirst for life, creation is uncompromising in her laws, yet ever accommodating in her organic resources, her ways of cooperative survival, and her willingness to "turn the other cheek" as she absorbs negative aggression, incursion, invasion, and skirmishes waged against her — both natural and man-made. Even in the most long-term and caustic of wars waged against her, nature is war's consummate "conscientious objector." Nonviolent resistance, sustaining life,

---

4. Nikitas Stithatos, "On the Practice of Virtues," 1.90, in *The Philokalia: The Complete Text,* trans. and ed. G. E. H. Palmer et al., vol. 4 (London: Faber and Faber, 1995), 79, 103.

encouraging growth, and reacting in modes of healing are her uncompromising strategies. Wars require a sense of entitlement, privilege, ownership, hierarchy, property, ideology, nationality, and closed systems. They are undertaken to acquire riches, seek revenge, accumulate status, enforce beliefs, and sustain power. Even when waged for values of democracy, safety, security, or defense, wars are soon perverted and contaminated by pride, self-righteousness, avarice, and greed. These are not the ways of peacemaking, nor are they the ways of blessing.

Creation certainly is full of conflict and violence, and can be deadly: a polar bear shredding a squalling seal pup, a venomous injection slowly dissolving the innards of a living insect so another can dine on the gooey mixture at its leisure. But these are not wars. Nature is "red in tooth and claw": violence is pervasive, and death frequently occurs. But violence and death in nature are part of the larger cycles of life. War as humans wage war against themselves and against creation does not respect or participate in these larger cycles of life. Blessed are the peacemakers. The Greek verb for "will be called" (κληθήσονται) reveals the intention of this Green Beatitude. It reveals creation's identity: creation will be called "children of God." "For all who are led by the Spirit of God are children of God" (Rom. 8:14). "He has destined us for adoption as his children through Jesus Christ" (Eph. 1:5). "And through him God was pleased to reconcile to himself *all* things, whether on earth or in heaven, by making peace through the blood of the cross" (Col. 1:20).

Listening to Nature: Human Wisdom

Nature delivers destruction and death, yet beneath this obvious cycle is a more sublime whisper, Wisdom's call: "peace." Listen and you will hear Wisdom raise her voice to peace. Peace is the name of the children of God.

THE EIGHTH BEATITUDE
"Blessed [happy] are those who are persecuted (δεδιωγμένοι) for righteousness' sake, for theirs is the kingdom of heaven" (Matt. 5:10).

Nature's Wisdom

Unfortunately, Christ could not suggest a more apt or timely Green Beatitude for creation today. In the fourth Beatitude, creation hungers and thirsts for righteousness. Perhaps not since the time of the age of Christian martyrs has anyone or anything been so persecuted as is the earth today. The persecution is often "justified" on the basis of some form of misguided righteousness. But whatever the form — self, economic, social — creation persecution is not God's righteousness, or even God's plan. The verb form of this Beatitude is also particularly apt for creation: it is a perfect passive participle, indicating a present state resulting from past action, in this case literally "those who bear the wounds of persecution." Regarding the earth, the past action has been long-term, continuing into today in such a way as to ensure that well into the future the natural world will bear the wounds of persecution from past actions as well. It is not necessary to enumerate once again the wounds of persecution that nature bears today. It is more helpful to realize that it is not overblown rhetoric to make the claim today that nature is not only persecuted, but is our contemporary martyr.

The second and third centuries of the Christian era became known as the age of martyrdom: many thousands were killed for their beliefs. In the early third century, Tertullian, the bishop of Carthage, wrote that "the blood of Christian martyrs is the seed of Christians," implying that the martyrs' willing sacrifice of their lives would sprout and grow into the conversion of many more Christians. Along with the first great period of persecution, there have been recurrent periods in which Christians willingly or unwillingly sacrificed their lives, shedding blood for Christ; they have come to be known as "red martyrs." During periods of lessened or no persecution, many Christians have sought to imitate the intentions of the "red martyrs," if not their fates. These Christians are often referred to as "white martyrs" in the sense that they "die" to the world. Today we have new martyrs: they are of our own making and can appropriately be called "green martyrs." Creation is hemorrhaging "green blood." Sadly, many Christians are nature's primary persecutors, and we can be sure that the Christian shedding of green blood is not seed for new Christians.

Listening to Nature: Human Wisdom as Creation-Care

What did non-Christians think of men and women willing to be tortured and killed in horribly violent ways rather than renounce their faith? It must have given them pause. We do not claim to know God's ways, but what do Christians *and* non-Christians today think of the green martyrdom of creation as she is wounded, tortured, and killed in violent, inhuman, and unnatural ways? It gives us pause. It forces us to ask what is holy, what is sacred, what is inviolable. Our own humanity requires that we stop the bloodshed and begin to act and live in environmentally sustaining ways. Perhaps — just perhaps — the green martyrdom of creation today *is* the seed that will grow in ways that will open our understanding and hearts to new ways of revering and honoring our green, earthly garden.

THE NINTH BEATITUDE

"Blessed [happy] are you when people revile (ὀνειδίσωσιν) you and persecute you and utter all kinds of evil against you falsely (ψευδόμενοι) on my account" (Matt. 5:11).

Nature's Wisdom

The eighth Beatitude ends with the same words as the first Beatitude, showing a literary parallelism within the first eight Beatitudes. With this ninth and final Beatitude, Jesus' statement changes to the second person (you) and does not have the same conditional form as the others: there is no if/then construction, only the blessing. The persecution Jesus refers to here is similar to that in the eighth Beatitude, but here in the ninth there is an added sense of verbal abuse. "Revile" or "reproach," equally good English translations for the Greek ὀνειδίσωσιν, both indicate verbal condemnation. And ψευδόμενοι (translated "utter falsely" in the NRSV) literally means to "speak falsely" or "lie." For the natural world, the verbal content of this persecution is significant and important. The verbal imprecations in a sense overturn, make chaotic, and de-create a creation that was initially and is continually *spoken* into being. As the Spirit of the Lord moves across the face of the deep (Gen. 1:2) — with Wisdom beside the Lord as a master-worker (Prov. 8:30) and with the Word through whom all things came into being (John 1:1-3) — God speaks, and creation *is,* and it is good, imprinted with Wisdom and uttered through the voice of the Son of man. This final Beatitude recognizes that reviling and false speech is a perversion of creation. Any time we revile or speak falsely of creation we, in a sense, de-center it from its original centering in the Word of truth. Does a word kill an elephant for its ivory? Yes, a reviling, falsely spoken word certainly does.

Listening to Nature: Human Wisdom and Creation-Care

Assimilating the Beatitudes as a way of life into the everyday means absorbing them into our marrow, having them become a part of hearts and minds, learning through them to purify our hearts, to mourn, to be gentle, poor in spirit, merciful, hungry and thirsty for righteousness, peacemakers. With the previous eight thus in our "marrow," humanity is compelled to see and hear this ninth Beatitude as a disquieting creation blessing: creation is reviled, spoken evil of, falsely accused, and abused. Is creation "blessed" as a result? As children of God — humanity as well as all creation — there is no reason that the same blessing could not emerge without the false accusation, the spoken evil. In other words, humanity can utter and "do" blessing toward creation, can speak the truth to and of nature, can be an agent of reform to and on this earth.

Through these Green Beatitudes humanity blesses and is blessed by creation now and in the future. These Green Beatitudes are practices for hearing, attending to, and responding to Wisdom's increasingly loud voice. Hearing with the ears of the Creator, being led along the paths of Christ, finding strength for confession and restoration in the Spirit, we can begin to hear a new word: *Blessed*.

The Green Beatitudes end with Jesus saying to the crowds, "Rejoice and be glad."

A brief reflection on salt is inserted between the Sermon on the Mount and Jesus' call to "rejoice and be glad." Imagine salt without its taste, as Jesus asks us to do. One could hardly think of anything more "useless." Salt without its taste is a degraded material, serving not even the function of dirt. It is, as Christ says, "no longer good for anything, and is thrown out and trampled underfoot" (Matt. 5:13). Jesus' point is partly that salt without taste will never again rejoice and be glad, will never be green.

Humanity has degraded large parts of nature: we have in effect condemned these systems of nature to being no more than salt without taste. What Jesus adds in these verses is haunting and chilling when it is placed in the context of ecological systems becoming more and more like salt without taste. He hints that some of what humanity has done to creation cannot be undone: "If the salt has lost its taste, how can the saltiness be restored?" (5:13b).

Through the Green Beatitudes, Jesus invites every man, woman, and child (and all the earth) to become like this most basic of minerals, to rejoice and be glad, to be glad as salt, to be as a simple salt of the earth: loving, joyful, peacemaking, patient, kind, generous, gentle, and self-controlled.

PRACTICES

Scripture's Green Designs

INTENTION The following practices use Scripture as a basis for fostering contemplative attention, seasoned discernment, reciprocal perception, the capacity to wonder, and moral response appropriate both to others and to creation. Each practice comes with a minimum of instruction or questions: the intention is that each reader and practitioner will find his or her own ways into Scripture's green designs and continue to experience creation as spiritual practice leading to contemplative attention and moral action — here — "on earth as it is."

PRACTICES The following practices consist of suggestions from Scripture on how to grow in ways that are congruent with Scripture's own green intentions. Some are much more than suggestions: they are gifts, ways of life, models for growth in communion and love of nature. Normally these suggestions are not applied to the natural world, but as you meditate on them in the context of nature, you will find that the application of these gifts and virtues to creation is more than appropriate.

"Joy" is one example from the list of "fruits of the Spirit" in Galatians. If we equate joy with praise, there is no question that many parts of creation are less in a position to praise than they once were and we, in turn, less able to pray as a result. But perhaps in another sense, green praise in the midst of a brown ecology reminds us that the Spirit groans in prayer when we cannot. As overwhelmed by ecological destruction as we may be, prayer still rises up from the earth — if not in praise, then in lament. This, too, may be a prayerful "gift of the Spirit."

For each of the following practices, allow yourself to wander or hike or stroll or sit or simply stand in the natural world — in a city park, along a beach, in a state park, into the wilderness, or in a garden — noticing and attending to each Scripture suggestion in turn as it helps you reflect on nature and what nature might be able to tell you. You may find, say, a gift of the Spirit in nature, or nature may show you a gift of the Spirit in yourself or others you have not noticed. Keep in mind that the lists and individual items are simultaneously ways of contemplating creation and paradigms for loving, caring action in nature.

- *Gifts of the Spirit: Galatians 5:22-26.* Where in nature do you find each gift? How does nature mediate the following gifts of the Spirit to you? Taken as a whole, how would practicing the gifts of the Spirit form the way we live in the everyday? Let nature share these gifts with you: "If we live by the Spirit, let us also be guided by the Spirit" (Gal. 5:25).
  - Love
  - Joy
  - Peace
  - Patience
  - Kindness
  - Generosity
  - Gentleness
  - Self-control

- *Gifts of the Spirit of the Lord: Isaiah 11:2.* Again, allow yourself to attend to these gifts in the natural world and to note how the natural world, in turn, shares these gifts with you.
  - Wisdom
  - Understanding
  - Counsel
  - Might
  - Knowledge
  - Fear of the Lord
  - Delight in the Lord

- *Spiritual gifts: 1 Corinthians 12:8-10.* The spiritual gifts of 1 Corinthians are in many ways shorthand for how the natural world forms and shapes identity. Perseverance and patience in perceiving these gifts in nature and receiving them through nature will slowly build your understanding of their function in nature.
  - Utterance of wisdom
  - Utterance of knowledge
  - Faith
  - Healing
  - Working miracles
  - Prophecy

- Discernment of spirits
- Various kinds of tongues
- Interpretation of tongues

- *Two kinds of wisdom: James 3:13-18.* James uses two kinds of wisdom. "Wisdom from above" is reminiscent of the Proverbs text: "Does not Wisdom call, and does not understanding raise her voice?" (Prov. 8:1). "Wisdom from below" gives insight into some of the human "foolishness" that contributes to ecological stress and degradation. Do you see "wisdom from below" in nature herself?

Wisdom from Above	Wisdom from Below
Gentleness born of wisdom	Bitter envy
Purity born of wisdom	Selfish ambition
Peaceable	Earthly [in the sense that it is self-
Gentle	centered, rather than God-
Willing to yield	centered, insubstantial]
Full of mercy	Unspiritual
Full of good fruits	Devilish
Without partiality	Disordered
Without hypocrisy	Wickedness of every kind
Yields a harvest of righteous-ness sown in peace	

- *The Ten Commandments: Exodus 20:2-17.* Though the Ten Commandments, like the other Scripture suggestions, are predicated on a contemplative attentiveness in order to help us see a situation or relationship clearly, they are a bit different from all the suggestions given previously. Unlike the previous lists, the Ten Commandments are a list of things *not to do* instead of a list of gifts or things *to do*. Both can be applied to the natural world; both help us to be conscious of how the natural world mediates Christ's guidance to us; both move from awareness to intention to action. Applying each, how do the Ten Commandments help you "hear" Wisdom's voice in creation? Some people prefer or find the Green Beatitudes more helpful; others will find that the following Green Ten Commandments speak more intimately and meaningfully.
  - You shall have no other gods before me.
  - You shall not make yourself an idol.
  - You shall not misuse the name of the Lord.
  - Remember the Sabbath.

 – Honor your father and your mother.
 – You shall not murder.
 – You shall not commit adultery.
 – You shall not steal.
 – You shall not give false witness.
 – You shall not covet a neighbor's goods.

- *New life in Christ: Colossians 3:2, 12-17:* The description of the new life in Christ given in Colossians returns us to the opening section of this chapter, summed up by Saint Hesychios in the epigraph to chapter 13: "Watchfulness is a graceful and radiant virtue when guided by Thee, Christ our God." Here the contemplative watchfulness and the life of virtue blend together, as both are guided by Christ. Do you find places in nature not bestowed with the garments of this new life of Christ? Why?
 – Set your minds on things that are above.
 – Clothe yourselves with:
   • Compassion
   • Kindness
   • Humility
   • Meekness
   • Patience
 – Above all, clothe yourselves with love.
 – Bear with one another.
 – Forgive one another.
 – Let the peace of Christ dwell in you richly.
 – Teach and admonish in all wisdom.
 – Sing psalms, hymns, and spiritual songs.
 – Do everything in the name of the Lord, giving thanks to God.

Nature as spiritual practice is engagement with Love:

Come, my beloved,
    let us go forth into the fields,
    and lodge in the villages;
let us go out early to the vineyards,
    and see whether the vines have budded,
whether the grape blossoms have opened

and the pomegranates are in bloom.
There I will give you my love.

Song of Songs 7:11-12

May nature turn the Beatitudes green for you. May you begin to read all of Scripture in a green way and encounter your God as green and greening.

APPENDIX A

What Are Christian Practices?

- They address fundamental human needs, longings, and conditions through practical acts.
- They involve us in God's activities in the world and reflect God's grace and love.
- They are grounded in Scripture.
- They sustain faithfulness to Christian tradition and doctrine.
- They are social in character.
- They are a gift and not a task.
- They knit the body of Christ in worship.
- They involve deep awareness and a profound, sacred way of knowing.
- They involve solitude as a practice, and practices are often done in solitude.
- They shape the people who participate in them.
- They nurture specific habits, virtues, and capacities of body, mind, and spirit.
- They have what is good as their purpose and goal (though they can become distorted and corrupt).
- Their basis is in experience, witnessed in service and social justice.
- They are missional in character.
- They foster devotion to the humanity of Christ and identification with the risen Lord.
- They correspond to contemporary religious experience.
- They enable relationships and dialogue outside the group: they are ecumenical and interreligious.
- They foster stillness.

- They develop love for and attachment to the things of God, and detachment from the "world."
- They initiate a habit of personal and social formation and transformation.
- They promote the consciousness of the presence of God.
- They result in a deepening connection to oneself, to others, to creation, and to God.
- They draw one ever deeper into the love of God.
- They foster a growing sense of holiness in and of all things.
- They add up to a way of life.

Multiple Intelligence Inventory

The following is a Multiple Intelligence Inventory based on Howard Gardner's seven types of intelligences.[1] Mark each statement that applies to you and count the number in each type of intelligence: the higher the number, the higher the likelihood that this particular form of intelligence is one you possess and use frequently.

Linguistic Intelligence

__ Books are very important to me.

__ I hear words in my head before I read, speak, or write them down.

__ I'd rather listen to the radio or the spoken word than watch television or film.

__ I enjoy word games like Scrabble, Anagrams, or Password.

__ People ask me to explain the meanings of words I write or speak.

__ English, social studies, and history were easier for me in school.

__ When driving on the highway, I pay more attention to billboards than to scenery.

__ I frequently refer to things that I've read or heard.

__ Recently, I've written something that has given me pride or earned recognition.

Logical-Mathematical Intelligence

__ I easily compute numbers in my head.

__ Math and/or science were my favorite subjects in school.

---

1. "Multiple Intelligences Checklist," from *7 Kinds of Smart: Revised and Updated Edition* by Thomas Armstrong, copyright © 1993, 1999 by Thomas Armstrong. Used by permission of Plume, an imprint of Penguin Group (USA) Inc.

__ I enjoy games or brainteasers that require logical thinking.

__ I like to set up "what if" experiments.

__ My mind searches for patterns or logical sequences.

__ I'm interested in new developments in science.

__ I think almost everything has a rational explanation.

__ Sometimes I think in clear, abstract, and wordless images or concepts.

__ I like finding logical flaws in what others say and do.

__ I feel more comfortable when something has been measured, categorized, analyzed, or quantified in some way.

Spatial Intelligence

__ I often see clear visual images when I close my eyes.

__ I am sensitive to color.

__ I frequently use a camera or camcorder.

__ I enjoy doing jigsaw puzzles, mazes, etc.

__ I have vivid dreams.

__ Generally, I can find my way around unfamiliar territory.

__ I like to draw or doodle.

__ Geometry was easier for me than algebra.

__ I can imagine easily how something would look from a bird's-eye view.

__ I prefer reading material that is heavily illustrated.

Bodily-Kinesthetic Intelligence

__ I exercise or play sports regularly.

__ I find it difficult to sit for long periods of time.

__ I like concrete activities like sewing, weaving, carving, carpentry, or model building.

__ My best ideas come to me when I am doing something active like walking.

__ I like to spend free time outdoors.

__ I use hand gestures or body language when talking.

__ I need to touch things to learn more about them.

__ I enjoy roller coasters and other thrilling physical experiences.

__ I would describe myself as well coordinated.

__ I need to practice a new skill rather than watching a video or reading about it.

Musical Intelligence

___ I have a pleasant singing voice.

___ I can tell when a musical note is off-key.

___ I frequently listen to music on radio, cassettes, or CD's.

___ I play a musical instrument.

___ My life would be poorer with no music in it.

___ Often I have an advertising jingle or other tune running through my mind.

___ I can easily keep time to a piece of music.

___ I know the tunes to many different songs or musical pieces.

___ When I hear a musical selection once or twice, I am usually able to sing it back accurately.

___ Often I make tapping sounds or sing little melodies while working, studying, or learning something new.

Interpersonal Intelligence

___ People come to me for advice or counsel.

___ I prefer group sports like volleyball, softball, or soccer to solo sports like swimming or jogging.

___ When I have a problem, I'm more likely to ask someone for help than to work it out on my own.

___ I have at least three close friends.

___ I prefer social pastimes like board games or bridge to video games or solitaire.

___ I enjoy the challenge of teaching others what I know how to do.

___ I consider myself a leader (or others call me that).

___ I feel comfortable in a crowd.

___ I like to be involved in social activities at work, church, or community.

___ I would rather spend my evenings at a party than stay home alone.

Intrapersonal Intelligence

___ I regularly spend time alone meditating, reflecting, or thinking about important life issues.

___ I have attended counseling or personal growth seminars to learn more about myself.

___ I am able to respond to setbacks with resilience.

___ I have a special hobby or interest that I keep pretty much to myself.

__ I have important goals for my life that I think about on a regular basis.

__ I have a realistic view of my strengths and weaknesses (born of feedback from other sources).

__ I would prefer to spend a weekend alone in a cabin than at a fancy resort with many people around.

__ I consider myself to be strong-willed or independent-minded.

__ I am self-employed or have thought seriously about starting my own business.

Some teachers speak of Gardner's "intelligences" as "smarts." Thus:

Linguistic intelligence = Word smart
Logical-mathematical intelligence = Logic smart
Spatial intelligence = Picture smart
Bodily-kinesthetic intelligence = Body smart
Musical intelligence = Music smart
Interpersonal intelligence = People smart
Intrapersonal intelligence = Self smart

Whether you find "intelligence" or "smart" more helpful, experiment with applying your own wisdom and attention to the wonders of the natural world.

The Meaning of "Nature"

Those readers for whom the distinctions and meanings of "nature" and nature's cognates (creation, earth, ecology, place, space, natural world, universe, cosmos) are important or of interest will find the following books and articles helpful. For a good, brief "ecological perception of place," in a book consciously evoking a Christian perspective, see Steven Bouma-Prediger, *For the Beauty of the Earth: A Christian Vision for Creation Care* (Grand Rapids: Baker Academic, 2001), 19-38. Philip Sheldrake, *Spaces for the Sacred: Place, Memory, and Identity* (Baltimore: Johns Hopkins University Press, 2001), 1-63, is also good at depicting distinctions among these words, especially in his chapters entitled "A Sense of Place" and "Place in Christian Tradition." A good exploration of how American sacred space is defined, produced, and contested, with an excellent introductory survey on these issues, can be found in David Chidester and Edward T. Linenthal, *American Sacred Space* (Bloomington: Indiana University Press, 1995), 1-42.

Since the beginning of the century, "environmental history" has been articulated variously by writers from a range of disciplines, including geographers, historical ecologists, ethnohistorians, ecological anthropologists, ecotherapists, various literary and landscape historians, and theologians and biblical scholars who have addressed the history of attitudes toward and practices within the natural world — often from preclassical times to the present. Informative representatives of some of these disciplines are the following. Conrad Cherry gives a good, short summary of philosophical and theological conceptions of nature by tracing the "symbolic-imaginative response to nature" from Jonathan Edwards to Horace Bushnell in *Nature and Religious Imagination: From Edwards to Bushnell* (Philadelphia: Fortress, 1980), 1-13. An accessible account of our scientific understandings of nature, with further commentary on how scientific understandings call forth reasonable and appealing religious responses, is Ursula Goodenough, *The Sacred Depths of Nature* (Oxford: Oxford University Press, 1998). For an excellent "environmental history" from a history of religions perspective that focuses on nature and its cognates and on humanity's ongoing relationship with nature from pre-Greek to contemporary times, see Rupert Sheldrake, *The Rebirth of Nature: The Greening of Science and God* (Rochester, VT: Park Street Press, 1991).

Though debated and refined by recent scholarship, the now classic work in ecology from a Christian, theological perspective, a study dedicated to uncovering the roots of the classical Christian traditions, including what we mean by "nature," is H. Paul Santmire, *The Travail of Nature: The Ambiguous Ecological Promise of Christian Theology* (Philadelphia: Fortress, 1985). Santmire's own more recent book, *Nature Reborn: The Ecological and Cosmic Promise of Christian Theology* (Minneapolis: Fortress, 2000), joins other scholars in refining his earlier work and definitions.

The theologian Sallie McFague has written extensively and incisively on nature, ecology, the earth, and their meanings. In her book *Super, Natural Christians: How We Should Love Nature* (Minneapolis: Fortress, 1997), 9-25, she introduces a "Christian Nature Spirituality," in which she gives definitions of "nature," "creation," and "earth"; her section on what she means by "nature" is by far the most comprehensive. For an excellent book on the intellectual "environmental history" that stands behind the meaning of these terms and that also gives a good introductory account of the meaning of "nature" or "natures of nature," see Peter Coates, *Nature: Western Attitudes Since Ancient Times* (Berkeley: University of California Press, 1998), 1-22. John Gatta approaches the meaning of these terms, also looking at "environmental history," specifically at the relationship between literature and religion in America, in *Making Nature Sacred: Literature, Ecology, and Environment in America from the Puritans to the Present* (Oxford: Oxford University Press, 2004). A good introductory text on the meaning of "nature" and its cognates given from the perspective of cultural geography is Steven Field and Keith H. Basso, eds., *Senses of Place* (Santa Fe, NM: School of American Research Press, 1996), 3-12.

Anne Whiston Spirn combines literary and landscape history, arguing that landscape is itself a form of meaningful and expressive language with a literature of its own, which in turn is in dialogue with the ambiguous meaning of nature itself, in *The Language of Landscape* (New Haven: Yale University Press, 1998), 15-83. The eminent biologist E. O. Wilson includes a chapter entitled "What is Nature?" in *The Creation: An Appeal to Save Life on Earth* (New York: Norton, 2006), 15-25. On the meaning of "nature" and "spirituality" from a cross-cultural perspective, see David Kinsley, *Ecology and Religion: Ecological Spirituality in Cross-Cultural Perspective* (Upper Saddle River, NJ: Prentice Hall, 1995), xv-xxi. Two helpful essays that contribute to the contemporary discussion about the meaning of "nature" in a Christian context are "Beyond Lynn White: Religion, Contexts of Ecology, and the Flux of Nature," by Christopher Hamlin and David M. Lodge, and "Christianity and Changing Concepts of Nature: An Historical Perspective," by Elspeth Whitney. Both essays can be found in David M. Lodge and Christopher Hamlin, eds., *Religion and the New Ecology: Environmental Responsibility in a World in Flux* (Notre Dame, IN: University of Notre Dame Press, 2006), 1-25 and 26-52.

Essential reading on the meaning of "nature" in the context of identity formation can be found in Susan Clayton and Susan Opotow, eds., *Identity and the Natural Environment: The Psychological Significance of Nature* (Cambridge, MA: MIT Press, 2003), especially the editors' introduction (1-24) and "Some Lives and Some Theories" (25-42), by Steven J. Holmes. W. David Hall teases out the equivalency (or lack of it) between "creation" and "nature" in "Does Creation Equal Nature? Confronting the Christian Confusion About Ecology and Cosmology," *Journal of the American Academy of Religion* 73, no. 3 (September 2005): 781-812. Finally, in a short introduction, John Hay sums up the core issue of the difficult process of defining "nature" in the aptly titled "The Nature Writer's Dilemma," in Daniel Halpern, ed., *On Nature: Nature, Landscape, and Natural History* (San Francisco: North Point Press, 1987), 5-10.

Bibliography

Abba Sisoes. *The Desert Christian: The Sayings of the Desert Fathers; The Alphabetical Collection.* Translated by Benedicta Ward, S.L.G. New York: Macmillan, 1975.

Abram, David. *The Spell of the Sensuous: Perception and Language in a More-than-Human World.* New York: Pantheon Books, 1996.

Alighieri, Dante. *Dante: The Divine Comedy.* Translated by John D. Sinclair. New York: Oxford University Press, 1961.

Allen, Diogenes. *Spiritual Theology: The Theology of Yesterday for Spiritual Help Today.* Cambridge, MA: Cowley, 1997.

Appleton, Jay. *The Experience of Landscape.* Revised edition. New York: John Wiley and Sons, 1996.

Aquinas, Thomas. *Summa Theologica,* vol. 2. Translated by Fathers of the English Dominican Province. London: Burns, Oates and Washbourne, 1921.

Athanasius. *De Incarnatione Verbi Dei.* In *Nicene and Post-Nicene Fathers,* 2nd ser., vol. 4. Edited by Philip Schaff. New York: The Christian Literature Company, 1892.

Augustine. *The City of God.* In *Basic Writings of Saint Augustine,* vol. 2. Edited by Whitney J. Oates. New York: Random House, 1948.

Basil the Great. *Hexaemeron.* Translated by Blomfield Jackson. In *A Select Library of Nicene and Post-Nicene Fathers,* 2nd ser., vol. 8. Grand Rapids: Eerdmans, 1952.

Bass, Dorothy C. *Practicing Our Faith: A Way of Life for a Searching People.* San Francisco: Jossey-Bass, 1997.

Bernard of Clairvaux. *Bernard of Clairvaux: Early Biographies.* Vol. 1. Translated by Martinus Cawley. Lafayette, IN: Guadalupe Translations, 1990.

————. *Life and Works of St. Bernard, Abbot of Clairvaux.* Translated by Samuel Eales. London: John Hodges, 1889.

Berry, Thomas. *The Dream of the Earth.* San Francisco: Sierra Club Books, 1988.

Berry, Wendell. *Given Poems.* Emeryville, CA: Shoemaker and Hoard, 2005.

Berryman, Jerome W. *Godly Play: A Way of Religious Education.* San Francisco: Harper, 1991.

Brower, Michael, and Warren Leon. *The Consumer's Guide to Effective Environmental Choices: Practical Advice from the Union of Concerned Scientists.* New York: Three Rivers Press, 1999.

Buber, Martin. *I and Thou.* Translated by Ronald Gregor Smith. Second edition. New York: Scribner, 1958.

Bunyan, John. *The Pilgrim's Progress from This World to That Which Is to Come.* Edited by James Blanton Warey and Roger Sharrock. Second edition. Oxford: Oxford University Press, 1960.

Callicott, J. Baird. *Earth's Insights: A Survey of Ecological Ethics from the Mediterranean Basin to the Australian Outback.* Berkeley: University of California Press, 1994.

Calvin, John. *Commentaries on the First Book of Moses Called Genesis.* Vol. 1 of *Calvin's Commentaries.* Translated by John King. Grand Rapids: Baker, 1989.

———. *Institutes of the Christian Religion.* Edited by John T. McNeill. Translated by Ford Lewis Battles. Philadelphia: Westminster Press, 1960.

Canadian Conference of Catholic Bishops. "A Pastoral Letter on the Christian Ecological Imperative": www.cccb.ca/Files/pastoralenvironment.html (accessed April 2009).

Carroll, John E. *Sustainability and Spirituality.* Albany: State University of New York Press, 2004.

Catherine of Siena. *Catherine of Siena: The Dialogue.* Translated by Suzanne Noffke, O.P. New York: Paulist Press, 1980.

Catton, William R., and Riley E. Dunlap. "A New Ecological Paradigm for Post-Exuberant Sociology." *American Behavioral Scientist* 24 (1980): 15-47.

Chard, Philip Sutton. *The Healing Earth: Nature's Medicine for the Troubled Soul.* Minnetonka, MN: NorthWord Press, 1994.

Chase, Steven. *The Tree of Life: Models of Christian Prayer.* Grand Rapids: Baker Academic, 2005.

Chenu, Marie-Dominique. *Nature, Man, and Society in the Twelfth Century.* Chicago: University of Chicago Press, 1983.

Chesterton, G. K. *Saint Francis of Assisi.* London: Hodder and Stoughton, 1924.

Chevalier, Tracy. *The Girl with a Pearl Earring.* New York: Plume, 2001.

Cioran, E. M. *Tears and Saints.* Translated by Ilinca Zarifopol-Johnston. Chicago: University of Chicago Press, 1995.

Clayton, Susan, and Susan Opotow, eds. *Identity and the Natural Environment: The Psychological Significance of Nature.* Cambridge, MA: MIT Press, 2003.

Clinebell, Howard. *Ecotherapy: Healing Ourselves, Healing the Earth.* Minneapolis: Fortress Press, 1996.

Combes, Allen J. *Trees: Smithsonian Handbooks.* Second edition. New York: Dorling Kindersley, 2002.

Densmore, Frances. *How Indians Use Wild Plants for Food, Medicine and Crafts.* Formerly titled "Uses of Plants by the Chippewa Indians." In *Forty-fourth Annual Report of the Bureau of American Ethnology to the Secretary of the Smithsonian Institution, 1926-1927,* 275-397. New York: Dover Publications, 1974.

DeWitt, Calvin B. "Creation's Environmental Challenge to Evangelical Christianity." In *The Care of Creation: Focusing Concern and Action,* edited by R. J. Berry, 60-73. Leicester, England: InterVarsity Press, 2000.

Diadochos of Photiki. "On Spiritual Knowledge." In *The Philokalia: The Complete Text.* Translated and edited by G. E. H. Palmer, Philip Sherrard, and Kallistos Ware. 1:253-96. London: Faber and Faber, 1979.

Dunne, John S. *The Reasons of the Heart: A Journey into Solitude and Back Again into the Human Circle.* Notre Dame, IN: University of Notre Dame Press, 1978.

Earth Charter Commission. *The Earth Charter: Values and Principles for a Sustainable Future.* Earth Council: http://www.earthcharter.org (accessed December 2008).

Edwards, Jonathan. *Personal Narrative.* In *The Works of Jonathan Edwards,* vol. 16, *Letters and Personal Writings.* Edited by George S. Claghorn. New Haven: Yale University Press, 1998.

————. *Typological Writings.* Vol. 11 of *The Works of Jonathan Edwards.* Edited by Wallace E. Anderson, Mason I. Lowance, Jr., and David H. Watters. New Haven: Yale University Press, 1993.

Egan, Harvey D. Introduction to Karl Rahner, *The Need and the Blessing of Prayer.* Collegeville, MN: Liturgical Press, 1997.

Ehrlich, Gretel. "On Water." In *Words from the Land,* edited by Stephen Trimble, 198-206. Las Vegas: University of Las Vegas Press, 1995.

Eiseley, Loren. *The Night Country.* New York: Charles Scribner's Sons, 1971.

Evernden, Neil. *The Natural Alien: Humankind and Environment.* Second edition. Toronto: University of Toronto Press, 1993.

Fern, Richard L. *Nature, God, and Humanity: Envisioning an Ethics of Nature.* Cambridge: Cambridge University Press, 2002.

Francis de Sales. *Francis de Sales: Introduction to the Devout Life and Treatise on the Love of God.* Translated by Wendy M. Wright. New York: Crossroad, 1993.

Francis of Assisi. "Canticle of Praise." In *Francis and Clare: Complete Works.* Translated by Regis J. Armstrong and Ignatius C. Brady. New York: Paulist Press, 1982.

Gertner, Jon. "The Future Is Drying Up." *New York Times Magazine,* October 21, 2007.

Gesner, Conrad. *On the Admiration of Mountains.* San Francisco: Grabhorn Press, 1937.

Goodenough, Ursula. *The Sacred Depths of Nature.* Oxford: Oxford University Press, 1998.

Green, Thomas H., S.J. *When the Well Runs Dry: Prayer Beyond the Beginnings.* Notre Dame, IN: Ave Maria Press, 1998.

Guenther, Margaret. *The Practice of Prayer.* Cambridge, MA: Cowley Publications, 1998.

Hamman, Jaco J. "Remembering the Dismembered: Teaching for Transformation and Restoration." *The Journal of Pastoral Theology* 16, no. 1 (Spring 2006): 44-59.

Hammerschlag, Carl A., and Howard D. Silverman. *Healing Ceremonies: Creating Personal Rituals for Spiritual, Emotional, Physical and Mental Health.* New York: Perigee, 1996.

Harrison, Robert Pogue. *The Dominion of the Dead.* Chicago: University of Chicago Press, 2003.

———. *Forests: The Shadow of Civilization.* Chicago: University of Chicago Press, 1992.

Hay, John. "The Nature Writer's Dilemma." In *On Nature: Nature, Landscape, and Natural History,* edited by Daniel Halpern, 5-10. San Francisco: Northpoint Press, 1987.

Heschel, Abraham Joshua. *God in Search of Man.* New York: Straus and Giroux, 1955.

Hesychios the Priest. "On Watchfulness and Holiness." In *The Philokalia: The Complete Text.* Translated and edited by G. E. H. Palmer, Philip Sherrard, and Kallistos Ware. 1:162-98. London: Faber and Faber, 1979.

Hildegard of Bingen. *Scivias.* Translated by Mother Columba Hart and Jane Bishop. New York: Paulist Press, 1990.

———. *The Book of the Rewards of Life.* Translated by Bruce W. Hozeski. New York: Garland Publishing, 1994.

Holmes, Steven J. "Some Lives and Some Theories." In *Identity and the Natural Environment: The Psychological Significance of Nature,* edited by Susan Clayton and Susan Opotow, 29-41. Cambridge, MA: MIT Press, 2003.

Homer-Dixon, Thomas. "A Swiftly Melting Planet." *The New York Times,* October 4, 2007.

Honoré, Carl. *In Praise of Slowness: Challenging the Cult of Speed.* New York: Harper One, 2004.

House, Freeman. *Totem Salmon: Life Lessons from Another Species.* Boston: Beacon Press, 1999.

Hugh of Saint Victor. *The "Didascalicon" of Hugh of St. Victor.* Translated by Jerome Taylor. New York: Columbia University Press, 1961.

Irenaeus of Lyons. *Against Heresies: Book I.* Translated by Dominic J. Unger. In *Ancient Christian Writers,* 55. New York: Paulist Press, 1992.

John of the Cross. *The Collected Works of St. John of the Cross.* Translated by Kieran

Kavanaugh and Otilio Rodriguez. Washington, DC: Institute of Carmelite Studies, 1979.

Johnson, Maxwell E., ed. *Benedictine Daily Prayer: A Short Breviary.* Collegeville, MN: Liturgical Press, 2005.

Julian of Norwich. *Showing of Love.* Translated by Julia Bolton Holloway. Collegeville, MN: Liturgical Press, 2003.

Kipfer, Barbara Ann. *The Order of Things.* New York: Workman, 2008.

Klassen, Abbot John, O.S.B. "Environmental Stewardship." St. John's Abbey: http://www.saintjohnsabbey.org/abbot/041116.html (accessed November 16, 2007).

Kluckhohn, Florence R., and Fred L. Strodtbeck. *Variations in Value Orientations.* Westport, CT: Greenwood Publishers, 1973.

Kohák, Erazim. *The Embers and the Stars: A Philosophical Inquiry into the Moral Sense of Nature.* Chicago: University of Chicago Press, 1987.

Ladner, G. B. *God, Cosmos, and Humankind: The World of Early Christian Symbolism.* Translated by Thomas Dunlap. Berkeley: University of California Press, 1995.

Lehrer, Jonah. *Proust Was a Neuroscientist.* New York: Houghton Mifflin, 2007.

Leopold, Aldo. *A Sand County Almanac: And Sketches Here and There.* Oxford: Oxford University Press, 1987.

————. "Wherefore Wildlife Ecology?" In *The River of the Mother of God and Other Essays,* edited by J. Baird Callicott and Susan L. Flader, 336-37. Madison: University of Wisconsin Press, 1991.

Lévinas, Emmanuel. *Ethics and Infinity.* Translated by Richard A. Cohen. Pittsburgh: Duquesne University Press, 1985.

Lewis, Charles A. *Green Nature, Human Nature.* Urbana: University of Illinois Press, 1996.

Liebert, Elizabeth. *The Way of Discernment: Spiritual Practices for Decision Making.* Louisville: Westminster John Knox Press, 2008.

London, Peter. *Drawing Closer to Nature: Making Art in Dialogue with the Natural World.* Boston: Shambala, 2003.

Lopez, Barry. *Arctic Dreams: Imagination and Desire in a Northern Landscape.* New York: Vintage Books, 1986.

Lorbiecki, Marybeth. *Aldo Leopold: A Fierce Green Fire; An Illustrated Biography.* Helena, MT: Falcon Publishing, 1996.

Louv, Richard. *The Last Child in the Woods: Saving Our Children from Nature-Deficit Disorder.* Chapel Hill, NC: Algonquin Books, 2005.

Luther, Martin. *Sermons on the Gospel of John* (Chapters 1-4). In *Luther's Works,* edited by Jaroslav Pelikan, vol. 22. St. Louis: Concordia, 1957.

Macy, Joanna, and Molly Young Brown. *Coming Back to Life: Practices to Reconnect Our Lives, Our World.* Gabriola Island, BC: New Society Publishers, 1998.

Martin-Schramm, James B., and Robert L. Stivers. *Christian Environmental Ethics: A Case Method Approach.* Maryknoll, NY: Orbis Books, 2003.

Maximus the Confessor. *Ambigua.* Translated by Andrew Louth. New York: Routledge, 1996.

May, Gerald G. *The Dark Night of the Soul: A Psychiatrist Explores the Connection Between Darkness and Spiritual Growth.* San Francisco: HarperSanFrancisco, 2004.

———. *The Wisdom of Wilderness: Experiencing the Healing Power of Nature.* San Francisco: HarperSanFrancisco, 2006.

McCarthy, Cormac. *The Road.* New York: Alfred A. Knopf, 2006.

McKibben, Bill. *The End of Nature.* Second edition. New York: Anchor Books, 1999.

Merton, Thomas, O.C.S.O. *New Seeds of Contemplation.* New York: New Directions, 1961.

Messervy, Julie Moir. *The Inward Garden: Creating a Place of Beauty and Meaning.* Boston: Little, Brown, 1995.

Metzner, Ralph. "The Psychopathology of the Human-Nature Relationship." In *Ecopsychology: Restoring the Earth, Healing the World,* edited by Theodore Roszak, Mary E. Gomes, and Allen D. Kanner, 55-67. San Francisco: Sierra Club, 1995.

Mills, Paul. "VA's Flower Therapy." *V.F.W. Magazine* 63 (November 1975): 36-37.

Moffitt, John. "To Look at Anything." In *Teaching with Fire,* edited by Sam M. Intrator and Megan Scribner, 124. San Francisco: Jossey-Bass, 2003.

Nash, James A. *Loving Nature: Ecological Integrity and Christian Responsibility.* Nashville: Abingdon Press, 1991.

National Museum of Natural History. "Basic Facts: Harm Done by Insects and Spiders." Smithsonian Institute: http://insectzoo.msstate.edu/Students/basic .harm.html (accessed October 7, 2007).

Newell, J. Philip. *Listening for the Heartbeat of God: A Celtic Spirituality.* New York: Paulist Press, 1997.

Nicholsen, Shierry Weber. *The Love of Nature and the End of the World: The Unspoken Dimensions of Environmental Concern.* Cambridge, MA: MIT Press, 2003.

Nikitas Stithatos. "On the Practice of Virtues." In *The Philokalia: The Complete Text.* Translated and edited by G. E. H. Palmer, Philip Sherrard, and Kallistos Ware. 4:79-106. London: Faber and Faber, 1995.

Oelschlaeger, Max. *Caring for Creation: An Ecumenical Approach to the Environmental Crisis.* New Haven: Yale University Press, 1994.

Oliveros, Pauline. "The Poetics of Environmental Sound." In *The Book of Music and Nature,* edited by David Rothenberg and Marta Ulvaeus, 133-38. Middletown, CT: Wesleyan University Press, 2001.

———. "Sonic Images." In *The Book of Music and Nature,* edited by David Rothenberg and Marta Ulvaeus, 131-32. Middletown, CT: Wesleyan University Press, 2001.

Painter, Christine Valters. *Illuminating Mystery: Creativity as a Spiritual Practice.* Seattle: Abbey of the Arts Press, 2009.

Palmer, Parker. *A Hidden Wholeness: The Journey Toward an Undivided Life; Welcoming the Soul and Weaving Community in a Wounded World.* San Francisco: Jossey-Bass, 2004.

Peattie, Donald Culross. *A Natural History of North American Trees.* New York: Houghton Mifflin, 2007.

Placher, William C. *The Domestication of Transcendence: How Modern Thinking about God Went Wrong.* Louisville: Westminster John Knox Press, 1996.

Plotkin, Bill. *Soulcraft: Crossing into the Mysteries of Nature and Psyche.* Novato, CA: New World Library, 2003.

Pope John Paul II. "General Audience Address on Psalm 19." Vatican City, Italy, January 30, 2002. Distributed by the Religious Campaign for Forest Conservation Information Service.

Preston, Richard. *The Wild Trees: A Story of Passion and Daring.* New York: Random House, 2007.

Pseudo-Dionysius. *The Divine Names.* In *Pseudo-Dionysius: The Complete Works.* Translated by Colm Luibheid. New York: Paulist Press, 1987.

Rahner, Karl. *The Need and the Blessing of Prayer.* Translated by Bruce W. Gillette. Collegeville, MN: Liturgical Press, 1997.

Richard of Saint Victor. *De arca mystica: De gratia contemplationis, seu Benjamin Maior.* In *Patrologiae Latinae* 196, edited by J. P. Migne. Paris, 1855.

Rilke, Rainer Maria. *The Sonnets to Orpheus.* In *Ahead of All Parting: The Selected Poetry and Prose of Rainer Maria Rilke.* Translated by Stephen Mitchell, 411-519. New York: The Modern Library, 1995.

Rogers, Pattiann. *Eating Bread and Honey.* Minneapolis: Milkweed, 1997.

Rolheiser, Ronald. *Against an Infinite Horizon: The Finger of God in Our Everyday Lives.* New York: Crossroad, 2001.

———. *The Shattered Lantern: Rediscovering the Felt Presence of God.* New York: Crossroad, 2001.

Roszak, Theodore. *The Voice of the Earth.* New York: Simon and Schuster, 1992.

Roth, Nancy. *Organic Prayer: A Spiritual Gardening Companion.* New York: Seabury Books, 2007.

Ruffing, Janet K., R.S.M., "'Flesh Is More Than Flesh': Sexuality and Spirituality in Spiritual Direction." In *Still Listening: New Horizons in Spiritual Direction,* edited by Norvene Vest, 171-82. Harrisburg, PA: Morehouse Publishing, 2000.

Santmire, H. Paul. *Nature Reborn: The Ecological and Cosmic Promise of Christian Theology.* Minneapolis: Fortress Press, 2000.

Savage, Candace. *Prairie: A Natural History.* Vancouver/Toronto/Berkeley: Greystone Books, 2004.

Shepard, Paul. *The Others: How Animals Made Us Human.* Washington, DC: Island Press, 1996.

———. *Man in the Landscape: A Historic View of the Aesthetics of Nature.* New York: Knopf, 1967.

Shore, Lesley Irene. *The Healing Art of Feminist Psychology.* New York: Harrington Park Press, 1995.

Silf, Margaret. *Roots and Wings: The Human Journey from a Speck of Stardust to a Spark of God.* Grand Rapids: Eerdmans, 2006.

Simkins, Ronald A. *Creator and Creation: Nature in the Worldview of Ancient Israel.* Peabody, MA: Hendrickson Publishers, 1994.

Skutch, Alexander F. *Harmony and Conflict in the Living World.* Norman: University of Oklahoma Press, 2000.

Sölle, Dorothée, and Shirley Cloyes. *To Work and to Love: A Theology of Creation.* Philadelphia: Fortress Press, 1984.

Sontag, Susan. Introduction to *The Temptation to Exist,* by E. M. Cioran, translated by Richard Howard, 7-27. Chicago: University of Chicago Press, 1986.

Spirn, Anne Whiston. *The Language of Landscape.* New Haven: Yale University Press, 1998.

Steiner, George. *Real Presences.* Chicago: University of Chicago Press, 1989.

Strehlow, Wighard, and Gottfried Hertzka. *Hildegard of Bingen's Medicine.* Rochester, VT: Bear and Company, 1988.

Tanner, Kathryn. *God and Creation in Christian Theology: Tyranny or Empowerment.* Oxford: Basil Blackwell, 1988.

Taylor, Barbara Brown. *When God Is Silent.* Cambridge, MA: Cowley, 1998.

Teilhard de Chardin, Pierre. *The Divine Milieu: An Essay on the Interior Life.* New York: Harper, 1960.

Thérèse of Lisieux. *St. Thérèse of Lisieux: Essential Writings.* Edited by Mary Frohlich. Maryknoll, NY: Orbis Books, 2003.

Thomas à Kempis. *The Imitation of Christ.* Edited by Harold Gardiner. Garden City, NY: Image, 1955.

Twain, Mark. *Life on the Mississippi.* New York: Library of America, 1982.

Weems, Renita J. *Listening for God: A Minister's Journey through Silence and Doubt.* New York: Simon and Schuster, 1999.

Whitman, Walt. "Song of Myself." In *Leaves of Grass.* Edited by Harold W. Blodgett and Sculley Bradley. New York: W. W. Norton, 1995.

Williams, Terry Tempest. *Red: Passion and Patience in the Desert.* New York: Vintage Books, 2001.

Index of Names

Abba Sisoes, 195-97, 199, 211, 257
Abram, David, 11, 71, 182-83, 185-86, 190, 257
Alighieri, Dante, 38, 125-27, 146-47, 257
Allen, Diogenes, 87
Appleton, Jay, 171-73, 257
Aquinas, Thomas, 7, 257
Armstrong, Thomas, 249
Athanasius, 3, 64, 257
Augustine, 57, 59, 89, 110, 257

Basil of Caesarea (the Great), 74-75, 257
Bass, Dorothy C., xv, 257
Basso, Keith H., 254
Battles, Ford Lewis, 42
Bernard of Clairvaux, 63, 86, 257
Berry, Thomas, 207, 218, 257
Berry, Wendell, 14, 64, 102-3, 134, 257
Berryman, Jerome W., xiv, 258
Bouma-Prediger, Steven, 253
Brower, Michael, 153n.8, 258
Brown, Molly Young, 135n.10, 136n.14, 261
Buber, Martin, 39, 258
Bunyan, John, 116, 258
Bushnell, Horace, 253

Callicott, J. Baird, 208-9, 258
Calvin, John, 11, 42-43, 64-66, 86, 95, 108, 185, 188, 190, 258

Carroll, John E., 218, 258
Cassian, 235
Catherine of Siena, 93, 187-88, 190, 258
Catton, William R., 21n.5, 258
Chard, Philip Sutton, 24n.10, 258
Chase, Steven, 94n.4, 102nn.7-8, 258
Chenu, Marie-Dominique, 86n.15, 258
Cherry, Conrad, 253
Chesterton, G. K., 37-38, 258
Chevalier, Tracy, 168, 258
Chidester, David, 253
Church, Frederick Edwin, 169
Cioran, E. M., 94, 258
Clayton, Susan, 21, 22nn.6-7, 255, 258
Clements, Frederic, 18
Clinebell, Howard, 206-8, 258
Cloyes, Shirley, 264
Coates, Peter, 254
Combes, Allen J., 35n.2, 258

Densmore, Frances, 78-79, 259
DeWitt, Calvin B., 212, 213nn.12-13, 259
Diadochos of Photiki, 235, 259
Dock, William, 259
Drunyan, Ann, 207
Dunlap, Riley E., 21n.5, 258
Dunne, John S., 149, 259
Dykstra, Craig, xv

p. 36 - pure in heart - unmuddied by self-concern

p. 84 - Words of God in nature are contempla. reversed .. God in contemp. seeking us.

p. 86 - We allow ourselves to be wooed

p. 61 - Scrip. sh. be read outdoors

p. 64 - Scrip. as lens thru which we read bk of crea. more clearly.

p. 85 - St. Therese - in seeking beauty in nat., she was being wooed by God contemplating her thru nat. Therese, loved by + loving nat., is formed by nat. as she herself became a living word.